Study and Communication
Skills for Psychology

@ Online Resource Centre

Study and Communication Skills for Psychology doesn't end with this printed book. Visit the book's Online Resource Centre at **www.oxfordtextbooks.co.uk/orc/parson/** to find a range of materials, prepared by the author and grouped by chapter, to help you master the concepts presented throughout the book.

The extra materials include:

• Exemplar essays, lab reports and theses to help you see how to implement the guidance given in the book

• 'Mark schemes' to accompany exercises given in the book, which ask you to assess exemplar essays and posters

• Exemplar poster templates

• Downloadable weekly timetable and academic calendar

• Crossword/wordsearch activities to help reinforce some of the key concepts covered in the book

Adopting lecturers can also register for access to the following teaching materials:

• Figures from the book, in electronic format

• Lecture slides covering the writing of essays, the writing of lab reports and giving presentations

• Handouts for use in class, covering various sections of the book

STUDY AND COMMUNICATION SKILLS FOR PSYCHOLOGY

Vanessa Parson
University of Sunderland

University of
South Wales
Prifysgol
De Cymru

Library Services

OXFORD
UNIVERSITY PRESS

OXFORD
UNIVERSITY PRESS

Great Clarendon Street, Oxford, OX2 6DP,
United Kingdom

Oxford University Press is a department of the University of Oxford.
It furthers the University's objective of excellence in research, scholarship,
and education by publishing worldwide. Oxford is a registered trade mark of
Oxford University Press in the UK and in certain other countries

British Library Cataloguing in Publication Data
Data available

Library of Congress Cataloguing in Publication Data
Library of Congress Control Number: 2011944052

ISBN 978–0–19–959348–4

Printed in Great Britain by
Ashford Colour Press Ltd, Gosport, Hampshire

Contents

1 Introduction   **1**

Why do I need this book?   1

How is university different from school?   2

The importance of being an independent learner   3

Time management: a skill best learned early   3

A final word   4

2 Time management: a skill best learned early   **5**

Term time juggling   6

Fitting everything in   7

Making your own timetable   8

Vacation juggling   9

Extra help for exam season   11

Checklist   13

3 Teaching time: making the most of it   **16**

What's the point of lectures?   16

Handouts—before and after the lecture   18

Asking questions—when is it okay to do so?   19

Where to find information if you miss the lecture   20

Small group teaching—tutorials and seminars   21

After teaching time is over—what then?   22

Checklist   25

4 Communication and learning with others   **27**

Online learning as an individual: virtual learning environments   27

Online learning with others: blogs and wikis   29

Online learning with others: Facebook™ and Twitter™   31

Online learning with others: discussion boards   31

Offline learning and sharing with others   32

Checklist   35

5 Before and after assessments: guidelines, criteria and feedback   **36**

Before your assessment is due—finding out what to do   36

After the assignment is returned—this thing called feedback   41

Checklist   44

References   44

6   Sources of information and their uses   **45**

What to look for in a textbook   45

Wading through journal articles   49

Critical analysis and thinking   50

How to use, and not use, the Internet   51

How can you tell whether the content of these sources of information is any good?   54

How to use what you've found in your assignments   56

Checklist   57

References   57

7   How to find and read a journal article   **59**

How to find an article to read   59

Getting to grips with the articles you've found   60

Checklist   68

References   69

8   Reading and evaluating text   **70**

What is evaluation?   70

How to think critically   73

Trying to remain objective   76

Checklist   77

References   77

9   So you think you can write good?   **79**

The building blocks of writing: types of words   80

The building blocks of writing: what is grammar?   80

The building blocks of writing: structure and organization   81

The building blocks of writing: squiggly symbols (aka punctuation)   82

The building blocks of writing: expressing yourself   90

Different types of writing style   91

Effective writing—how to communicate your thoughts clearly and precisely   93

Checklist   93

References   94

Useful sources of information   94

10   Writing essays   **95**

Structure—the basic essay format   95

Addressing the question   96

Structure—introductions and conclusions   101

Demonstrating understanding   104

Developing an argument   106

Developing your argument from the essay title   108

Using and evaluating evidence in your essays   109

Checklist   110

References   111

**11 Writing practical reports: how to write   112
up an experiment**

What are psychological reports?   112

Abstract   113

Introduction   114

Methods   118

Results   121

Discussion   125

References   127

Appendices   127

Qualitative versus quantitative reports—what's the difference?   128

Checklist   129

References   130

Useful sources of information   130

12 Plagiarism   131

What is plagiarism?   131

Collusion   131

Avoiding plagiarism—it's easy when you know how   132

Can you plagiarise from yourself?   135

Checklist   136

References   136

13 What is referencing?   138

How to reference   139

Referencing in the text   139

Referencing at the end of your report   141

How to reference from the Internet   145

Primary versus secondary referencing   147

The Harvard system   149

Checklist   152

References   152

Useful sources of information   153

14 Presentations and posters   154

Presentations—standing up in front of people and   154
talking to them intelligently

Posters—presenting your work with minimal talking to people!   164

Checklist   171

15   Your dissertation and thesis: what you need to know   172

Final year dissertations—your empirical project   172

What is a thesis and how is it different from a dissertation?   177

Checklist   180

16   Revision and exam tips   181

Tips for helping you remember course material   181

Active revision versus passive revision   183

Different revision methods   183

Doing past papers is like doing practice exams: practice makes perfect!   187

Tackling different question types   188

Coping with stress during exam periods   192

What to do *after* the exam   193

And finally—common sense tips   194

Checklist   196

References   196

Answers to exercises   197

Index   209

Chapter 1

Introduction

Over my years of teaching a few things have consistently frustrated me about why intelligent undergraduates frequently fail to do as well as they are able to. Students who can verbally communicate in an articulate way in class suddenly lose their communication skills when it comes to written work, and cannot produce good, well-thought-out essays; students who grasp the complexities of statistics beautifully are, for some reason, unable to get the reference and methods sections of their written assignments correct. There are always a few who perform well in all areas of the course, but there are many more who could do so much better if only they had a better grasp of the basics required in psychology—basics such as accurate referencing, setting out coherent arguments in essays, displaying critical thinking skills and demonstrating the ability to write well-formatted laboratory reports.

As an undergraduate, you have a lot to think about at university, and the subject matter alone can pose many problems for students trying to retain so much information. The difficulty you, as students, face is that no matter how much you know about a subject, and no matter how much you write, you won't get good grades if you can't communicate your knowledge and understanding effectively.

Knowing how to present information is a skill that you started to learn at school and college. 'Started to learn' is key here: you don't stop learning how to communicate when you leave school or college. Instead, it is a skill that you need to continue to learn and improve upon if you want to do well at university. There is no such thing as the perfect essay, report or presentation; if you keep trying to do better every time you produce one then you will continue to achieve your potential while at university. Hopefully this book will enable you, as a psychology student, to fulfil your potential and produce work which accurately reflects your abilities.

....

Why do I need this book?

You will have acquired and developed many skills from your education so far (whether you realize it or not!). However, every course and subject comes with its own fresh challenges and requirements, and psychology is no exception. With this in mind, this book is designed to help you manoeuvre your way through all the lectures, seminars and assignments you will be required to do throughout your studies in higher education. Many of you will have studied psychology before, written essays before, made posters, done presentations and written reports. In psychology, we place a large emphasis on doing these things correctly and in a specific manner. While you may already know the basics, there is no harm in revising and getting better.

Many universities have formal study and communication skills programmes in place, while others have materials available for you to use more informally to learn the basics and improve your study skills. All of these resources and programmes are of a high standard and you should take advantage of whatever your university provides. However, the term 'study skills' is a fairly generic one and different degree programmes at different universities vary in terms of what is, and what isn't, covered. By contrast, this book seeks to bring some cohesion to the development of study skills by bringing together in one place the various aspects of these skills taught in psychology programmes at different universities, helping all students to learn the key requirements for psychology to the same high level. This text should complement any study skills course your institution has to offer and will provide you with a helpful resource throughout your studies at undergraduate level.

This text is also aimed to be a key resource for postgraduate students and there are distinctions made throughout this text about elements which may relate only to postgraduates. In addition, a lot of the skills covered in this book aren't applicable only to undergraduate or postgraduate study. Instead, they are just as valuable post university: they are a collection of transferrable skills which you will be able to apply to most of the jobs available once you have a degree.

How is university different from school?

Students typically find university challenging as it is the first time they are responsible for their own learning. There are numerous routes to university, but they all involve clearly directed learning where students are taught from a highly prescribed teaching specification. Consequently, there is limited opportunity for elaboration and independent learning: whatever you do is organized and monitored by those teaching you.

It doesn't take a first year undergraduate long to realize that the university experience is quite different. There is no longer anyone telling you when to do work, or what bits you should learn next—and nobody chases you up if you miss one lecture. Now you are learning to learn independently. It is now your responsibility to work as hard as you like in order to pass the course.

The importance of being an independent learner

It's all very well saying that you now have to become an independent learner, but students are often confused about why this is the case. After all, you are paying for an education so why are the lecturers not teaching you more often and why are you set so much to do by yourself? The answer is a simple one. Beyond university you will no longer be in a position where you are told what to do, what to find out and how to do it. Employers will be looking for a series of specific skills from anyone with a degree and, no matter what the nature of the business you go into, they will expect independent learning to be one of those skills. While at university, you need to learn to run your learning by yourself or you will struggle when you get into the workplace. Psychology is a particularly good subject when it comes to including a wide variety of transferable skills within its remit; it is up to you to take advantage of the opportunities for learning these skills while at university.

It would probably help here to define what independent learning is. An independent learner is someone who can work out for themselves what information they need to solve a particular problem or answer a question. They can then find it, understand and assimilate it, apply it to the problem at hand, then report back on that information in relation to the current problem and find answers which allow conclusions to be drawn about a particular topic. All psychology courses will teach you how to do this by the time you leave. The only thing you have to do is be motivated to work hard by yourself as well as in structured class time. Throughout this book I make reference to the fact that you don't *do* a degree, you *read* for a degree. This tells you what you need to be doing to improve: to read information. A multitude of sources will be provided for you on reading lists throughout your degree, but these are only ever a guide. The best students read materials outside these lists, which they have found themselves.

What we try to teach you at university—beyond the material you need in order to get your degree—is how to be an independent learner: how to accomplish your tasks and assignments to the best of your ability. In this way you will then be prepared when you enter the workplace as a psychology graduate.

Time management: a skill best learned early

There will be many students who are good at time management, but I for one was not one of them. So if, like me, you always seem to be running to catch up despite the best intentions and motivations, you will probably find the chapter on time management useful. However, all students can benefit from improvement in the skills which will help them get work done on time, and to a standard that reflects their ability.

Many of you will find the first few weeks at university hugely confusing. You have a timetable you don't understand, assignments you can't fathom, and you can't work out how to write down everything a lecturer says when they are talking to you. On top of all this, there are people telling you about what social events are happening in the evenings, all of which sound far more interesting than the preparation you don't understand for the seminar in which you don't want to speak to people you don't yet know. Many of you will be able to juggle all the things you *need* to do as well as all the things you *want* to do. However, some of you may find the distractions too great and others may eschew the distractions in favour of working night and day on your studies.

The best way to get through university is to get organized. This way you will have time to study *and* have fun (the two things are not mutually exclusive!). None of your lecturers will expect you to study around the clock, and none will exhibit any surprise should you appear a little bleary-eyed the morning after the local 'student's night' in town, although they may be a little cross if you don't show up at all! The chapter on time management is one that you should read very early on: it will give you lots of tips on how to get organized so that you can make the most out of your studies and your time at university.

A final word

This book is not designed to be read cover to cover. There are some chapters that you will not need to read until your course introduces the concepts involved: for example, you won't need the chapter on laboratory reports until you need to write one. You should treat this book as a resource you can dip in and out of whenever you need it. There are also online resources which you can use to practise the skills presented in this book, in addition to the activities and exercises given in the book itself. (Further details about the online resources are given at the very start of the book, on page ii.) As I've said, the concepts here are skills to be learned or improved upon, so when you read a chapter I do advise you try the exercises provided. The old adage 'practice makes perfect' is a true one—if you do something more often you really do get better.

Your time at university should be rewarding and fun—and hopefully this book will help ease some of the tension you will feel about not always knowing what is required of you while you are studying. I wish you the best of luck in your studies and I hope this book helps.

Chapter 2

Time management: a skill best learned early

All students start off their university career with the best intentions: you will all be thinking you will get all of your studying done, and have a great social life at the same time. Then, every year, thousands of students end up rushing around, finding that they are late for assignment hand-in dates, unprepared for classes, finding the book they wanted is already checked out of the library and going out every night, then wondering why they're behind in their study and haven't done the reading. There are many ways to avoid this situation: hopefully this chapter can ensure that you are never late for an assignment again, that you do manage to get that book from the library, you are prepared for classes and you do manage to find that elusive work–life balance which is right for you.

I will use the word 'term' during this chapter as UK universities work on three basic terms even when the academic year itself is split into two semesters. The semesters begin at the start of the year and each includes 50% of the teaching load for your year. The vacations relate to traditional holiday periods and so are used to split the year into the three terms. The exams come either at the end of each semester or at the end of the year, but these do not relate to when the vacations are, meaning you should expect to do revision in the 'holiday' periods. So if you have two exam sessions for your course, the first set of exams will fall just after the Christmas vacation, and the second set of exams will fall a few weeks after the Easter vacation. If you just have one exam session, then these will fall in the exam period a few weeks after the Easter vacation.

Time management is a term bandied around by people from all walks of life, professionals and academics alike. It is also a term you will have heard before, so you've probably got a pretty good idea about what it means: managing your time effectively so you get everything done. It is all very logical; essentially the idea is that you probably shouldn't watch the *Star Wars* movies back to back when you have an essay deadline the next day. However there's a bit more to it than that. As a student you will have different workloads at different times of the year, and there will be many different requirements made upon you with minimal supervision. The result is that you have a big and scary pile of work during term time and no orders from lecturers other than to 'get it done'. The situation is even more difficult outside term time: there is reading to do but term feels like months away so it gets put to one side and forgotten about. The end result is that even those organized individuals with the best intentions in the world are not always up to date with reading and assignments. However, it is relatively easy to keep on top of your workload as long as you keep track of everything you are doing—and this includes when you're going to the pub as well as when the next assignment is due!

Term time juggling

During term time, you have a lot of individual courses to take, with assignments for each, tutors to see, and reading lists to get through. It can feel like there is a mountain of work to do when all you want to do is socialize with your friends who all seem to have finished their work. If you add in time for any paid jobs you do, time to sleep, meeting your tutor and study group, going to the supermarket, doing the household chores, etc., it can feel as if there are not enough hours in the day. We'll cover the more obvious things shortly, but we'll cover the counter-intuitive stuff first: visual cues and aids are as relevant to time management as is the tip that you probably shouldn't spend all day every day in the pub drinking if you want to get your work done!

Visual cues and aids to time management

1. Write things down clearly

Do you remember the student at school who used lots of different coloured pens in their work and always wrote everything down? There are several of these in every school, and they are rarely the ones who forget to do their homework and don't know what's going on. It may seem like common sense, but just writing down what you need to do is a good first step towards getting your assignments done on time. However, writing down what you need to do on a scrap of paper which then ends up on the floor or in the bin is self-defeating and won't help at all. Make sure you write down what you need to do in a diary, on your notes from class, or put it in your smartphone if you have one.

- If you forget to write things down, make sure you know where to look so you can find the information later on. Many a student hour has been lost looking for information which tells them what they should be doing. If you know where to get information about courses, assignments and reading lists then you won't waste time rushing around trying to find things.

2. Get a diary

Most *academic* diaries have spaces for timetables, assignment dates and notes pages. They also span the academic year (rather than the calendar year) so you don't need to find another diary and transfer all the information in it every January. Once you have a diary you need to make sure you actually check it regularly: a diary that you don't open isn't much good.

3. Wall planners—big poster diaries for your wall

Did you get an academic wall planner amongst the various pieces of paper you got at registration? If not, there is a picture of what the wall planner looks like in this book on page 15. Wall planners are much better than any facilities provided by electronic gadgets because the information is there all the time in front of you—you don't have to consciously look for it. There are various things that work well with wall planners:

For a copy of the academic planner, see page 15 or go to www.oxfordtextbooks.co.uk/orc/parson/

- Colours—this is where highlighter pens come into their own. Take tips from the students at school who used different colours for their notes. Using brightly coloured pens to highlight when you have assignments is a really good way of not forgetting them.

- Crossing days off as you go past them. This is a bit like a countdown until the holidays, which always feels nice; in practice, though, it helps you keep track of what day you're on. This way, you'll be able to work out how much time you've got to do the assignments you've highlighted in bright colours.

- Don't just block out the vacation/holidays as 'free time'. While you're at university you do actually have to do some academic studying outside of term time, so you should not assume that a third of your year is actually vacation/holiday. Even though many of you will use time outside of term for paid employment, you will need to try to find some time to do reading necessary for your course. As we covered in the introduction (and will cover again throughout the book) you *read* for a degree—you don't get taught every tiny thing, so you have to find some things out for yourself through reading the material you're directed to.

4. Gadgets, smartphones and watches

While wall planners might be great for keeping track of workloads, most students are outside their rooms for a good deal of their time at university, so another method of keeping track of what is going on is by using phones, smartphones and watches. Having reminders set up in the calendar on your phone/smartphone is a good way to not forget to hand in assignments and, if you can be bothered to programme them all in, when your lectures are. Alarms can also be programmed into some watches, although this is more a daily method and is not as useful as the phones/smartphones available.

Fitting everything in

The number of taught hours you have at university will vary according to your institution and which stage of your studies you are at. However, whatever the taught content of your degree, there is a significant proportion of non-contact content which needs to be fitted in as well as the contact teaching time, be that preparation for classes, going through your notes, or doing the extra reading on the topics taught. As a general rule, around twice as much non-contact time is necessary for successful completion of your course than contact teaching time.

Working out how to fit everything in can be a challenge, as the majority of people entering university have always had their timetables worked out for them at school. However, it's straightforward enough: you just have to be prepared to: (a) study outside lecture times during the day, and (b) stick to a timetable you produce.

Making your own timetable

For a blank timetable, go to www.oxfordtextbooks.co.uk/orc/parson/

There is a blank timetable in this book (see page 14) and online for you to use. The idea is that you fill in all your lectures, seminars, tutorials and so on, then you fill the remaining space during the day with the private study hours you need to do. If you treat these times as official study hours, just like in any other school or job, then you will keep on top of your studying and not fall behind, plus have plenty time to have fun.

It is important to schedule time off in your timetable too. Having fun and relaxing is important, not just because it's part of life at university, but also because if you study all day every day you will burn out—you will be too tired mentally to study efficiently. If you have nothing planned on a night you have scheduled off, try to relax instead of study. As long as you have been sticking to your timetable you will find you have plenty of evenings free to do with as you please. How much time you schedule as free time and how much as study time will depend on the stage of your university career: first year students will have significantly more free time than final year students.

Last minute changes

It is all very well planning your study times and making a schedule, but everyone knows that best laid plans frequently go wrong. It is highly likely that something will come up suddenly on an evening on which you'd planned to study so that you want to go out instead—for example, on someone's birthday. You have three choices here: firstly, you can stick to your timetable and stay in; secondly you could go out but move that evening's study to another day when you would ordinarily have gone out; finally you could get your work done quickly and then go out afterwards. Which option you chose will depend on the situation you face. For example if it's your friend's birthday and you have an assignment due the next day which you've almost finished, you would choose option three and meet them a little later after you've finished your assignment, but if you haven't started you probably ought to choose option one and go out another time. If you've no assignments due then my advice would be to pick option two, mark it clearly on your timetable and work out when to do the work you'd planned to do, then go out and have fun.

Weekends

Weekends pose a problem for most students, as typically most will go out and relax. Unfortunately this means they then panic on Monday morning as they didn't manage to do the studying they needed to do. One solution to this is to keep the equivalent of one day free over the weekend, so that you study for two half-days, but have the afternoons and evenings free. Another solution is to study for one day and then have the other day off. Finally, a third option is to study alternate weekends: so one weekend you prioritize studying, and the next weekend you prioritise socializing.

Vacation juggling

The term 'vacation' makes more sense at university than the more commonly used term 'holiday'. The word 'holiday' conjures up images of sandy beaches, and relaxing by a pool; in other words, it is not a word that is synonymous with doing a great deal of work. The word 'vacation', however, is better as it simply means a break from whatever it is you do on a typical day (in your case, going to lectures). This makes it much easier to visualize doing some studying while you're away from university. If you are on a postgraduate programme where the vacation time is not preordained, this section simply relates to the weeks leading up to a vacation, whenever that may be.

Work it out before you go

It helps to have an idea about what you want to accomplish in the vacation between each term at university—whether that be revision, reading or the completion of assignments. Whatever you plan to do in each vacation you need to work it out before you go: if you need any resources or help from tutors the best time to act is at the end of term rather than after the vacation has started. Unlike students, if academics are away in vacation time it means they're generally taking annual leave and this probably *does* mean a holiday, so you cannot guarantee a response from your tutors during vacation periods. If you get information *before* the vacation then you won't waste valuable hours of your vacation hunting for information in order to do your work.

- REVISION: make sure all your notes are up to date and you have all the books you need.
- READING: make sure you have as much of the reading lists as possible printed out or saved on your computer. You may not be able to access some of the material on it outside of term time, particularly if you live a considerable distance from your university.
- ASSIGNMENTS: ensure you know what you are supposed to be doing and by when; make sure you get all the required reading, and check you understand the assessment

We discuss assessment criteria in Chapter 5.

criteria. If you have any doubts about an assessment then find your tutor before you go: they can help with any problems you may have and ease potential frustration with non-comprehension during the vacation.

Get back what you need

Most students lend their notes and books to friends on their courses. However, if you live a long way apart during vacations, it can be very frustrating when you forget to get them back before you head off on vacation. So, make sure you collect back anything you need for that particular vacation before you go. If you're someone who has borrowed material from a friend and needs to return it, make sure you make notes of what you need and give it back to them: you don't want to be the subject of resentment at the start of the next term!

Plan time to have fun!

During your vacation, make sure you work out how long you need to complete the tasks you have set yourself. This will vary according to what you want to achieve, but you should always factor in some time for rest and relaxation as well. Contrary to student mythology, lecturers at university do not expect you to study your socks off throughout your vacation time: they do expect you to rest. Nobody can perform at their highest level and achieve their potential if they are worn out and tired. By the end of a term everyone is tired, including the lecturers and everyone needs a break.

A large number of you will be in paid employment over vacation periods, so you'll need to use the same tools as in term time to make sure you get your academic study done but also have chance to relax and have some time off. There are many possible methods for making sure you are well rested while also completing your study schedule by the time you return to university. There are two aspects to your vacation: work time (academic and paid employment) and holiday time. If your academic aims are assignments or reading, you probably want to fit work in around your paid employment and/ or holiday time. If your aim is revision then you will need to fit holiday time around your paid employment and/or revision time. The way in which you approach academic study over the vacation period is a matter of personal preference: if you are not sure what may suit you best then try these different methods in turn and see which works best for you. For all of these options, if you're in paid employment, factor that in as well, and follow the gist of the methods given here. If you are in paid employment over the vacation periods, it is especially important to make sure you factor in some relaxation time as well as study time.

- Sacrificing 50% of your holiday to study, preferably the first 50%. If you wait until the end of your vacation to work you'll never get started! If you calculate how long you have off and then spend the first half working, you have the remainder to do what you like with. For example, if you have a four-week break, spend the first 14 days getting all your study done that you need to do, and then you have the remaining two weeks to rest and relax. This is rather a difficult option and requires a lot of will power: others will want you to go out and spend time with them now you are on 'holiday'. This method is particularly advised for when you have assignments to complete.

- Spend a few hours each day studying and relax for the rest of the day. This method is most useful when revising or trying to get through a reading list. Work out a timetable of what you are doing on which day and make sure you do it. A few hours each morning are generally more productive when you're revising as you don't get too fatigued or distracted. Make sure you set your alarm: if you oversleep too much you'll lose out on study time and end up not having enough time to do it. With this method it is easier to do study in the mornings: you then have all afternoon and evening to do what you like. If you oversleep every day and *then* do three hours work, you'll feel like you're spending all your vacation studying. At this point you'll end up taking days off because you need a break. A little discipline, and an effective alarm clock, will give you back your holiday time without encroaching on your study time.

- When you go on holiday, take reading material with you. If you will be spending time by a pool or on the beach, take reading material with you: get a tan while you study! If you can't study in the heat, spend an hour in the morning/evening studying and then relax the rest of the time. It is important with this method not to aim to do more than around an hour a day: you're on holiday and if you end up studying all the time people you are on holiday with will resent it, plus you'll wonder why you bothered to come on holiday in the first place!

Whatever method you employ during the vacation to get your study done, make sure you take the first weekend of your vacation off to rest and catch up with friends and family. Unless you have had the easiest term ever, there is no way you can launch straight into studying hard without some form of rest. A weekend where you sleep and socialize will rejuvenate you for the study plans you have during the rest of the vacation.

Anyone who celebrates religious holidays should factor those into their schedules, and those who aren't particularly religious will probably want to take into account traditional national holidays such as Christmas and New Year.

Extra help for exam season

During the exam season, which does include Christmas/Easter holidays, you will want to be extra strict with yourself. Most of time management tips here involve how you stay focused and approach these times of the year, and how you organize your time.

It is particularly difficult when revision time starts during vacation time. Try to be realistic about revision, but try to employ the tips listed earlier about having a break and not studying all the time. If you treat revision like a job, i.e. 9am to 5pm, you'll find you get a lot done and still have time to relax, so it will still feel like you've had a holiday. It is likely that exams will not start up the moment you get back to university, so it is as well to get a break first and then you can launch into revision full time feeling refreshed and eager to do well.

Don't get bored!

After you've been studying and revising for a while you start to suffer from a lack of focus. If you realise you've been staring at the same page for the last 15 minutes and don't remember reading a word of it you should probably take a break from that particular topic and move on to something fresh.

The problem many people have when they take a break is that they spend too long having that break and never quite get back to studying—they assume that they have done enough for the day and their brain is 'tired'. This is not the case: the brain does not get 'tired' as such; all it wants is a change. What you should do is take a break for as long as it takes to have a comfort break or make a cup of tea, then go straight back to studying—but on a different topic. If you are 'zoning out' (daydreaming and thinking of anything but revision, or simply staring at something without thinking) you are bored—and bored people don't work. If the brain is bored it does something about it in the form of daydreams.

The trick is not to get bored. If you are really interested in something you can spend all day quite happily doing it, but if you're not interested in a topic then every moment you spend reading about it will be incredibly hard work! As I say above, the trick is to change topic regularly. You should never try to spend an entire day on just one subject. This rarely works for anyone. Spend an hour on a topic and move on: you can always come back to it later on or even alternate two topics throughout a day. However you manage it, change is as good as a rest where the brain is concerned. So, make sure you write your schedule with that in mind.

How to organize revision around exams

Organizing revision around exams can be problematic for students: there are multiple exams happening at different times, all with different material to be learned. The most important tip is that when you have an exam, only revise the material for that particular exam the half-day beforehand. This becomes a little more difficult when you have two exams on one day. In this situation allocate half of one day to each exam, in the order in which you'll take the exams, as shown in Figure 2.1. There is a good reason for this: if you revise in the same order then you will find it easier to remember information in that order. The white spaces in-between exams and revision that you'll see in Figure 2.1 can be used for eating lunch and allowing yourself time to adjust to a new topic. The white space in the evening before the exams indicates that an early night is necessary! This will be covered in more detail in the section on revision tips.

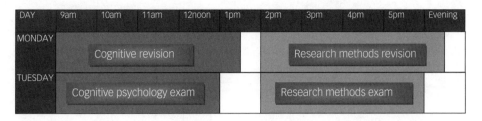

Figure 2.1: Revision schedule option when you have two exams on one day.

Don't panic!

Many students panic at the volume of information they are expected to assimilate. Unfortunately, though, this is counterproductive. The more stressed you are, the less productive your revision will be and the less you'll remember. It is much better to go into revision thinking 'It will all be fine, I'll get it all done eventually', even if you can't see how that can happen. At least this way you have a chance to optimize your revision process. A small amount of stress is good for us and is a great motivator; but a large amount of stress is something that will only hinder your revision by making you uncomfortable mentally and will lead to panic. If you do start to panic try to remind yourself like your course and that you chose it because you were interested in the subject matter: at this point it is hardly an arduous task to read about a topic you enjoy. There are plenty of revision tips in Chapter 16, which will help you reduce your stress levels considerably.

✎ Checklist

Check you've understood the key points covered in this chapter by seeing if you can answer the following questions:

- ✔ Can you name at least three ways to manage your time effectively?
- ✔ What are they and how do they work?
- ✔ Why should you call breaks between terms at university vacations instead of holidays?
- ✔ What should you do when you start to 'zone out' while studying?
- ✔ How should you manage your time during term time?
- ✔ How should you manage your time during vacations?
- ✔ What extra things should you remember during exam time?

DAY	9am	10am	11am	12noon	1pm	2pm	3pm	4pm	5pm	Evening
MONDAY										
TUESDAY										
WEDNESDAY										
THURSDAY										
FRIDAY										
SATURDAY										
SUNDAY										

Weekly timetable

This weekly timetable can also be downloaded from www.oxfordtextbooks.co.uk/orc/parson/

	Sat	Sun	Mon	Tue	Wed	Thurs	Fri	Sat	Sun	Mon	Tue	Wed	Thurs	Fri	Sat	Sun	Mon	Tue	Wed	Thurs	Fri	Sat	Sun	Mon	Tue	Wed	Thurs	Fri	Sat	Sun	Mon	Tue	Wed
September	1	2	3	4	5	6	7	8	9	10	11	12	13	14	15	16	17	18	19	20	21	22	23	24	25	26	27	28	29	30			
October			1	2	3	4	5	6	7	8	9	10	11	12	13	14	15	16	17	18	19	20	21	22	23	24	25	26	27	28	29	30	31
November	29	30				1	2	3	4	5	6	7	8	9	10	11	12	13	14	15	16	17	18	19	20	21	22	23	24	25	26	27	28
December	1	2	3	4	5	6	7	8	9	10	11	12	13	14	15	16	17	18	19	20	21	22	23	24	25	26	27	28	29	30	31		
January				1	2	3	4	5	6	7	8	9	10	11	12	13	14	15	16	17	18	19	20	21	22	23	24	25	26	27	28	29	30
February	28						1	2	3	4	5	6	7	8	9	10	11	12	13	14	15	16	17	18	19	20	21	22	23	24	25	26	27
March	28	29	30	31			1	2	3	4	5	6	7	8	9	10	11	12	13	14	15	16	17	18	19	20	21	22	23	24	25	26	27
April			1	2	3	4	5	6	7	8	9	10	11	12	13	14	15	16	17	18	19	20	21	22	23	24	25	26	27	28	29	30	
May	30	31			1	2	3	4	5	6	7	8	9	10	11	12	13	14	15	16	17	18	19	20	21	22	23	24	25	26	27	28	29
June	1	2	3	4	5	6	7	8	9	10	11	12	13	14	15	16	17	18	19	20	21	22	23	24	25	26	27	28	29	30			
July			1	2	3	4	5	6	7	8	9	10	11	12	13	14	15	16	17	18	19	20	21	22	23	24	25	26	27	28	29	30	31
August	29	30	31			1	2	3	4	5	6	7	8	9	10	11	12	13	14	15	16	17	18	19	20	21	22	23	24	25	26	27	28

Academic calendar 2012/2013

This wall-planner can also be downloaded from www.oxfordtextbooks.co.uk/orc/parson/

Chapter 3

Teaching time: making the most of it

Teaching time is the main crux of going to university: the lecturers and tutors are there to guide you in your learning and help you achieve your potential. Note that I've used the word 'guide' in that sentence; there is no 'spoon-feeding' at university, no passive absorbing of information. You are expected to participate in your education now rather than simply learn everything you are told, and should expect your learning to be active.

Lecturers and tutors put a lot of effort into producing your taught material, and it is in your best interests to make the most of this. It's easy enough to turn up and sit through your lectures and seminars; most students go to lectures, listen, and write down notes based on the slides and most of what is said by the lecturer. Then they leave that topic, never to return to it until they need the information for assignments or exams. At this point, their brief notes provide, at best, a superficial coverage of the material—and certainly less detail than is needed for achieving a good grade in assessments. To close this gap in detail, there is then a whole pile of extra reading to do during exam preparation, when what you should be doing is consolidating what you have already learned throughout the course. A few small, easy steps, between the lecture and the exam as outlined below can prevent this, and lead to you getting better marks.

What's the point of lectures?

The point of a lecture is fairly obvious on the surface. The lecturer is there to tell you information about the subject you are studying you don't already know. The mistake that students frequently make is to assume that this lecture contains all the information on a topic area. This is a mistake because the lecturer cannot possibly hope to include every piece of information about any given subject area with the time allotted to them. A lecture is, therefore, just the highlights and key information of a particular topic. This means that you need to gather other information to gain a fully rounded view of the topics covered, and this is where small group teaching time and private study come in. We'll cover these shortly, but first we'll concentrate on lectures themselves.

How do you write everything down that fast?

Quite simply, you cannot write down everything the lecturer says during the lecture, so you need to make shortened notes to make sure you get all the key information down. It is a fairly common observation from lecturers that students, generally, do not take notes effectively. As a rule, you rarely get the opportunity to learn to take notes before university. This is unfortunate as effective note-taking is the only way to get all the key information down during a lecture.

Effective note-taking involves writing down the gist of what is being said rather than recording every word, and using shorthand symbols to ensure you capture the maximum amount of information (see Figure 3.1). This does mean that you need to go through your notes the same day as the lecture in order to make sense of them—if you leave it for weeks and then come back to them they will not make sense. You can only ever write down the gist of what a lecturer says: it would be almost impossible to write down every word. A mistake students often make is to write down information that is on

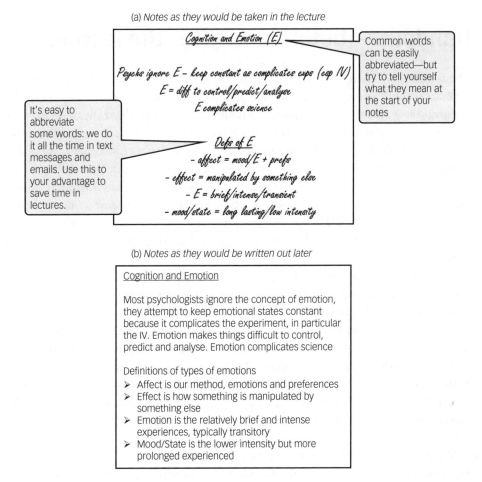

Figure 3.1: Example of note-taking.

the slides provided by the lecturer—information which is frequently provided after the lecture via the university VLE (virtual learning environment), for example Blackboard. If you find it helpful to write out what is on handouts and slides, then that's great, but you should do this after lectures rather than during. Sometimes information doesn't sink in just from reading, most of you will find that you need to write and use the information in order to make sense of it. Taking notes in lectures on what is *said* and then revisiting those notes afterwards and expanding them provides a really good opportunity for you to embed this information into your memory (see Figure 3.1). This essentially means that you'll be doing revision from lecture 1, giving you a huge advantage when you come to exam time.

It is also possible to record the lecture. For those of you who write slower than average, it might be useful to invest in a Dictaphone. Ideally this should be digital so you can put the files straight onto your computer. Most lecturers do not mind being recorded while they talk, but make sure you ask them first. Some lecturers may already be recording their lectures, in which case this step is not necessary.

Handouts—before and after the lecture

The availability of handouts will vary between institutions and lecturers, but you will have access to them at some point, usually before the lecture starts. Occasionally, lecturers feel you would not be quite as attentive if you already have the notes in front of you, so they don't provide them until after the lecture. By contrast, others feel that you benefit from not having to write as much down. Either way, there are good reasons for when a lecturer provides their handouts, but they will provide them and you will have access to them at some stage. Generally I think it is better that handouts are provided after a lecture: students do concentrate more if they do not have pre-prepared notes in front of them, and they are also not going to be reading ahead before the lecturer has finished making the point they're trying to make.

The form these notes will come in varies, but generally you'll find that PowerPoint slides are provided in handout form (see Figure 3.2), but that this will only mean bullet-point notes about the topics provided. In the example provided, you can see that there is minimal information about the topic (face perception in the example provided here); there are not as many details as you would need for any assignments or exams you might get. This is because the lecturer will only put headings and small details in slides, as they are verbally providing the rest of the information. Generally, what you would be expected to do is to make notes on what the lecturer was saying in addition to the PowerPoint slides, and then add to your notes after class from your reading around the subject matter.

Slides are helpful as they show you the key issues that the lecturer would like you to focus on. You can then use the slides to embellish your notes when you go through them after the lecture, and they can also help in guiding your further reading. Sometimes you

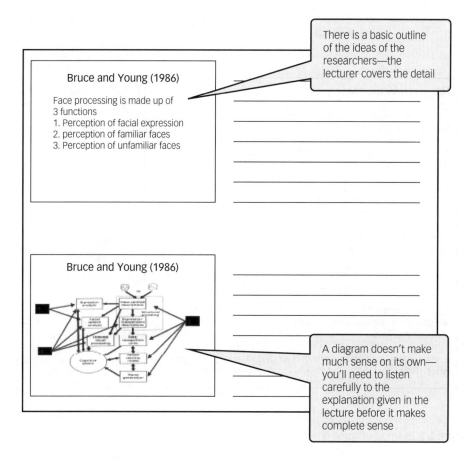

Figure 3.2: Example of PowerPoint slides and notes.

might be given abbreviated notes of what your lecturer has said if they haven't used PowerPoint (see Figure 3.3).

Asking questions—when is it okay to do so?

It is always acceptable to ask questions. As one of my lecturers once said to me, "There is no such thing as a stupid question." As long as you are listening and paying attention, you will find that lecturers do not mind being asked to rephrase or clarify points if you didn't understand them. You should never feel that you cannot ask a question. If you don't want to ask your question within the lecture scenario then write it down and ask them at another time. This could be after the lecture while students are filing out, by email later on, or during the lecturer's office hours.

> You can see that there is minimal detail in these notes. The lecturer will have provided the rest of the information during the lecture.

Monocular Visual Cues

Interposition (occlusion/overlap)—This is where one object obscures another from full view.

Ariel perspective (atmospheric perspective)—Objects which are further away appear less clearly than those closet to you.

Shading and lighting—In natural situations light comes from above, a constant with whcih the visual system bases its judgements of depth perception.

Elevation—Objects which are further away tend to appear higher in the visual field than those which are closer to us.

Linear perspective—As objects stretch away from us lines they are made up of appear to converge and come together.

Texture gradient—Most surfaces have a visible texture which appears to be stretching away from us or towards us when the surfaces is angled.

Relative size—The distance between you and other objects varies, which means that the size of the objects on your retina varies.

> There is no context to these notes, so you need to make sure you see the lecturer, and read the textbook if you cannot attend the lecture.

Figure 3.3: Example of typed notes.

It is worth noting that lecturers are generally not used to being simply interrupted (by contrast, school students frequently simply interrupt their teachers whether they should or not, and this practice occasionally spills over into higher education). The advice here would be not to simply interrupt the lecturer: put your hand up and wait for them to address your question when they are ready and are in a suitable place to pause their lecture. There are many students in a single lecture, and only a few will want to ask questions during the lecture itself: it is essentially impolite to interrupt the lecturer and disrupt the lecture.

Where to find information if you miss the lecture

Obviously it is best to go to every lecture, but sometimes justifiable absences are unavoidable. In this case you need to find out what happened in the lecture, and the information that was covered that you now need to look at. There are a few options here: get a friend's notes or get the notes from the VLE.

Your friends are a good source of information about lectures, as they were there and experienced first-hand what was said and what happened. This is helpful because no matter what notes you get from other sources, they may not contain every single thing that happened in the lecture (as we have already seen).

The VLE is the 'virtual learning environment'. Most (if not all) universities subscribe to a VLE; it is where you can find all your course information and lecture notes. It provides many other resources in addition, but these are covered in the next chapter. The lecturer will upload the notes from the lecture, be they PowerPoint slides or typed notes, either before or after the lecture. You will then be able to download these if, for any reason, you have to miss a lecture. Some lecturers may even provide audio files of the lecture, which means that you will be able to listen to the lecture and get the benefit of the lecturer's expertise in explaining the tricky concepts you're learning. These 'podcasts' are great if you get them, as you can listen to material many times and hopefully increase your understanding.

➠ See Chapter 4 for more detail about VLEs.

It is even more important to review and expand on available notes if you weren't actually ion the lecture, as you've not listened to the information first-hand so you've got more ground to catch up in terms of your understanding. If you do find you're struggling after looking at your friends' notes and the information on the VLE, then you should go and see the lecturer in their office hours to ask them to go through some of the material with you. They won't go through the entire lecture again with you, but they will answer questions that you have about specific topics.

Small group teaching—tutorials and seminars

Small group teaching time is incredibly valuable time while at university, and you should make sure you take as much advantage of this as possible. Generally, seminars allow you to explore in greater detail the topics covered in lectures, and provide far more opportunity for discussion and elaboration between students and lecturers. It is a very rich form of knowledge provision, and will always give you greater insight into the topics being covered.

Preparing for a small group teaching session

Obviously it is always helpful to have been to the lecture associated with the small group session, as the session will be based on its content. Sometimes you will be given readings to do before a session—for example, articles or specific passages in books. You may even be asked to check out a website or two. Whatever you are asked to do prior to a small group session, you should do it. Never assume that you'll pick up everything you need at the session; you will only be able to make the most of it if you have read everything that came before it.

How to make the most of the session

It's easy to tell people to make the most of a teaching session, be it large or small group teaching time; but it is rare that the person you are telling actually fully understands what 'making the most of the session' actually means. In practice, it means taking part in every activity, concentrating throughout, and getting involved to the best of your ability. If you sit back and take a much more passive role, you are much less likely to absorb any additional information, or understand more clearly the topics covered in lectures.

You probably won't be with your closest circle of friends in the session, and this can be quite intimidating for many undergraduates in particular. However, you should make sure you engage with and take a full part in, the session.

Interaction and being brave

This section is really for those of you who are not that happy to speak up in groups of strangers. Small group sessions generally involve talking in depth about topics with people you barely know—a situation that fills many people with dread and fear.

To get the most out of the session you will need to conquer your fear and dive right in. This is made significantly easier if you've been to the lecture and have read the notes prior to attending: you will understand the concepts involved and have more confidence that you can respond appropriately. Talking and listening go hand in hand. You will also find that it is perfectly acceptable to ask other students, or the tutor, to clarify what they're saying if you don't understand. Nobody will expect you to understand everything first time: it is always okay to ask for clarification if you're not quite sure.

Don't be afraid to contradict other people, even if there seems to be massive support for their ideas. If you've read the background material and disagree with what they're saying then be brave and say so. (If nothing else, this may stimulate the tutor to explain something in more detail so that, if you—or other members of your group—didn't quite understand something (hence having different opinions) you might get that extra little bit of explanation needed to help something make sense.) Equally, don't be afraid to support other people who appear to have limited support within the group.

After teaching time is over—what then?

So, you've been to the lectures and seminars, so you must have learned all the lecturers want you to learn. This would be the common assumption that students have of teaching time, and it's a mistaken one. Teaching time is just the start of the process: there is a lot more to do yet. Generally, around one-third of your studies are spent actually being taught at university; these sessions produce notes which need embellishing. The other two-thirds of your course requirements are described as either 'directed learning' or 'private study'.

Private study/directed learning

Around two-thirds of your course requirement is entirely up to you. Part of your studies at university is actually to learn to motivate yourself to work independently. Some people find this easier than others, but most people find this difficult initially. Your first year is probably the most important year in terms of directed learning; it is this portion of your degree where you learn what is expected of you in terms of learning. Around halfway though the second year, most students finally work out that they probably need to do significantly more work than you have been doing. One of the aims of this book is to help you get a jump on this, and prevent the delay in the realization of what is involved at university.

The main thing with directed learning is reading 'around' the subject matter of your courses. 'Reading around the subject' means reading the information provided for you, and then finding additional information of your own, to supplement or augment what you've already been told. You will find that you have a reading list for each module you are taught, alongside which there will be various recommended readings for each lecture.

Many of you will find that the reading lists are split into 'essential' and 'recommended'. The essential list will contain key textbooks and journal articles directly related to what is covered in the lectures; it is from this list that your lecture materials will be drawn so it is very important that you read the contents of this list. You shouldn't need to buy every book on this list: the university library is a much under-used resource. Some universities even have books from reading lists available to read online, thus negating the problem of not being able to get hold of a physical copy.

The contents of the 'recommended' list are more variable. Generally this will contain books and journal articles (these are original research studies and papers) that are linked to topic, but have not been used in the preparation of lecture material. It is a good idea to read at least some of these. Try focusing first on the books as these will give you a general overview of your topic area, and then move onto the journal articles, which will give you a lot more specific details about key aspects of the topic area.

Embellishing your notes

So, you've got your notes from your lectures, now you need to add to them. How do you go about this? University study was traditionally called 'reading for a degree', which gives a clear clue to what students were expected to do: students had to read a lot about a subject and answer questions based on what they'd read. University teaching has not changed much, and you are still expected to read a significant amount of material; the only difference now is that you get considerably more help from lecturers.

A standard complaint from undergraduates when confronted with the concept of directed and independent learning is: "If it's not in the lecture then we shouldn't be tested [examined] on it." Actually, what you get legitimately tested on while at university is everything you may have been directed towards learning. So you should view directed study material as essentially containing a whole lot of examination material which you must learn for yourself. This is how universities are able to test motivation. Those students who are motivated, and willing to learn, are those who will do the directed reading and will then out-perform those students who just looked at the lecture material. If directed reading is not done, and additional reading on lecture topics is not done, there is only one person at fault if the end test scores are lower than desired—and it's not the lecturer who set the work in the first place.

When you flesh out your notes, you need to add in any material which the lecturer did not cover. As we have already found, it is a mistake to think that the lecturer will cover all the material in class: they simply won't have time for this. Lecturers cover key points in their lectures, but they may not have time to go through every key point of a theory; time constraints mean that depth is sometimes sacrificed in favour of breadth. So lots of detail is still in the books for you to find, you can treat it as an academic treasure hunt. The 'map' is the lecture, and the 'treasure' of details is for you to find. Students are frequently confused as to how far in depth they are supposed to go in their reading. This is a difficult one to answer, as students of different ability need different answers. The best tip I can give is to read the material provided and try to understand the concepts you have been directed to by your lecturers as fully as you can. You won't have been introduced to anything beyond your academic level, and no books will be recommended which are not suitable for your year group. However, there are some additional recommendations for the different year groups:

- *Level one*: concentrate on the books, then pad out your knowledge with the recommended journal articles. You probably won't do a huge amount of journal article reading in level one but you should definitely introduce yourselves to it so that you are ready to expand this in level two.
- *Level two*: you should be using books as a basis for your journal article searches now, introducing more original material into your learning so that you can get more in-depth knowledge of the topics.
- *Level three and above*: the main focus of your reading should be journal articles now, books should only be used sparingly as a 'check point' for topic details.

So your job is to complete the task of finding out information for that topic. If you do this at the same time as you write out your notes from the lecture, you will find that you remember much more later on; this process consolidates the information in your memory and aids the integration of that single session into the topic you are studying. Generally you will need to look in the 'essential reading' section to find the books you need to flesh out your notes, and then the 'recommended reading' to get an advantage in terms of understanding the concepts involved.

Finding the rest of the information you need

It's easy to talk about reading lists, but most of you will probably be wondering where they are. Generally they are available in three places: in your course handbook, the lecture notes, and the VLE (virtual learning environment). If you can't find your reading lists then ask your lecturer; they will be thrilled to provide you with a reading list!

Reading lists usually contain books and articles that will be available within the university itself; you should not need to go outside, as most libraries make sure they have copies of anything lecturers recommend to students. You may want to buy key textbooks so that you have them at your disposal all the time. However, I would generally recommended that you wait a few weeks before doing this, just to make sure you know which books are really important, and which you should just borrow when you need them from the library. You could always team up with friends and split the books you need between you, this way you don't spend as much but always have access when you need it.

➠ We discuss VLEs in more detail in Chapter 4, and will explore the types of information sources listed in reading lists in Chapter 6.

Reading around the subject—why is this important?

Reading helps to place the core information gathered from lectures in the context of the wider subject of psychology: while an individual topic might make sense at the time of the lecture, it is often difficult to see how it fits in with the rest of the literature as a whole. Psychology is an integrated subject—it is made up of various themes (social, biological, developmental, cognitive, etc.), which all come together to form the discipline as a whole. When you study it, however, there is a distinctly non-integrated sensation. Each discrete module feels very different from every other module, making it hard to feel as though you are studying a single subject.

Reading in each topic area helps to expand and integrate your understanding of the information you're given, and embed it within the context of psychology as a whole. If you read material that is linked with, but not directly relevant to, the module itself, you will find that your understanding of psychology as a whole topic will improve, as will your sense of integration. You will also find that your understanding of all the other modules will improve.

✎ Checklist

Check you've understood the key points covered in this chapter by seeing if you can answer the following questions:

✔ Why is university learning active rather than passive?

✔ What does 'reading for a degree' mean?

✔ And why is reading important?

✔ What is the difference between contact time and non-contact time?

✔ What should you do with the notes you've made during lectures once the lecture has finished?

✔ When is it acceptable to ask your tutor questions?

✔ Where can you find lecture notes if you missed the lecture?

✔ What are the pros and cons of the different types of handout?

✔ And why should you always add to them?

✔ What should you do before small group teaching sessions?

Chapter 4

Communication and learning with others

While you're at university the last thing you should try to do is to cope by yourself, without looking for support from others, and from teaching and learning materials that are available to you. There is a lot of information out there, and there are numerous resources provided to help you find your way.

In this chapter, we'll focus on two general types of activity that you should engage with—those that are delivered and carried out electronically (online), and those that are delivered and carried out in other ways—that is, 'offline'. We will also consider activities that you can undertake independently (as an individual), and those that should be undertaken with others. Much of the guidance given in this chapter focuses on the general theme of finding information—helping you to track down what's likely to be most helpful to you from all the different information sources that are out there.

Online learning as an individual: virtual learning environments

All universities have internet-based provision in place to help you access information relevant to your course. However, the degree to which this happens varies from institution to institution. The standard method is to provide a virtual learning environment (or VLE) that contains information about lectures, assignments and all course information. If you use your university's VLE regularly, you will find that you are always up to date with the latest information.

Types of VLE

There are some major players in the VLE area that have been taken up across the country, predominantly Blackboard and Moodle. Some universities may have systems developed by in-house technicians that are based on older VLEs such as WebCT (for example *SunSpace* at Sunderland). But many have, or are in the process of, moving over to a newer

VLE (such as Blackboard or Moodle) which are easier to use and have more features. These VLEs can be altered to fit the needs of the individual universities, and the in-house technicians will be in charge of it. Chances are the VLE where you are studying will be called something other than Blackboard or Moodle, for example Hull has *Portal* and York has *Yorkshare* (both versions of Blackboard).

Whichever VLE your university uses, you will become very familiar with it over the course of your years with that university, and you can expect certain things to be provided for you. A VLE makes the whole process of finding information at university far easier, as everything is literally at your fingertips.

What you will find on a VLE

- Information about modules and assignments:
  - Details of what your modules will cover, and what assignments will be about, usually in a folder labelled with the name and code of the module
  - Timetables and lists of 'learning outcomes' that you should have achieved at the end of the course
  - Along with this you will find out about your independent learning requirements are for your courses: what we expect you to do (in terms of independent studying).
- Reading lists:
  - You should be able to access a list of materials you should be reading. This may be split into 'essential', 'recommended' and 'suggested' lists. Start with the 'essential' reading and work your way through the 'recommended' and then onto the 'suggested' reading lists; this hierarchy indicates the relative importance of the individual items and, hence, the order you'd be best to tackle them in. While you may want to buy copies of the key texts, nobody expects you to buy all the items on the reading list; this is what the library is for.
  - You may find that some items in the library are not available. However, if the item you're looking for is a textbook, you don't necessarily have to wait until it's returned. There are plenty of textbooks out there on the same topics; you've only been recommended a particular one because the lecturer liked it. Other books on the same topic will have very similar information in them, so just use one of those. It's probably best to use the more recent editions of books though: if you find a book that's looking rather old and faded, it's probably not a good idea to use the information in it, as most likely it is out of date. (If you're uncertain, always check the copyright page at the front of the book. This will tell you the year of publication, and will give you a sense of how up-to-date (or otherwise) a particular edition is.)
- Announcements from lecturers regarding your modules:
  - Your university will probably use various facilities within its VLE to provide announcements to the students. These facilities can include pop-up information panels, or highlighted information on your home screen; alternatively, your

institution may post colourful messages on the weekly list for your module. Which-ever format is used, the VLE will be the primary vehicle for highlighting any impor-tant changes. These changes may include:

- Changes to lecture/seminar locations
- Any lecture or seminar cancellations
- Hints about assignments
- Important things to bring to seminars/lab classes
- Information about assignments
  - For example any changes in deadlines and when marks are available

  – Many universities are implementing systems to contact students via text-message or email when a lecture is cancelled. However, these are still very much in their infancy and you may still find that the piece of paper waiting for you on the door of the lecture is all you are given. Frustrating as this may be, use the time to get some directed or independent study done in the library so that your time is not wasted in the café or pub (unless you're discussing work over those coffees and pints that is)!

- Lecture notes and PowerPoint slides:
  – These may be uploaded before or after the lecture/seminar, depending on when the lecturer is able to do so
  – Occasionally you may find that some lecturers wait until the end of the module to upload material rather than doing it on a weekly basis. This is because they want to make sure you attend their lectures/seminars. However, the typical requirement is that staff should upload material weekly.
- Seminar information and materials:
  – Information such as articles to read prior to attending, or directions to particular information that will be needed in the seminar itself
  – It is important that you do these things prior to actually attending the seminar as the session itself will usually be to discuss what you have read—something that is difficult if only two people out of a larger group have done the reading.

Online learning with others: blogs and wikis

Blogs and wikis are methods of communicating and collaborating with other individu-als. They are both web-based concepts and are run and maintained by the individuals who use them, without any outside interference. If you set up a blog or a wiki then only you and the individuals you choose to share it with can comment on the information on it. Anyone will be able to read it, but they'll only be able to *edit* (make comments) with your permission.

Creating a blog or a wiki is definitely one for the more technically minded individuals. If you are still finding computers and the internet a little daunting then please feel free to skip this section and read the rest of the chapter.

Blogs

A blog is simply a website, or part of a website, maintained by the user, where you can write about your thoughts, have discussions and upload material. Most blogs are text-based and can be used academically for having detailed discussions about aspects of a course or the literature. They can be created by individuals, or existing ones can be utilized for a particular purpose.

We discuss study groups, and other revision tips, in Chapter 16.

A method of using blogs to help with your studies is linked with the idea of forming study groups. You can discuss assignments, specific reading material, or indeed any manner of things related to your course in a blog. It's a bit like having an instant message conversation with your entire group, in detail, while having constant access to the entire blog available so you can see what has already been said.

Wikis

A wiki is essentially a web-based document-editing facility. Wikis of varying format are on the internet, and all serve the same purpose—to allow you to access and edit documents with a group when you are all in multiple locations. Wikis are different from blogs in that you can only access what you have permission to see, they're not open-viewing like blogs are. If you want someone to be able to access material, you need to share it with them. Some of the more popular ones are GoogleDocs™ and Skydrive™, both of which have blog options built into them so you can write notes to people working on the documents when you have time. Dropbox™, while not being strictly a wiki, is a facility whereby you can share access with designated people to a folder of materials online. Of course, a word document could serve as the internal *blog* here so that a running commentary of your discussion is available; this is rather more prone to *editing* by individuals, however, and may not be the preferred choice.

A wiki is useful for group assignments as you can upload a document, give your group access, and everyone can work on the document in their own time instead of trying to get into university for meetings with the group. This method is particularly useful for those with families or with jobs which take up a lot of their time. Internet-based access is available around the clock, so group work can realistically be fitted in around life, rather than the other way around.

All these are excellent facilities which make working in groups over distances a lot easier. In universities today the norm is to have students from across the globe working and learning together in one place. However, working together over vacation periods is rather more difficult when your group is scattered across the UK or the rest of the world. Wikis and Dropbox™ can aid this and make it considerably easier.

Online learning with others: Facebook™ and Twitter™

This chapter would not be complete without mentioning Facebook™ or Twitter™. Most students will use one or both of these and many universities are taking advantage of this. These social communication tools were not designed as learning platforms, but they were designed as communication and contact facilitation platforms, meaning that learning can occur if they are used in the right way.

Many universities will have their own *group* on Facebook™, membership of which is restricted to university members. These groups are maintained by academic and technical staff within the university, who are able to post announcements about everything from assignment information and announcements of results availability to notices about lecture cancellations and date changes. You will also find interesting information about conferences and student meetings being posted, so you can feel really involved with your course and your university. Rather than distracting you from your studies, Facebook™ if used in the right way, can actually aid them and help you be on top of all the latest information. The same people who maintain the Facebook™ groups will keep the Twitter™ feed going, typically with the same information. In this way, information is directed at the majority of students who are at university.

If you're reading this and thinking that you don't use either, so how will you get this information, don't worry. All the information posted on Facebook™ or Twitter™ will probably be posted on the VLE as well. Universities are increasingly reliant on technology to communicate with students, but this is something that you will have to embrace rather than shy away from. If you're quite shy of technology it might be worth seeing if there are any short courses and tutorials where you are studying so that you can make the most of the resources available to you throughout your degree.

Online learning with others: discussion boards

Many VLEs have discussion boards where you can ask other students and lecturers question. Any distance learning courses use them a lot; they allow everyone to interact far more than they would be able to otherwise. Discussion boards are fairly similar to blogs, except that they are the domain of the university, so anyone with access to your module on the VLE can access and comment on them. You will find that some lecturers monitor them, providing answers to questions and removing unsuitable content.

Discussion boards generally work by someone posting a question and then other people answering the question (see Figure 4.1). This creates what is known as a 'thread'. You can search through existing threads to see if your question has already been asked, and answered. As you go through your studies, and as you get more confident in your abilities and knowledge, you will find it easier to actually provide answers rather than asking the questions. They are a great way of finding out information about assignments, many of you will get stuck on what to include in your early assignments in particular. Posting a question on a discussion board means other students and the staff involved with the assignment can look and you can get answers to your questions very quickly, resolving any confusion. Of course, this is only going to work if you use it early on, rather than waiting until the last minute to do your assignments which, as we've already covered in Chapter 3, is not a good approach to university work.

You can access the discussion boards via your VLE at any time of day, so you can post a question at any time. Of course this then means that you may have to wait for a response as there is no guarantee that others will be online at the same time as you. However, they are very useful means of finding out information and discussing the more difficult concepts on your course.

Lecturers will sometimes be involved, depending on the institution, and they will check every few days to see if there is anything they need to help with. You will find that announcements may also be posted in the discussion boards, as well as on the VLE and noticeboards.

Offline learning and sharing with others

There are going to be times when you don't want to deal with a faceless computer and the internet, and you feel you need to work with another human being directly. This is an equally important part of your degree, as communicating and cooperating with different people are important skills to learn. There are two avenues, and I've presented them in order of priority in terms of which avenue to follow first: other students are a mine of information, so they should never be underestimated. When this avenue fails to help, lecturers and tutors are automatically your next contact point.

Other students

Your fellow students should be your first port of call for all questions you might have. It is easy to miss little bits of information when so much knowledge is being thrown your way; you will find that other students know the bits of information you don't, or they will have information about where you can get it. You can ask your fellow students wherever you find them; in class, the cafeteria and the library. You can also find them on the discussion boards and the VLE.

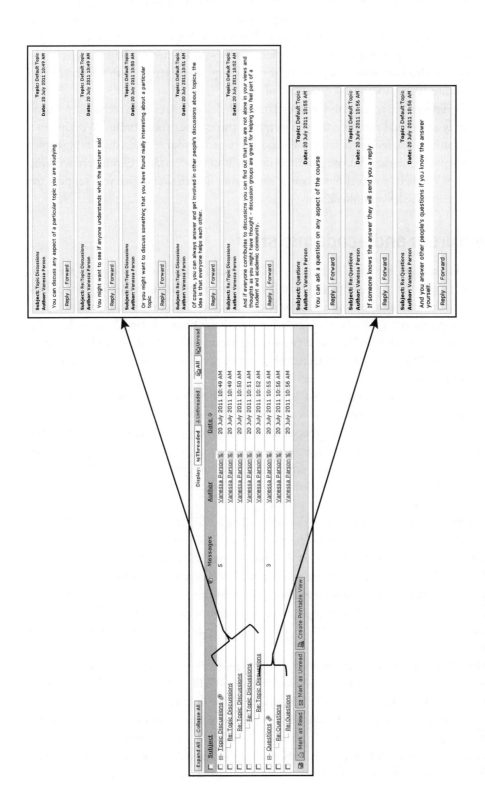

Figure 4.1: Example of a discussion board.

After you have got comfortable at university and have met a fair number of your fellow students you can set up study groups. Study groups are sometimes seen as a bit 'geeky', but they are actually very effective. The idea is that you form a group to do the directed and independent study that has been set by your lecturers. The group then provides you with an academic support network and a group of people with whom you can discuss difficult topics and ask questions of.

Study groups are covered in Chapter 16, which discusses revision techniques. However, they are a good resource for you to utilize throughout your studies. Working in a group can help you feel more integrated and interested in your studies; discussing topics can help you highlight what you definitely do, and don't understand. Ultimately, working in groups can help you feel more confident in your abilities, and give you support for what you may be less confident with.

Lecturers and academic staff

As mentioned in Chapter 3, your lecturers are typically available for a limited period of time per week, so take advantage of that. If you have questions during lecture or seminar time, ask them then, when you are in the room with them. Lecturers will always want to help you get the most out of your degree, but they won't know specifically what help you might need if you don't tell them. If you're stuck or unsure then ask, either in person or via email. (Be mindful that most lecturers get many emails each day, so it's unreasonable to expect an instantaneous response!)

All lecturers have what are called 'office hours'. These will be displayed clearly in the department, in introductory lectures of modules and/or on office doors. There is a common myth among students that office hours are when they *can't* be disturbed. In fact, the opposite is true: office hours are the times when they *are* free to answer any questions or queries you might have—it is this time where they can guarantee they will be in their offices and are available for you to ask questions. You can turn up on the day or you can book an appointment with them in advance.

Regardless of the types of resource employed on a VLE, the easiest way to get in touch with lecturers outside of their designated contact time (their office hours) is to email them directly. Many will interact on discussion boards, contribute to wikis or use the VLE messaging systems, but the vast majority of lecturers will be simply too busy to do this on a regular basis. If you want to get a quick answer, send an email and your lecturer will reply as soon as they can. If you don't get a response by the next office hour, turn up and try again. Most lecturers will respond as quickly as they have time however, so be patient.

Emails for university staff are really easy to find: every psychology department will have its own section of the main website. Here you will find a staff list for the department, and all your lecturers' contact details should be up there.

Another way of finding out email addresses is to refer to the individual module guides for the subjects you're studying. Every module will have a guide, written by whoever is in charge of the module that year. This guide will almost certainly include the contact details for everyone involved for this course, amongst other things.

Personal tutors

You will all have a personal tutor assigned to you, a member of the lecturing staff who will be your first port of call throughout you degree if there are any problems or issues. You will be assigned a personal tutor at the start of your studies and will be scheduled to meet with them a couple of times a year (either through formal timetable slots or via an email from your personal tutor) so they can check on how you're getting on; but you can contact them at any time if you need to discuss anything with them. If you have any unexpected personal circumstances, or you are struggling for any reason with any aspect of your course, you should go and see your personal tutor as soon as you can, they will be able to minimize any impact on your studies.

....

✎ Checklist

Check you've understood the key points covered in this chapter by seeing if you can answer the following questions:

✔ Do you know which VLE your department uses?

✔ Have you visited your VLE and explored what you can access on it?

✔ Do you know how to work as a group using the internet?

✔ If you are on Facebook™ or twitter™, have you found the *group/feed* and signed up?

✔ Do you know where to find the online discussion boards and have you tried using them?

✔ Do you know which of your friends is most likely to have the answers about your course?

✔ Have you formed a study group yet?

✔ Do you know the email addresses of your personal tutor and lecturers?

✔ Do you know when your personal tutor and lecturers have their office hours? And do you know how to find out?

Chapter 5

Before and after assessments: guidelines, criteria and feedback

The transition from school or college to university is a big change in many ways. In addition to changes in lifestyle and teaching, there are differences in expectations to deal with as well. These changes in expectation concern what lecturers are looking for in assignments, and what it is that students are expecting to be assessed on.

Once they have been assessed, students frequently put their work to one side and leave it alone, thinking that it's done and nothing more can be gained from it. This is not the case, we spend time telling you how to improve—this is called feedback. Reading it carefully can help you work out how to do much better next time.

Before your assessment is due—finding out what to do

There is much confusion among students about what lecturers are actually looking for in assignments. While some of it may be obvious, there are many occasions where the feedback and marks don't tally with what students were expecting. This confusion is shared by lecturers, who feel that it should be obvious what is being asked for in assignments, mainly as they're generally fairly clear in the assignment guidelines provided with each individual assessment, sometimes in the form of a marking guide, and usually stated explicitly in the module guides. These guidelines tell you what you need to think about when doing your assessments, they tell you what criteria your lecturers are going to be using to mark you work and they tell you what are the most important things to think about when you're doing your assignment. It is important to read these guidelines as without them you're pretty much flying blind in your assessment, relying on what you think rather than what the lecturers are telling you. Surprisingly for many, these do not match, as you'll see a little later in this chapter.

So how do these misunderstandings arise? Assignment guidelines tend to end up under a pile of books while students are writing essays; just as it is very easy to stray off the central theme of an essay and get a bit lost, it is equally easy to forget about particular things lecturers might be looking for. Students usually expect certain things—such as content—to be assessed. By contrast, lecturers rate understanding as being far more important (Norton, 1990).

➽ For tips on writing essays, see Chapter 10.

This chapter will hopefully demystify assessment criteria and help you understand the most important aspects of university assessments. It will also help you learn where to find the criteria for each assignment you do.

What are assessment criteria?

Assessment criteria are a set of guidelines used by lecturers to mark your work. They are usually written by the lecturers themselves, although sometimes they are set by the department or, in the case of lab reports, the British Psychological Society and the American Psychological Association. There are good reasons why lecturers use assessment criteria:

1 We need to work out what level of achievement your piece of work represents in relation to degree classifications. All work is marked to degree classifications while at university, so the days of getting As, Bs, and so on is long gone. Generally, if you start your degree getting percentages in the 50s, you're doing well. (We cover this further at another point.)

2 We need to give you feedback on how well you've done in a particular assignment—both what you've done well, and the aspects of the assignment where you need to look to improve.

3 Next, we need to give you feedback on how to go up a grade in your next assignment. For example, if you get percentages in the 50s, the comments you get are aimed at helping you get percentages in the 60s, a 2-1 in terms of degree classification.

4 Finally, we need all of this to help us decide if you are able to progress to the next year of study. It might be straightforward enough to get a basic level of marks to enable you to progress to the next year of your course, and most students become aware fairly quickly that they need only 40% overall during their first year to enable them to progress to the second year. However, what many students don't realize is that progression from year 2 to 3 is *also* conditional on attaining particular grades. Indeed, the passing of some courses is a prerequisite for getting into the final year of your studies. For example, many psychology departments have a research methods and statistics course in year 2 that you have to pass in order to be officially 'capable' of doing the final year. You cannot complete your research project/dissertation if you have not done this course for example. If you don't pass then your progression to the final year of your studies is on hold until you have passed this one module. While this is absolutely not a problem for the vast majority of students, a few don't do enough work during year 2, but instead assume they'll make up for it in year 3. This

is risky: if you do badly in year 2 (less than 40% in many modules, for example) then your department has every right to make you repeat the year, or in extreme cases remove you from the course altogether. Neither option is good, for either you or your bank balance.

Assessment criteria are designed to help you do the best that you can, giving you all the information you need to get the best marks possible in each of your assignments.

Different types of criteria

Standard criteria

These are the criteria which are important in every essay and lab report you do while at university. These 'standard' or 'core' criteria can be found in Table 5.1 (see Exercise 5.1).

....

Exercise 5.1

This exercise is designed to help you really get to grips with the important criteria given in Table 5.1. Fill in the right hand column of the table with what you think the criteria actually mean—in other words, what you are actually being asked to do. For the answers, see 'Answers to exercises' at the end of the book.

....

TABLE 5.1 What do the standard criteria mean?

Standard criterion	What it means
Answering the question	
Structure	
Evidence of understanding	
A clear argument	
Use of evidence	
Critical thinking	
Appropriate use of language and writing style	

Adapted from Elander et al. (2006).

Specialist criteria

These are the criteria which are important for particular pieces of work. For example, a particular lab report may put more weighting on the marks for the method and results sections, whereas another lab report may put more weighting on the introduction and discussion.

Example 5.1: Specialist criteria for an essay on social influence

- Focus on the methods and ethics of the studies.
- Try to think objectively about whether the methods are actually shocking when taken out of context of the results.
- In terms of the ethics, consider whether the results justify the methods used to get them: do the ends justify the means?

Many students don't know where to find specific criteria, but they are very easy to get hold of, and are often less confusing than the title makes them sound. In the example above, the lecturer is trying to make the students think objectively about a subject which is typically considered in a subjective manner and is frequently vilified in terms of ethical procedures. The aim is clearly to remain focused on what the researchers actually did and not go off on an ethical 'rant'. Any student who does produce an ethical *rant* will find they will lose marks, because the guidelines specifically asked for objectivity—which always leads to more reasoned conclusions than any subjective analysis.

So, where do you find all these different types of criteria?

- The assignment itself: the specialist criteria for each of your assignments will probably be found on the assignment guidelines themselves, be they in handout form or verbal form direct from your lecturer.

- Your lecturer or tutor: make sure you write down any hints your lecturer gives you. They will be specifically looking for some things and they will always tell you what those are.

- Virtual learning environment (VLE): all assignment guidelines are put up on the departmental VLE, so anything you might have missed in the lecture will be there in the space allocated for the module the assessment is for. Each module space on the VLE will have an electronic copy of the module guide and all the details you need for your assignments, plus lots of announcements from lecturers with any last-minute hints.

⮕ We discuss VLEs in more detail in Chapter 4.

- Ask: if you don't remember anything being said in the lecture and can't find anything uploaded onto the VLE, go and find your lecturer or tutor: ask them what they are specifically looking for in the assignment; they will be happy to tell you.

Which criteria are the most important?

Many of you may have found that you produced a piece of work, which was in line with standard guidelines, but which was not marked as highly as you might have liked, and you can't work out why this might be the case. Usually, the reason is that lecturers and students have very different ideas of what is more or less important in assignments. Exercise 5.2 will help you find out what you consider to be important in essays, and then you can see how lecturers rate the same items. For the answers, which come from data collected by Norton et al. (2002), see 'Answers to exercises' at the end of the book.

....

Exercise 5.2

Rank each of the criteria shown in Table 5.2 from 1 to 9 (1 being the most important and 9 being the least important aspect).

....

TABLE 5.2 Relative importance of standard criteria

Answering the question	Structure	A clear argument
Use of evidence	Evidence of understanding	Critical thinking
Referencing	Spelling	Appropriate use of language and writing style

Why can't I get hold of a standard set of guidelines?

The problem with standardized guidelines is that they leave no room for variation between different pieces of assessment. There are a lot of different subjects within psychology, more so than most other subjects. This means that there are many different requirements for each area within psychology: for example, social psychology has fairly obvious got different requirements than biological psychology. An assessment in social psychology will be looking for more discussion and argument within essays, whereas there will be far more emphasis on factual information within biological psychology. In addition, there are different types of assessment. A laboratory report will not assess the same things as an essay or a presentation, yet all are an important part of your university assessment.

➠ We discuss lab reports in Chapter 11, essays in Chapter 10, and presentations in Chapter 14.

Consequently, it is simply not possible to get a standardized set of criteria, because every piece of work demands something slightly different. Instead, the simplest achievable criteria will combine the standard and specialist criteria detailed above. As long as you follow the standard criteria for all assignments, and incorporate the specialist criteria for each individual assignment, then you will match the assignment guidelines and stand a good chance of getting a decent grade in your assessment.

Applying assessment criteria to your own work

There are a number of tools you can use to improve the focus within your work and help you apply assessment criteria successfully. To start with, much of this book is specifically targeted at your assignments and what you need to comply with both standard and specific criteria. This book contains a considerable amount of relevant material for different types of assignment and a careful reading of these chapters will help enormously with all your assignments.

Tips for applying assessment criteria:

- Make sure you find out the specialist criteria for the particular assignment you are completing.

- Keep a list of the standard and specialist criteria handy when you're writing your assignment, and keep referring to it.

  - Don't get distracted and misplace your focus in the assignments.

- Re-read your essay or lab report at least 12–24 hours after you've 'finished' writing it.

  - Always a good tip whatever you're trying to improve: re-reading after a period of time helps you see exactly what needs improving, rather than reading what you 'think' you've written.

  - You need to make sure you finish your assignment a few days before the deadline for this to be an effective tip so many of you will have to read Chapter 2 on time management, beforehand!

- If you can stand it, ask a friend who is doing the same assignment to read it for you—and offer to do the same for them. A fresh set of eyes and opinions are always helpful, and they can frequently pick up things you haven't noticed.

What not to do

A lot of books may suggest you ask your lecturer to look over your work before you hand it in. This is something that is probably not the best idea any more. There are likely to be between 100 and 600 students in a year group at any university, and no lecturer is going to want to read all those assignments twice. They will, however, answer your questions and concerns so make sure you email them as soon as you have a question. If you have a genuine concern about your assignment, by all means go and see your tutor or lecturer in their office hours, but unless this is the case, stick to emailing your questions rather than your assignment itself.

After the assignment is returned—this thing called feedback

Most of you will know what feedback is: it is information provided to you on work you've done that will help you improve your work in the future. Feedback can be obtained in various contexts: from your tutor or lecturer directly, in seminars or practical sessions, on returned written assignments or as part of generic feedback given to an entire cohort of students.

- Feedback on returned written work

  - All written work you produce while at university will be returned to you with a multitude of comments written on it. Your tutors and lecturers have spent many painstaking hours writing these comments to help you improve your work, which makes it fairly frustrating when students make the same mistakes over and over again: it implies they haven't read our comments and that we've therefore wasted our time. It is your responsibility to read the comments provided to you and learn from what you are being told.

- It is important to view feedback in a constructive manner. After all, we all learn from our mistakes (so we are often told). As such, those essays that are perhaps not the best in the world are a goldmine of useful guidance, which you can use to improve future assignments. But you need to make the time to read the feedback to get any value from it.

- If you are in any doubt about comments on your work, or cannot read your lecturer's writing, you should arrange a session with them.

• Feedback in seminars or practical sessions

- During seminars and practical sessions you will have access to lecturers and/or tutors and academic assistants. These teaching sessions are interactive and require work from you plus feedback from staff members. Such sessions provide feedback that is directed and immediate, so you should take full advantage of them. The feedback you'll receive during these sessions will be tailored to specific aspects of the course and your work, and be structured around exactly what you are doing in the session. You will also find that staff teaching the session will be able to give you feedback about other aspects of your course as well. However, academic staff will only be able to help if they are involved with other aspects of the course.

- The only way to get the benefit of this type of feedback is to attend practical sessions and seminars. It may seem obvious to attend taught sessions, but many students skip things which aren't lectures. Actually, you get more benefit from these small group teaching sessions, so it is doubly important to attend them.

• Generic feedback

➠ We discuss VLEs in Chapter 4.

- Sometimes lecturers or tutors will provide generic feedback on your assessments and exams. This will either be a Word document posted on your VLE or verbally in your lectures.

- Generic feedback is simply information on how a group as a whole has performed on a piece of work and will usually comprise a list of things done well overall and, more importantly, a list of things that didn't get done quite so well overall. It is important to note that generic feedback relates to everyone who did the assignment or exam: it's not directed at any one student.

- Reading generic feedback can actually be quite motivating as you often find that you did better in relation to the group than you thought. Of course, if your mark is the other end of the scale, then you might feel as though the comments are targeted at you; in this instance please remember that this simply means you are not alone in making the mistakes you did, and lots of people now have to make the same corrections.

- Individual tutor/lecturer feedback
  - This is the least common format in most universities for getting feedback. You'll only get direct, one-on-one feedback if you make an appointment with you tutor or lecturer to discuss your work.
  - Some universities hold individual feedback sessions as a matter of course and they are formally encouraged. If you are one of the lucky ones who gets this then make the most of it: tailored feedback like this is incredibly valuable to your learning.
  - Most universities, however, offer individual feedback as an option. All lecturers and tutors are willing to help students individually, but the onus is on you, the student, to ask for this help. Email your tutor or set up a time to speak to them and you will get this valuable form of feedback.

Using feedback to improve your work

It is a common complaint up and down the country that students don't read their feedback. Lecturers and tutors can often be left wondering why they spend so much time writing detailed comments on student work only to find the subsequent piece of work contains the same errors because their earlier comments haven't been read.

The best way to use feedback to improve your work is to go through your assignments when you get them back after being marked. There are a number of steps you can take to help utilize the comments most effectively to improve future work.

1 Go and see the person who marked your essay (or your tutor if the marker is not available or you don't know who they are) and go through it with them. Discuss where you went wrong, how you could improve it and what steps you might take to improve your next piece of work.

- It's quite easy at this point to get upset if your perceptions and those of the marker/your tutor differ wildly in terms of your performance. It's important to not get upset, however. Try to bear in mind that, while you may have performed brilliantly pre-university, studying at university is a very different experience with a whole new set of requirements that you're still learning. Any mismatches in perceptions can be sorted out early on if you are prepared to work at learning what the new requirements are rather than carrying on doing what you've always done.

2 Find your original essay and re-write it, taking into account the comments which the person marking your work has made.

3 Ask a friend to have a look at this new version.

- Get them to compare the two essays and give you feedback on how much they think you've improved it.
- You can offer to do the same for them.

4 Ask your tutor to read this new and improved piece of work; ask them what mark it would have obtained.

- Hopefully you will have improved your level of writing sufficiently that the piece of work is of a higher standard. Bear in mind your mark is not going to change from the original; this is merely an exercise to make sure you are on the right lines for your next piece of work.

5 Make a list of mistakes you seem to keep making and keep it handy for your next assignment.

- That way you will hopefully not make the same mistakes again.

....

Activity 5.1: Giving essay feedback

Pick one of your recent essays and imagine it was written by a friend. If you've not written any university essays yet, try writing one on a topic you enjoyed in a lecture. What feedback would you give them and how would you explain how it could be improved?

....

....

✎ Checklist

Check you've understood the key points covered in this chapter by seeing if you can answer the following questions:

✔ What are assessment criteria?

✔ What are the standard criteria relevant to every assignment?

✔ What are specialist criteria?

✔ Where can you find the specialist criteria?

✔ Which criteria are more important in your assignments?

✔ How can you apply assessment criteria to your work?

✔ What types of feedback are there?

✔ Where can you get feedback?

✔ How can you use feedback to improve your work?

....

📖 References

Elander, J., Harrington, K., Norton, L., Robinson, H. & Reddy, P. (2006). Complex skills and academic writing: a review of evidence about the types of learning required to meet core assessment criteria. *Assessment & Evaluation in Higher Education*, 31(1), 71–90.

Norton, L. (1990). Essay writing: what really counts? *Higher Education*, 20(4), 411–442.

Norton, L., Clifford, R., Hopkins, L., Toner, I. & Norton, J.C.W. (2002). Helping psychology students write better essays. *Psychology Learning and Teaching*, 2(2), 116–126.

Chapter 6

Sources of information and their uses

There are many different types of resource available to you when you're writing your assignments; you will use some types more than others. Lecturers and tutors will refer to appropriate sources of information, but what actually counts as an *appropriate* source of information to use in your work might not always be clear. This chapter is designed to help you learn how to filter out quality source materials from less useful materials. All resources are not created equal, and this chapter will help you understand how each type is useful, and the pitfalls you should be aware of.

Within this chapter we will consider the different types of appropriate sources of information (appropriate evidence)—that is, the kind of material that it is appropriate to refer to, to give credence to an argument you are presenting. What constitutes 'appropriate evidence' can vary between subjects. However, there are some general rules you can follow to ensure you have good information, and some good evidence to discuss, in your assignments.

There is a huge amount of information available to you during your studies and we'll go through the main ones here so you know what to look for when you're trying to establish whether or not a source is going to be useful to you. There are some clear guidelines which you can follow, but they vary slightly for each type of information source; we'll cover books, journals and the Internet here, as these are the main sources of information you will be using during your studies.

There is a section towards the end of the chapter which deals with evaluating the content of the sources of information and how you can use in your assignments all the information you've found.

⏭ We find out more about essay-writing and writing lab reports—two key types of assignment—in Chapters 10 and 11, respectively.

What to look for in a textbook

Most of you will be very familiar with reading books; you've encountered more than a few (of all varieties) throughout the course of your scholastic career so far. In fact, most of you will be using textbooks as your main resource for essays and lab reports during your first year. There are several mistakes students make when using textbooks, however. While most psychology textbooks will be great, and many general texts will contain everything you need to know during your first year of studies, not all textbooks will be equally suitable or relevant to your studies. There are several things to consider when choosing whether to use a book you've found. Most books you come across in the library are going to be relatively up to date and suitable for use, but it's helpful to consider the following tips in any case.

1. Don't use A level textbooks!

During the first year a common mistake made by students is to use the A level textbooks they already have. So why is this a mistake? Because A level textbooks are great for A level, but they're not remotely detailed enough for degree level work. To give you some idea, the topics in an A2 (Year 13) textbook each have an entire book dedicated to them for first year university studies—so one chapter is definitely not going to be enough to give you sufficient detail in your assignments: you will invariably need use other textbooks to get higher marks. You won't get anything more than basic marks on essays and lab reports if you use just A level books so look at your reading list for approved textbooks. As you all obviously want to do the best you can, use your A level textbooks as forms of reference only (perhaps just to refresh your memory at the start of your degree), not as core sources of information for your studies.

2. Is the book up to date?

You can tell this by looking at the back of one of the first pages of the book—the so-called copyright page. This contains all the publication information you need to assess whether the book is up to date. The date of publication (and of any reprints) will be there. Also, if the book is a new edition (second or third edition, for example) the copyright page will often list the year of publication of all editions, including the current one (see Figure 6.1). Remember that a reprint is not the same as a new edition: a reprint is literally another printing of a current edition, without any content changes. A new edition is a revised edition, in which content changes will have been made to bring the book up to date. You will probably find that most textbooks you encounter are new editions, as completely new first editions are published relatively rarely.

Anything written in the twenty-first century will be fine and can be considered up to date. However, books that were written in the twentieth century may be out of date: including those written in the 1990s. There is a good reason for stating this: books contain information from research, which is continually being carried out and is continually updating what we know in psychology. On top of this it can sometimes take years for a book to be published, meaning that any information it contains is already a few years older than the date of publication. So, the more recent the book, the more likely it is that the information is up to date.

As a subject, psychology is defined by other people's ideas—ideas that are continually changing as we learn more about how people behave. If you use out of date information in your assignment then you could run the risk of writing something that is no longer accepted as accurate in the academic community (which includes your lecturers and tutors who are marking your work).

OXFORD
UNIVERSITY PRESS

Great Clarendon Street, Oxford OX2 6DP

Oxford University Press is a department of the University of Oxford.
It furthers the University's objective of excellence in research, scholarship,
and education by publishing worldwide in

Oxford New York

Auckland Cape Town Dar es Salaam Hong Kong Karachi
Kuala Lumpur Madrid Melbourne Mexico City Nairobi
New Delhi Shanghai Taipei Toronto

With offices in

Argentina Austria Brazil Chile Czech Republic France Greece
Guatemala Hungary Italy Japan Poland Portugal Singapore
South Korea Switzerland Thailand Turkey Ukraine Vietnam

Oxford is a registered trade mark of Oxford University Press
in the UK and in certain other countries

Published in the United States
by Oxford University Press Inc., New York

© Graham Hole and Victoria Bourne, 2010

The moral rights of the authors have been asserted
Database right Oxford University Press (maker)

First published 2010

British Library Cataloguing in Publication Data

Data available

Library of Congress Cataloging in Publication Data

Data available

Typeset by MPS Limited, A Macmillan Company
Printed in Great Britain by
CPI Antony Rowe, Chippenham, Wiltshire

ISBN 978-0-19-923570-4

1 3 5 7 9 10 8 6 4 2

Where the book was published

The copyright holder, and the year in which this book was published

Date of first publication is the same as the date above - which means this particular book is a first edition

Figure 6.1: Example of a copyright page. Copyright pages are particular to individual publishers, and will vary from the example shown here.

3. Does the book use secondary sources or is it a primary source?

Primary and secondary sources are explained in more detail in Chapter 13. Briefly, a primary source is one written by a researcher, which describes their own original research; a secondary source is written by someone other than the original researcher, and simply reports what the original researcher found—in other words, it relies on other peoples' research to draw conclusions.

There are pros and cons to using both types of information source: a book containing the authors' ideas has a great deal of detail about a specific topic, but can be prone to bias as it may be reflecting just one viewpoint. By contrast, a textbook referring to multiple primary sources provides a balanced viewpoint across an entire topic, but at the expense of a little bit of depth. Single author, primary source books are less common, but can be extremely useful in the same manner that journal articles are: high depth and detail of information.

At the back of the textbooks you will find an index, naturally, but just preceding that should be a list of references for the entire textbook (sometimes you find these at the end of each book chapter). This reference list will provide full source information for everything cited in the textbook, just like you are shown in Chapter 13. The idea with this is that you can go and find the original sources if you want to learn more about that particular study in depth.

4. Is the book a popular book, a textbook or an academic, scholarly book?

There are several types of book, and you'll encounter all of them during the course of your studies. You will all recognize textbooks, such as the ones on your reading lists or those lining the shelves of the psychology section of the library, very easily by now and these will likely be your main source of information during the first year of your studies. Older textbooks were written fairly formally, but now they are written more informally so that they are more accessible to students. Do not be fooled into thinking this is an appropriate style of writing for your assignments however; the more conversational style of some textbooks is not appropriate for formal academic assignments so make sure you don't emulate the writing style of textbooks in your own academic writing. For example, in this book I use the words 'I' and 'you' frequently, but you cannot use these in your academic work because it's informal and conversational.

We discuss the topic of writing style in more detail in Chapter 9.

Academic or scholarly books contain a lot of highly complex and detailed information. They are usually aimed at academics, so they're a little more difficult to read than regular textbooks. You should expect to start using these in the second year of your studies, and all postgraduate students should use these as a large part of their reading during their studies/research. Scholarly books are usually collections of research by several authors (or just one), in a great deal of detail, and will use many different sources for their information, although their primary source of information is original journal articles. For example, *Visual attention* by Wright (1998) is a collection of chapters on the intricacies of visual attention. It's not a light, easy read, but it contains detailed and specific information distilled from many journal articles on the different aspects of the subject of visual attention, each chapter having a different focus.

More popular books are usually those which are a little easier to read and have a more relaxed writing style. These types of books tend to fall into two categories—the light-hearted but detailed approach to specific subjects, and the first person experiences of the authors themselves. An example of the first category is *Why zebras don't get ulcers* by Sapolsky (1994). This is a fairly detailed and humorous approach to the effects of stress and how we cope with it; it is an easy read but manages to convey some extremely complex points in a very accessible manner. An example of the second variety of popular book is *The jigsaw man* by Paul Brittan (1998), a detailed account of his own clinical and forensic case studies over the years, including the case of Jamie Bulger in the early 1990s. This is an easy and really interesting read; it is a primary source of Brittan's own experiences, containing almost no psychological theory and minimal external sources of information.

More popular, less academic, books such as these may contain less depth of information. As a result—and while still useful to your studies—they are more helpful when trying to grasp the basics of a topic rather than when trying to learn the precise details of a subject.

For intricate details of any subject you need to use academic textbooks. Make sure you don't make the mistake of just using the less academic popular books. The point being made here is that you should always use academic books when writing essays and assignments, but the less academic popular books are good for aiding understanding and backing up the academic texts.

5. Is the reference list substantial?

This tip really refers to textbooks, both large and small: and what matters is the relative rather than absolute number of references. You would expect a smaller textbook to have smaller reference list than a larger one, simply because there is less content. If there is a substantial reference list relative to the size of the book then you can be sure that the book is well researched and it isn't likely to be biased towards one particular standpoint.

All decent textbooks will have a big reference list, which typically covers several pages: this can be found next to the index at the back of the book. Some textbooks split the references between the chapters, in which case look at the end of each chapter. If the textbook has only a few references, less than a page, or they are missing altogether, then you might want to find another textbook. If there are limited or no references, there is a risk that the book is not well researched and may be biased towards one particular point of view. So, the general rule of thumb is this: more references mean less bias, which means a better source for you to use.

Wading through journal articles

In social sciences, just like the natural sciences, our most valuable source of information comes from articles in journals. The drawback to books, as stated above, is that the information is long out of date as the book takes time to write and get published. Articles are published much more quickly, in anywhere between six and 18 months. The information in journals is far more up to date—and using current ideas and information is very important in science. You can find journals in your university library or online.

Most journal articles undergo what is known as the peer review process. During this process a submitted manuscript is reviewed by other academics in the field to assess how good it is. The process ensures that only high-quality research is published. As with many aspects of life, there is a hierarchy with journal articles in terms of their quality, although this is more likely to be of significant importance to those doing postgraduate degrees, and is something you will learn about during the course of those studies.

Chapter 7, on reading and assessing journal articles, will help you to get the most out of journal articles. However, there are a few pointers that apply to this chapter too.

1. If the journal has been recommended by one of your tutors, take the hint and read it!

On the whole, lecturers and tutors will only pick those articles that complement your studies, or are central to a particular argument. So if a tutor or lecturer recommends that you read a particular article, the best advice is to read it.

2. Don't worry if you don't understand it all—use only the bits you do understand

Very few students, undergraduates *and* postgraduates, understand every word of the articles they read: this is only achieved if you've been reading journal articles for years and are an expert in your field. Nobody expects you to be an expert in everything related to what you're studying as you have yet to obtain a complete understanding of the field your studies are in. If you think an article might be especially useful but aren't sure what it means, ask your tutor to go through it with you. If you understand the gist of the article but not the details, don't worry—this is a big achievement, particularly early on in your studies. Use what you do understand and if you find you need to use some of the information you're not clear on, ask your tutor or lecturer to go through it with you.

3. Focus on the method: if the article isn't very good, this is typically where you'll find the problem

In journal articles which are reporting experiments, the method is a very important section: it tells you exactly what the author of the article did. Obviously, review articles won't have a procedure section (as reviews are *distillations* of research articles; they don't present the research first-hand), but for regular experimental journal articles you need to pay close attention to this method section. For example, ask yourself: are there any problems that you can see with the experiment? By the time you've done your first year you are more than equipped to look for genuine flaws in other peoples' work; all that you have learned in your research methods course will equip you to analyse another method section critically. Don't assume that something is high quality (and therefore perfect and there's nothing wrong with it) just because it is published; this may be accurate most of the time, but it's not always the case. Things you might pay close attention to are possible order effects, inappropriate sampling methods, cultural bias, poor validity and practice effects. These terms are found in your research methods courses, so if you're reading this at the start of the first year of your studies don't worry just yet, come back to this point after the winter vacation once you've learned a few of the basics.

Critical analysis and thinking

Reading with a critical eye will help you take an appropriately critical approach in your own writing. Students are frequently confused when confronted with the concept of

---

Box 6.1 Checklist: thinking critically about sources

1. What is this piece of writing about?
2. What is the author's angle? How do I know?
3. What is the argument?
4. What evidence is given?
5. Is this evidence relevant? How do I know?
6. Have I heard/read anything similar or dissimilar? What was it?
7. Do I agree or disagree? Why?

---

critical analysis, as they think it means they should criticize what they are reading. When reading something that you are considering using in your next assignment, ask yourself a series of questions (see Box 6.1).

The answers to these questions should help you figure out if the material is relevant to your purposes and how to use it in a critical manner in your essay.

➡ There is a more detailed section on critical thinking in Chapter 10.

Activity 6.1: Thinking critically about sources

In this activity, use the list of questions in Box 6.1 to critique the piece of prose in Figure 6.2 (the first page of an article by Reddy & Parson, 2007). Make sure you concentrate carefully while reading; don't be tempted to skim-read the passage: errors and misunderstandings occur only when something isn't read carefully. When you've finished reading the prose, go through the questions in Box 6.1 and answer them as best you can.

How to use, and not use, the Internet

If used correctly, the Internet is a vast mine of information; however, it is really important that you don't rely on the Internet as your primary source of information at university. It is important to remember that the majority of websites contain material that is not peer reviewed, so you have no guarantee of information quality. This is problematic: unless you use appropriate websites, you are going to run into trouble with your lecturers and tutors. The Internet is also used, however, for distributing journal articles, reviews, reports and newspaper articles, all of which are valid sources of information. These are peer-reviewed and/or published by recognized publishers and organizations, and are suitable for use in your assignments.

The underlying problem with the Internet is that anyone can publish anything they like, so you need to take care which information you use as a source of information in your writing: you need to make sure you have reliable and accurate information with which to write your assignments. In particular, Wikipedia™ appears to have the answer to everything, but while it is monitored carefully, it is modifiable by all those who create an account and want to change information. So, while much of the information it contains may be perfectly accurate and be based on peer-reviewed sources, it is not peer

---

Psychology Learning and Teaching 6(2), 154-159

Student response to a pub quiz style first year psychology assessment

PETER REDDY[1] AND VANESSA PARSON
Aston University, UK

The deterioration in staff-student ratios in UK higher education has had a disproportionate impact on assessment and feedback, meaning that contemporary students may have fewer assessments and much less feedback than a generation ago (Gibbs, 2006). Early use of a quiz assessment may offer a blend of social benefits (social comparison, shared problem solving leading to engagement, belonging and continuation), academic benefits (early formative assessment, immediate feedback) and administrative benefits (on-the-spot verbal marking and feedback to 230 students simultaneously). This study sought student views on the acceptability and contribution to learning of the quiz. Social benefits were apparent but difficulties in creating questions to elicit deeper reasoning and problem solving are discussed and the quiz had limited pedagogic value in the eyes of participants. The use of assertion-reason questions are considered as a way of taking the table quiz to a higher level and extending its pedagogic value.

INTRODUCTION

UK higher education (HE) has expanded and university per capita income has fallen, leading to growing class sizes and a deteriorating staff-student ratio (Gibbs, 2006). Class contact hours rather than marking load is the principal unit used to calculate staff workload in many UK universities, and the result has been that staff have less and less time to spend on assessment and especially on marking and feedback. Gibbs and Simpson (2003) argue that assessment regimes, including the speed and accessibility of student feedback, powerfully direct student learning and their approach to study. Arguably the result is a crisis in assessment and learning, with contemporary students having fewer assessments and much less feedback than a generation ago.

To help address this, a first year formative assessment was sought, that was suitable for early use and fast feedback with 230 students, offered little opportunity for plagiarism and was economical in staff time. Inspiration was found in the UK pub quiz tradition.

A pub quiz is a social event, typically in a public house, village or school hall, where informal groups of five or so compete to answer general knowledge questions. Answers are given after each round of questions and results and prizes are given at the end. The speed of response is in sharp contrast to the usual speed of academic marking and feedback. The quiz is divided into themed rounds and participants decide on group answers, within a time limit, to questions read out or on paper. Traditionally a mix of types of question is used, with at least one picture round on paper (naming people or objects, or matching them to a list). Answer papers are swapped with other teams at the end of each round,

and the answers are read out. Disputes or uncertainties are resolved by adjudication before moving on to the next round and the answer papers are collected for marking to be checked. This allows for participant interaction, a pleasing variation in activity and for interim results and team positions to be announced. The friendly competition, immediate feedback, round-by-round availability of scores, social interaction and public identification of the winners seem to be the factors making the pub quiz a popular entertainment.

Would a pub quiz style event be suitable as an academic assessment? An immediate problem was with the name. 'Pub quiz' is a shorthand that communicates the essence of the event and the details of its organisation to those familiar with the term, but may be unfamiliar or troubling to students who prefer to avoid pubs and alcohol. Simple 'quiz' was settled on.

Numbers also posed a problem. We had four or five times the number of participants usual for a pub quiz, and needed a room able to seat 230 students in 46 groups of five around small tables, with enough staff to achieve near simultaneous collection and distribution of question and answer sheets. Extra expense was incurred in hiring the Students' Guild hall, extra tables and chairs and in laying out the room.

The biggest problem was thought be the content of the quiz. General knowledge might be reducible to short answers for entertainment, but could a psychology quiz be made to fit the pub quiz format and still be a valid assessment? Answers to questions needed to be short and definitive in order to be read out. Asking students to write a hypothesis to a study would not work, but they could be asked to identify an independent variable or the appropriate test of significance.

Figure 6.2: Extract from Reddy & Parson, (2007). Reprinted with permission.

reviewed itself and is therefore very much frowned on as a reference and source of information in your assignments, as the content is simply less reliable. There will typically be a list of references with each entry, so use these instead of the original entry in Wikipedia™.

In short, this type of website is never acceptable to cite within your university essays: lecturers take a dim view of material from non-peer reviewed sources. Indeed, you may already have come across teachers at school who forbade you from using it. Use sites like this for a quick revision tool to remind you about a particular topic by all means, but use books and journal articles in your assignments.

Another problem with the Internet is that websites come and go: relatively few are constant and accessible months or years from when you first accessed them. This is the reason that in Chapter 13 we made a big deal about putting the date and time you accessed the information. This ensures that, even if the website is no longer accessed, the reader can be made aware that at the particular point in time you accessed the material, it existed and was a tenable source of information.

The Internet can be used to find useful information, but typically students simply search in Google™ and assume that whatever appears on the first few pages is correct. Actually this is not the case: what appears on the first few pages is the most popular, the most accessed sites, and this is a very different set of information to what is considered *correct* or *appropriate* information to use. Here are some tips you can follow to make sure you are using appropriate websites for information.

1. Use Google Scholar™ rather than Google™ itself

Google Scholar™ will only look at academic sites, reviews and articles on the Internet: all the extra junk that usually appears is automatically filtered out. This way you don't get side-tracked by interesting but ultimately non-suitable material.

2. Is there an author or a date when the site was last updated?

This might sound a little odd, but in a staggering number of websites no credit is given to anyone, and no details of updates are present. They are simply a list of information with no option of checking the source. If you can find an author's email address to contact the author, and a date when the site was last updated, then you probably have an appropriate source of information. If the site was updated, when was it last updated? If it hasn't been updated for a few years then you may want to find a new website that's a bit more recent. Some websites are perfectly valid and reputable, and so never get removed from the Internet, but haven't been updated for a while for various reasons. There is almost certainly more recent information around, so keep searching.

3. Check the URL: does it work when you delete bits off the end?

This might sound a bit odd, but if the website is from a reputable organization or source, the first part of the URL will work independently of the full URL you can see in the menu bar—for example, it will take you direct to the organization's home page. Checking the links on a website will also give you a clue: if some of them don't work then you're probably looking at a site that is having all links to it cut by others—an indication that the site is probably not one you want to use.

4. Is the purpose of the website to inform, sell or promote? Is it educational or populist?

There is a point to all websites, whether it's to provide information, sell a product or promote a particular point of view. If the purpose is to inform then keep reading the website. If the purpose is to sell a product or promote a particular point of view then you may want to avoid that particular website, so keep searching.

5. Should you use the website in your writing?

If, once you've gone through the checklist of points above, you're still not sure about a website—don't use it. It is far better to be safe than sorry. If you are in any doubt at all, stick to books and journal articles.

How can you tell whether the content of these sources of information is any good?

Typically, you should concentrate on empirical research findings reported in journals and textbooks. There is a series of things you need to think about when evaluating a book, article or Internet source as suitable for you to use in a particular assignment:

1. Don't assume that just because it has been published, it is automatically of a high quality!

Most people assume that, if something has been published somewhere, it must be a reliable, accurate and high quality source of information. The published world can be just as erratic, in terms of quality of information, as the Internet undoubtedly is; it is worth bearing in mind that you should judge each individual published work on its own merits. There is a lot of information out there, and this chapter will hopefully help you understand how to weed out the good from the bad.

2. Does what you're reading have value to the assignment you're trying to write?

➠ Look at Chapter 5 on assessment criteria, for more guidance on how to be clear about what you need to concentrate on in assignments.

This is the primary question you need to be asking yourself when getting information together for your assignments: is the source of information you're looking at adding something to what you need to write or do? If the answer is no, then you need to put it to one side and concentrate on another source of information. It takes practice, but you will fairly quickly find that it becomes quite easy to distinguish useful sources of information from less useful sources. Having a really clear idea about what you need to concentrate on in your assignment is a big first step to getting this right.

3. Is what you are reading consistent with the theory you already know?

You will have received some teaching sessions on the topic you will be assessed in, so you'll already have some idea about the theories which are directly relevant to what you are looking at.

4. Is what you're reading at the cutting edge of research or is it more than a few years old?

As has already been noted in the previous sections, information which is new or only a few years old is fine to use as it will contain the latest (or at least up to date) information. Books which are five or more years old and journals which are ten or more years old should be treated with caution—and replaced with more up to date, equivalent sources of information. Information in the academic community is constantly being updated and reviewed; you will be taught the most recent versions of theories in your lectures, so you need to make sure you're also using the most recent versions of information in your assignments.

5. What alternative points of view are there in other sources of information?

Psychology, as we've already covered, is a collection of ideas about how people work. As with any other collection of people and ideas, there are going to be disagreements so there are essentially lots of points of view which you need to consider. Sources which have multiple points of view in them are great to use, but you will find that these are mainly textbooks. All journal articles will have a less than balanced point of view, as they are all presented their ideas as the right ones. Very few journal articles are completely unbiased, despite appearances to the contrary. So, when you're looking at information to use in your assignments, you need to make sure you have a selection of points of view, preferably in multiple sources of information.

6. Are alternative ideas presented in this source?

(If there aren't, this means you're reading a biased piece of work, which is fine as long as you can find another source of information to balance the argument in your assignment.)

There is a checklist (see Box 6.2) you can work through when evaluating a source of information. It may sound like a lot of hard work to go through this checklist every time you try to read a source of information, but you'll find that it's actually second nature to do this once you get the hang of how psychology works as a subject. Typically psychology is a 'questioning' science: we like to find out what is going on, but crucially we like to find out *why* as well. This approach leads to many debates and arguments in the

---

Box 6.2 Checklist: deciding whether to use a source

1. Is the source a high quality one and suitable for your assignment?
2. Does what you're reading add value to the assignment you're trying to write?
3. Is what you are reading consistent with the theory you already know?
4. Is what you're reading at the cutting edge of research or is it more than a few years old?
5. What alternative points of view are there in other sources of information?

literature, so it becomes second nature to be critical of what you read the more you develop your own opinions about different topics.

How to use what you've found in your assignments

Using what you've found out is relatively straightforward, but is a task which confuses many undergraduates. Most of what you need to know regarding using what you've found in your assignments is discussed in Chapter 9. However, the following pointers will help—although I recommend reading Chapter 9 fully, to really help your writing skills.

- Integrate the information you've found from the notes you made while reading it thoroughly, make sure it links in with the points you're trying to make. Then make a plan of how you want to present this information.

- Don't simply list the bits of information you've found and be under the illusion that this constitutes an essay. Most of you won't ever fall into this trap. However, there are some who do perpetually list information rather than write an essay. Such an approach looks as though you haven't really understood what you've written (regardless of whether you have or haven't), and aren't exactly sure about what the essay is asking so are simply listing everything you think is relevant. If you think a bit more beforehand about how the information all fits together then you will do much better. There is more information on this in Chapters 9–11.

- You should not assume that the piece of information you have found automatically fits into your essay as it is. All information, no matter how relevant, needs to be carefully worked into your essay; you cannot just place it in and think that will be enough. There needs to be a clear reason for it to be there; it must be integrated and the explanation for its inclusion should be very clear.

- Try not to describe the information you have found in excessive or insufficient detail. Excessive detail, where you describe every last detail of the study or theory, wastes words and isn't necessary. You only need to include the parts of the study or theory that are going to directly support the point you are trying to make. At the other end of the scale, insufficient detail means that you won't be able to make your point at all, as there won't be enough details to back it up. Never assume that simply mentioning a study or theory is enough: you will need some details to support your ideas and show that you understand what you're writing.

In Example 6.1 the subject matter is covered appropriately, and the study supporting that information is used at the end in as much detail as is necessary for the argument presented, and then backed up by the sources of information.

Example 6.1: Integrating evidence and explanation

Terms are stated but not defined—to do so would move the focus from binocular feedback and onto other aspects of vision

In binocular feedback there are several types of cues available, such as stereomotion, diplopia and retinal disparities. Important information about the hand's trajectory could, therefore, be provided by the moving hand. It is necessary to establish whether binocular vision contributes anything to the online control of prehension or whether monocular vision will do just as well. Previous studies, notably Servos et al. (1994), have found that monocular visual cues are less effective than binocular cues for the online control of manual prehension.

Overall, generic conclusions are presented from other studies and a single reference is given as evidence of this. Note there is no huge detail about what the studies involved.

✎ Checklist

Check you've understood the key points covered in this chapter by seeing if you can answer the following questions:

- ✔ What assumption should you remember when reading books?

- ✔ Why should you not use your A level textbooks anymore?

- ✔ How many tips can you remember about how to check whether a book is a reliable source?

- ✔ What is the difference between academic and popular books?

- ✔ How do you know whether a journal article is any good?

- ✔ How do you search for information that is relevant, reliable and valuable to your assignment on the Internet?

- ✔ Why should you never use Wikipedia™ as a source in your assignments?

- ✔ Once you've found your information, how do you use it?

- ✔ Do you know which chapters in this book will help you most with your writing skills?

📖 References

Brittan, P. (1998). *The jigsaw man*. London, UK: Corgi Books.

Reddy, P.A. & Parson, V.J. (2007). Student response to a pub quiz style first year psychology assessment. *Psychology of Learning and Teaching: Conference Special Report*, 6(2), 154–159.

Sapolsky, R.M. (1994). *Why zebras don't get ulcers.* New York, USA: Freeman and Company.

Servos, P. & Goodale, M.A. (1994). Binocular vision and the on-line control of human prehension. *Experimental Brain Research,* 98, 119–127.

Wright, R.D. (Ed.) (1998). *Visual Attention.* Oxford, UK: Oxford University Press.

Chapter 7

How to find and read a journal article

This chapter focuses on how to hunt for relevant material for your essays and reports; it also addresses how to simplify the reading of journal articles, helping you get the most out of the complicated material you will be faced with. Full text articles are available on the book's website for you to read and practice the skills you will learn in this chapter.

▶ See www. oxfordtextbooks. co.uk/orc/parson/

Finding and reading journal articles is not as easy as you might think. They tend to be written about highly specific aspects of a given topic, and use a lot of technical language and refer to things you probably have never heard of. Fortunately, reading articles is a skill like any other: one you can master. A secret that is rarely broadcast by academics is that they themselves rarely understand the entirety of any article first time around—everyone needs to read the more complicated papers a few times before they understand them properly. So you're not alone if you read a paper and don't understand what you've just read. Practice makes perfect, and the more articles you read, the easier it will be to understand the bulk of what you are reading.

Although academic papers don't make life easy for anyone who is not a specialist in the particular field being covered in the article, academic papers have consistent structuring and labelling—features that help enormously with working out what is being discussed, and which help you find what you need.

How to find an article to read

Journal articles are very easy to find. The trouble comes when trying to identify the one you actually need to read. There are a lot of articles floating around, and your university will probably not have access to all of them. There are two types of access: electronic and paper. It would be logical to assume that a university and its library would have both versions available to you. However, this is not always the case. You need to be prepared to go hunting around the library to find articles you need; not everything you need during your degree will be conveniently online. The good news is that all university library catalogues come complete with an electronic database you can access from anywhere, so you can check online and get a list of relevant articles to find before even setting foot in the library. This saves you a huge amount of time.

You are also likely to get guidance on how to use article search engines such as PsycInfo, PsycArticles and Science Direct. Alongside these, you have the option of using Google Scholar™, which is a really easy way to find reports, articles and all manner of scholarly information. Google Scholar™ looks only at academic-style material and filters out all the general websites that Google™ normally searches through. An advantage when using Google Scholar™ is that you can specify years and keywords, making your search far more efficient. While this is very helpful for academics in general, search results are reported in the same way as Google™, with the most popular articles, reports, and so on are listed first. So be prepared to go through a couple of pages. You should be able to download directly anything your university has access to.

For undergraduates faced for the first time with journal articles, the process of working out what to read is usually made a little easier by your reading lists. These are provided for all courses and contain lists of books and articles that you should be reading. Sometimes assignments have lists of articles included in them to give you a head start and help focus your search. Use the tips provided below to find related articles and widen your reading in that manner. For postgraduates, you will pretty much be left to your own devices, and will be expected to find articles online without too much support.

Getting to grips with the articles you've found

The main reason you are reading an article in the first place is to find out information from it that will help you in your studies or projects. There are a series of elements in every journal article that you need to be familiar with; these elements are the key aspects which you need to understand to be able to work out if the article is going to be useful for your studies (as well as interesting!). I suggest breaking down the reading of these elements into stages. You will find that you will be able to follow these stages automatically as you get more used to reading journal articles: your search techniques will improve and you will get better at discriminating important information from the less important information.

Stage one: extract the aims and hypothesis

Every paper you read will have stated somewhere what the authors intended to study and what they expected to find out. The former is the *AIM* and the latter is the *HYPOTHESIS*. These are stated in two places normally, in the abstract and at the end of the introduction.

Aim: What did they want to look at?

This is an important statement to include when writing up a study as it tells you, the reader, what the authors were trying to do with their experiment or study, and helps you work out if they achieved their goals in the experiment. Stage one of taking a critical perspective about the article (to help with critical thinking) is always to work out if the aims of the experiment were met. Example 7.1 contains an aim and a method which clearly relate to each other.

Example 7.1: Linking the aim and the hypothesis (taken from student work based on Loftus & Palmer, 1974)

Aim

The aim of the investigation was to see whether different adjectives would influence the recall of 16–18 year old students.

Method

The experiment compared five groups of participants. Each group were given the identical questions to answer, with the exception of the critical question. The independent variable was the manipulation of the strength of an adjective in the critical question referring to the speed the car was traveling upon collision with the other in a film clip. The dependent variable was the speed estimate of the car given by the participants. Forty participants were recruited from a local school for convenience took part. They were aged between 16 and 18 (both male and female). Participants were randomly assigned to an experimental group. The materials used were the question sheets containing six questions (including the critical question relating to speed where the adjective was different for each group). A film clip of a car crash (2 minutes and 46 seconds in length), which the memory recall questions were related to, was displayed on a 21" analogue television. Procedure: participants were taken into the experimental room and presented with consent forms. The participants watched a video of a car chase and then had 10 minutes following the video to answer some questions relating to its content. All questions were identical on the sheets bar the critical question: *"How fast was the car going (in miles per hour) when it_____ into the bins?".* The adjective used to fill the gap was one of the following: smashed, collided, hit, bumped, contacted, touched.

Hypotheses: What did they think they would find?

The hypothesis is frequently easier to identify as authors tend to write 'We hypothesized that …' in their papers. However, working out which type of hypothesis has been used is slightly more difficult generally, but is an equally important piece of information.

▥▶ To learn more about different types of hypothesis, see Chapter 11.

If an author has provided a directional hypothesis then it indicates there is evidence that suggests a particular pattern of results and the author has spotted this. If a non-directional hypothesis is provided, the literature possibly shows evidence for multiple patterns of results, or the study is an exploratory one in which there is limited literature to draw on to create a directional hypothesis. In practice, though, it is most likely that the authors will have provided a directional hypothesis as these provide a stronger basis for analysis and discussion.

Individuals are subject to reconstructive errors in the recall of events (Bartlett, 1932), especially when presented with misleading information. Loftus and Palmer (1974) wanted to discover whether the memory of events actually changes as a result of misleading questions or if the existing memory is merely supplemented. They showed their participants a film clip of a car accident and then asked them a series of questions, and found that a simple word change affected the answers given by participants; leading them to conclude that leading/misleading questions can manipulate recollection of an event. This study reproduces this classic study by Loftus and Palmer, with the intention of repeating this result on a modern-day selection of participants. It was hypothesised that changes in adjective will elicit changes in responses given. Forty individuals, aged 16–35, from a school in Birmingham were tested in five different groups in an empty classroom. Participants watched a film clip of a car crash taken from a movie, followed by six questions. Each group were given identical questions apart from the critical question, where the strength of an adjective varied. The results showed that the stronger adjectives produced higher speed estimates. Leading questions can manipulate and affect the accuracy of recall of events.

Figure 7.1: An abstract (taken from student work based on Loftus & Palmer, 1974).

The first place you can find the aims and hypotheses is in the abstract. The aims and hypotheses will be described in more detail later in the article, at the end of the introduction, but it's typically easier to work out what a study is all about by having a quick look at the abstract. You don't want to waste time reading huge chunks of an article, only to find out it doesn't apply to what you are studying. If an article is relevant then you should read it all the way through, and carefully.

....

Exercise 7.1: Aim and hypothesis extraction

Read the abstract in Figure 7.1 and see if you can work out what the authors were aiming to look at and what they hypothesized would happen. Answers are at the end of the book.

....

Stage two: evaluate the method: what did they do?

Whenever you read an article, the only way to truly understand what the authors have found and concluded is to read the method section: you will only ever have a partial understanding of the conclusions without the context that being aware of the methods adopted brings. A brief mention of the method is in the abstract. However, the best way to understand what happened in the experiment in the article is always to read the full method section in the article itself.

You may read some reviews that contain no formal method section. In this case, check the studies mentioned in the paper to see if they contain a review of the methods used, and read them if so.

If you are reading an article other than a review, and it has no formal methods section, make sure you make notes as to the particular methods used when you read the entire paper. Not all method sections are clearly delineated; the vast majority only include some section headings. The example in Figure 7.2 employs this technique; look at this

The experiment employed a repeated groups design. The independent variables were the series of consonant trigrams and the counting task completed during the phase between viewing and recall of the trigram. There were 3 levels of the counting tasks: counting backwards, counting forwards and not counting at all. Each participant did each level of the independent variable, but the order was counterbalanced across participants. The number of trigrams recalled correctly by each participant was measured for each condition. There were 36 participants, mean age 17, selected via opportunity sampling from a sixth form centre in Birmingham. There were an equal number of males and females. The experiment was done on a computer, using PowerPoint. Each consonant trigram was presented sequentially on a separate slide.

Procedure:
The experiment was conducted within a secure, isolated room away from any distractions. Participants were shown the trigrams 3 times, to incorporate the three distraction tasks, over seven stages, using PowerPoint. Each stage had an increase in time of 3 seconds, beginning at an instant recall for the first round, 3 second delay for the second round, followed by rounds of 6, 9, 12, 15 and 18 seconds. The three counting techniques employed were counting backwards in 3's, counting forwards in 3's and not counting at all. Different trigrams shall be used each round to prevent potential recall being formed from repetitive use of the same trigram. The experimenter recorded the answers.

Figure 7.2: A method section without the expected headings (taken from student work based on Peterson & Peterson's (1959) experiment).

figure to get some practice at differentiating the different aspects of the method without the need for sub-headings.

....

Exercise 7.2: Understanding the method

In this exercise you need to read the method section in Figure 7.2 carefully and work out what the experiment was all about. Try and work out which bits are the design, participants and materials sections. Make a note of anything that is not clear and you can't quite understand. For the answers, see 'Answers to exercises' at the end of the book.

....

Stage three: interpreting the figures

Figures are visual representations of content of any description, be they pictures, graphs or timelines. Most of the figures you see will be easy enough to interpret. However, some of the more complex figures can be a little trickier. Pictures can save a lot of words when used appropriately, and can provide a huge amount of information.

Figure 7.3 shows something called a timeline. Timelines are commonly found in psychophysics articles and are designed to show exactly how the experiment worked and at what times each element appeared. Figure 7.3 is an example of just how much information you can get from a picture. In this example you can see that, in this particular experiment, a fixation point appeared for varying times between 500 and 700 milliseconds. It then disappeared and a cue appeared, remaining on screen for 300 milliseconds.

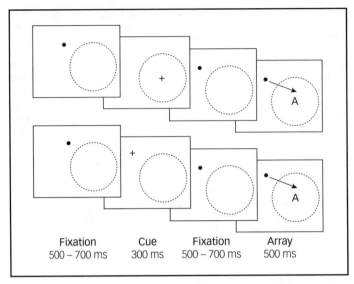

Fixation | Cue | Fixation | Array
500 – 700 ms | 300 ms | 500 – 700 ms | 500 ms

Figure 7.3: this timeline shows the two active conditions and the placement of items in the visual field.

Figure 7.3: The timeline.

The fixation point again appeared for a time between 500 and 700 milliseconds before disappearing to make way for some form of target array, which remained onscreen for 500 milliseconds. You can also see from Figure 7.3 that the cue was a cross, located at one of two points on the screen, while the target was a letter, located at a single point on the screen.

Figure 7.3 shows you that the authors had looked at whether placing a cue in a different location to the target affected response times in anyway, even after drawing attention back to the prime location of the fixation point. The first cue location was priming the target location and results might be expected to show response facilitation, in the form of quicker reaction times to the target array. The picture is also far easier to understand at a basic level than the paragraph you've just read, making the experiment obvious to all straight away.

Table 7.1 shows ratings by participants of levels of aggression in a series of video clips. The caption underneath tables and figures is your first port of call when you're trying to figure out what they mean, as they contain all the description of what the table or figure is all about. The caption for this table provides a detailed description of what happened in this study and what participants were asked to do.

Table 7.1 shows the results of a study looking at peoples' ratings of aggression. Three videos were shown containing different levels of aggression and participants were asked to rate from 1 to 7 how aggressive they thought the content was.

The graph shown in Figure 7.4 shows you another method of how the data could be presented in the paper you might be reading. Graphical representations of data are generally a little easier to understand than tables. In Figure 7.4 you can clearly see the relationship between the levels of aggression depicted in the videos as rated by the

TABLE 7.1 Mean ratings for levels of violence witnessed in videos shown to participants

Rating of violence in video	Mean	Standard deviation
Video showing high aggression	5.25	1.15
Video showing mild aggression	4.53	1.19
Video depicting no aggression (neutral)	3.14	1.12

participants and the videos' actual content. You can see just from looking at this that participants rated the videos in the order you might expect from the descriptions provided on the *x* axis.

Stage 4: interpreting the results

Now you understand what the experiment is all about, the next challenge is to understand what the authors found. A variety of methods are used to show the reader what the results are; the previous section looked at interpreting tables and graphs while this section deals with the main presentation of the results. A section is always included that describes, in prose, the results in detail. You can't just look at the tables and figures; you need to read the words too.

In Figure 7.5 you will see an extract of the written results from a study into attendance and performance among undergraduates. This particular study involved doing correlations, which you'll learn about in your statistics classes. You can see from Figure 7.5 that there was a positive correlation in the data: as attendance increased, the marks increased as well. You can also see that this correlation existed for both males and female students, but that males benefitted from attendance even more than females did. You can also see from the size of the correlations that there is still a lot of what statisticians call 'variance' left unaccounted for. This means something other than just performance is improving

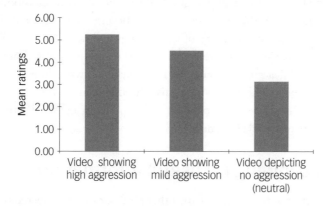

Figure 7.4: Graphical representation of the data in Table 7.1.

Overall there was a significant positive correlation between attendance and marks achieved ($r = 0.244$; $n = 327$; $p<0.001$), with marks increasing as attendance increased. This was mirrored for both males ($r = 0.332$; $n = 111$; $p<0.001$) and females ($r = 0.167$; $n = 111$; $p<0.02$), although this is more dramatic for males than females. This indicates that males benefit more from increased attendance than do females.

Figure 7.5: Results from a study into attendance and performance.

attendance, but at this moment in time you have not been given an explanation for what that might be. This sort of information is usually found in the discussion, where authors typically speculate on what else might be happening to account for the results they've got.

Stage 5: understanding the discussion

A discussion is simply that: a discussion of the results and how they fit in with our current understanding and knowledge as captured in the existing literature. Generally you'll find that the discussion takes you through various stages. These stages are detailed in Chapter 11 and your practical methods courses. This common sequence of stages is the reason we teach you how to write in such an ordered manner: by doing so, your writing follows the same format as everyone else's and discussions are easier to understand, regardless of how complicated the study itself may be.

Discussions start by summarizing the results before showing the reader how this relates to the authors' ideas about what they intended to do initially. This is followed by an explanation of how the results link with the ideas provided in the introduction; links are made with previous research and new evidence may be brought in to support or contradict evidence already provided. There is typically a discussion about what the authors think about the research they have done; the discussion then tends to move onto suggestions for future research and finally, the conclusion finishes it off.

Stage 6: comprehending conclusions

The conclusion should be a short paragraph at the end of the discussion, or a separate section immediately after the discussion. This section tells you a great deal of information. It provides a succinct summary of the findings and how they fit in with previous experiments and theories. It also tells you what the author thinks about the research they've just finished describing. Generally the conclusion will summarize clearly what the discussion has been addressing; it will also directly relate to the original question of the article. Figure 7.6 shows you a typical conclusion from a journal article and how to break it down into its useful elements.

Stage 7: Following up useful information

In any given article, the full details of any other study or theory referred to in the article are never given so you need to look out the original source of information if you want to

Title of paper: An exploratory investigation into the validity of student podcasting as a valid form of assessment

Conclusions:

Link to background research

Podcasts have great utility within an educational context (Carson, 2006). Group assessment is a valuable assessment practice for higher education, involving the learning of various skills and teachings students to work as part of a team; creating podcasts is a means by which group assessment can successfully be carried out without any detriment to students. This study shows that creation of podcasts is an equable and motivational form of assessment, which produces equivalent results to more traditional forms of group assessment.

What the author thinks

What the author found (relates directly to the title)

What the experiment involved

Figure 7.6: Deconstructing a conclusion.

learn more. As you will see in Chapter 10 (on essays) and Chapter 11 (on laboratory reports), authors provide references so that you can access this information.

When you have read a paper and found it interesting, relevant and want to find out more about that topic, you can look in the paper itself to find the information that was used—the references. Using references given in an article is one of the most effective methods of finding articles that directly relate to what you're studying.

When you read an article, you should try to make notes about those key points you're reading about that are of interest to you (see Figure 7.7). Most key points will be referenced, unless the authors have directly made those points themselves based on the evidence they're presenting: the article itself (the text) will indicate who came up with that key point in the first place, and the year they did so. If you then look at the end of the article you will see a list of the references that have been cited throughout the paper, enabling you to find the original article in which that key point was first proposed.

We learn more about referencing in Chapter 13.

Section from an Introduction:

The Justice system requires statements from witnesses about the incident in question. A significant amount of convictions are assisted by witness's recall of events. Thus, psychologists are inevitably concerned with how people can be manipulated by misleading information in these scenarios. Bartlett (1932) believed that memories are not stored passively but distorted or reconstructed by the individuals' prior knowledge and expectations. It appears that both adults and children are subject to reconstructive errors in the recall of events, especially when presented with misleading information. One argument, as presented by Bartlett, is that it is these 'schemas' that lead to said reconstructive errors. However, it is clear from research that misleading information can have a great impact on how people recollect events.

An article looks like it could be important: so check the reference section at the end of the article and do a search on the reference you find there

Reference list at the end of the article:

- Bartlett, F.C., (1932). *Remembering*, Cambridge: Cambridge University Press.
- Loftus, E.F. & Palmer, J.C., (1974). Reconstruction of automobile destruction: an example of the interaction between language and memory, *Journal of Verbal Learning and Verbal Behaviour*, 13, 585–589.

Figure 7.7: Finding interesting information.

Occasionally you won't find what you're looking for in the reference list in the article you're reading, but you'll still want to find out if there is any more recent work on the subject you've been reading about. In this instance you use the keywords located at the start of the article to search for more articles. You can restrict your search to only those articles published in the same year or later than the article you've just read. There is no guarantee that the author/s who wrote the paper you've just read managed to find and use every last article relevant to their paper so it's always worth having another look.

Keywords for the article in Figure 7.1 Memory, eyewitness testimony, misleading information, recall

Looking at the keywords for Figure 7.1, you can see that there is a specific set of ideas the paper is looking at, and a specific set of words you should use in your searches for more articles on this topic. When searching for more articles you should look at all of the keywords, and use different combinations to locate articles that are more specifically related to your topic of interest. Remember to read the abstracts rather than the titles if you want to know whether or not you can use an article: titles are too brief to give you much more than an indication of relevance, whereas the abstract will summarize the paper for you and give you all the information you need to determine whether it will be useful.

✎ Checklist

Check you've understood the key points covered in this chapter by seeing if you can answer the following questions:

- ✔ Do you know how to find out what the authors were trying to find out?
- ✔ Where do you find what authors actually did?
- ✔ Are you confident that you can compare the method with the aim to find out if the authors actually addressed the question they were asking?
- ✔ Do you think you could work out results just from looking at tables and graphs?
- ✔ Would you be able to work out what the written results section means?
- ✔ Do you know what the different sections of a discussion are and in which order they typically come?
- ✔ What can you find out from the conclusion?
- ✔ Do you know where in this book to find information about how a journal article is put together?
- ✔ Do you know where to find journal articles?

📖 References

Bartlett, F.C. (1932). *Remembering*. Cambridge: Cambridge University Press.

Loftus, E.F. & Palmer, J.C. (1974). Reconstruction of automobile destruction: an example of the interaction between language and memory. *Journal of Verbal Learning and Verbal Behaviour, 13,* 585–589.

Peterson, L.R. & Peterson, M. (1959). Short-term retention of individual verbal items. *Journal of Experimental Psychology, 58,* 193–198.

Chapter 8

Reading and evaluating text

One of the most difficult things to do when you're studying is to evaluate other peoples' work. You find yourself wondering how you can possibly critique what a professional researcher has done when you're still studying yourself. However, you are more than capable of evaluating someone else's work as well as your own as long as you've paid attention in your classes. This chapter will focus on how to evaluate your own and others' work, as well as how to obtain and use feedback from others. While you read, try to bear in mind that psychology comprises opinions based on evidence from experiments; not everyone agrees with each other and, indeed, scientific progress can be made when people actually disagree. You are in a unique position during your degree where you have preconceptions about what you expect to read in the literature on your various topics, which means that you are unbiased and are actually perfectly positioned to be able to critically evaluate objectively.

What is evaluation?

You'll probably find it quite intimidating as an undergraduate to have to look at a published piece of work and evaluate it. On top of this, the concept of evaluation has been warped by requirements at A level so much so that many students feel that they should list evaluation points in order of strengths and limitations rather than discuss the evidence as it is presented to them. Unfortunately the prescriptive formula taught prior to your degree will never allow you to effectively evaluate a piece of information. As a result, when you read other people's writing you evaluate in terms of what you are used to, rather than actually seeing what is there.

How to evaluate other peoples' work

Evaluation is more subtle and complex than simply producing a list of pros and cons about a study. It involves looking at how the information in a source fits within the wider framework of that particular topic, how the information it contains relates to that topic area, and how robust the study itself is—in other words, it asks the question 'can we rely on the information this source contains?'

Tips for evaluating articles/reports/essays from others

Here are five tips to help you be effective when evaluating articles and other sources of information from others.

1. Know the area

- Knowing an area means you need to do reading on the topic to make sure you understand the concepts involved. If you are reading an article about magic and misperception you will need to be familiar with the literature on information it contains—most likely topics such as change blindness, choice blindness, inattention blindness, visual perception and related theories.

2. Read carefully

- Many people are guilty of skim-reading articles and books, and so missing the minutiae of what is actually being said. Nobody can skim-read research articles unless they've been in the field a long time, so you should not expect to do anything but read every word carefully.

- Make notes to aid your later recall of important pieces of information. If you are working with a photocopy you may want to highlight, underline or make notes on the copy itself. Otherwise you will want to write notes clearly on paper. For the latter method, make sure you know which aspect of which source each section of your notes is referring to. There is nothing worse than spending hours disentangling and interpreting an article or topic, only to find you have no points of reference for all the notes you've made.

3. Know your research methods and statistics

- This applies to research articles rather than information from books

- Admittedly, research methods and statistics are not the most interesting subjects in the world. However, they are invaluable if you want to be able to evaluate properly.

- You will need to be able to evaluate whether the correct statistical procedures were used to analyse the data collected during the study. On top of this you need to be able to understand why they used the methods they did and how they compare with what others in the topic area have done.

- Things such as order effects, practice effects and cultural bias can all detract from the value of what you're reading. IQ tests, for example, are very culturally biased as they were developed in a Western culture so have no applicability to cultures outside of this. You also need to consider how representative the sample was: were there enough participants to be able to produce reliable results, for example? Psychophysics papers are a conundrum to many undergraduates: they frequently have fewer than 10 participants and yet are considered to be highly replicable. Psycho-physics involves testing a few participants in thousands of trials to produce data which has practice and individual effects reduced to a level whereby the results are generalizable.

• If you can establish that a methodology or analysis is inaccurate to some degree then the results presented can suddenly be questioned and the conclusions considered in a new light.

4. Think about what you've read

• Don't put things to one side when you've read them. Think about what you've just read and try to make some more notes. You should find that spending a few extra minutes doing this will help you make links with the literature you've already read on the topic and help you pull out discrepancies or consistencies.

How to evaluate your own work

Evaluating what you write yourself is perhaps the trickiest thing you have to do during your degree. Most students go to one extreme or the other when they evaluate their own work, at least to start with, being excessively positive or negative about what they have written. We all want to do the best we can, and we can become rapidly biased about our own work. As a result we find it very hard to be rational and objective when we're essentially marking our own work.

The first tip I will give you is always to do your work well in advance of the deadlines. By doing so, you will have time to follow the tips provided here.

1 Put your piece of work to one side for 24 hours.

• This may seem counter-intuitive, especially when you have multiple deadlines and you need to get your work handed in. However, when you write any lengthy piece of work you end up being so close to what you've written that you read what you *think* you've written rather than what you've *actually* written. This is a quirk of your perceptual system and your schemas. Giving yourself a break and doing other work and activities removes this quirky process and enables you to read what you *actually* wrote, enabling you to remove inconsistencies and errors.

2 Read your work out loud (or get a friend to do so).

• You may feel very silly when you're doing this. However, it's a really useful trick which can help your piece of work flow much better. When you or other people are talking you are generally aware if you can't follow what is being said, if you don't understand, or if you generally get lost. If you feel this way when you listen to your piece of work being read out then you have some work to do.

• This method will highlight most punctuation and spelling errors as you're reading every word and using the punctuation to read the phrases and rhythm of the writing. It will also show you where your argument is muddled or missing and whether you've answered the questions posed or not. It's a really useful trick to improving written work.

3 Go through your piece of work with a red pen and highlight all the things that need changing. Imagine it's someone else's piece of work and you're marking it for them. This will help you remain objective about what you've written.

4 Re-write your piece of work.

You should never hand in the first draft of any piece of work. By its nature, the above process will stop you from doing this, while also helping you be more objective and rational about your own work.

How to think critically

Thinking and writing critically is something you will need to learn to do well if you are going to achieve a good degree. Reading carefully and critically can help you be critical in your own writing while at university; the more you read critically the better your written critical analysis will become. When you read a source of information, be it a book chapter, a journal article or something on the internet, you need to focus on the question you are currently trying to answer. The question may be your essay title, the subject of your laboratory report, or a general question you have thought of yourself about the literature you've been reading.

When you read critically you typically look at and evaluate the material in front of you on three levels: the paragraph, the argument, and the evidence. We'll cover each of these in turn.

The paragraph

You need to consider each paragraph individually. If you read Chapter 9, on writing tips and tools, you will see that a paragraph is a collection of sentences that address a single point. As you read, you should be evaluating the individual points captured by each paragraph, while also evaluating the entirety of the material you're reading: all of the paragraphs collectively. Read carefully: you won't be able to understand the whole source if you cannot understand each of the individual paragraphs. The collection of paragraphs makes up your source and they combine to create the argument the author is trying to present.

Activity 8.1

We'll use the following student essay for three activities. In this first activity, look at each of the paragraphs and answer the following questions:

- What does the paragraph say?
- Is the evidence clearly presented to support what this paragraph is trying to say?
- Are the paragraphs clearly linked?

The main difference between cultures in pro-social behaviour is that more communal cultures are heavily based on interdependence, and independent culture on self-dependency. Miller (1994) compared a dependent Indian (Hindu) culture with an American individualist culture in terms of helping others, and found that Hindu Indians feel a need to respond to others' needs, whilst Americans are more likely to help family or friends only. In test of these assumed culture behaviours, Nadler (1986) compared attitudes to helping with urban Israelites and those living on a kibbutz. Communally raised people were more likely to seek and give help than Israel people living in urban area, especially when helping benefited their communal group. Nadler (1986) later compared these two groups with a group of American immigrants to Israel, and a group from the Soviet Union. The kibbutz dwellers were still those most likely to help, and the US and urban dwellers less likely. Those from the Soviet Union were far less likely to ask for help from others, rather they relied on family and were quite socially withdrawn. This further narrows the idea of interdependence, to include only those individuals that can offer reciprocal help when needed.

Yang (1994) found that guanxixue (the Chinese custom of exchanging gifts with others) formed a large network of obligatory people, who were more likely to help. They were specifically more likely to help if they deemed help necessary (as conducted by Chinese social rules) and if it was of a benefit.

Tower et al (1997) compared British and Russian participants in term of their use of equity and equality rules when sharing rewards after a shared task. British participants were expected to base the reward on levels of task performance, and Russian participants to be influenced by levels of task performance in a stranger (when with friends, they would give equal reward regardless of the amount of work.) The results supported this, with Russian participants awarding themselves with more of the reward if their co-worker was a stranger. Also, British participants gave almost identical rewards to themselves regardless of friendship status.

On the other hand, although this research supports the idea that communal cultures give more help and act pro-socially, it is an assumption. It has been theorised that rural communities would be more reluctant to act pro-socially in certain circumstances, such as in-group favouritism, making them less likely to help outsiders.

In terms of reciprocal help, there are several differing factors within each culture. For instance, Eisenberg et al (1991) discovered that girls are more likely to give pro-social help, though research findings are not always consistent. An idea to explain this is because of differences in social roles typically adopted by males and females. Eagly (1987) suggested that the uneven distribution in social roles is determined by gender-role differences. Piliavin et al (1969) supported that men were more likely to help in dangerous situations, as males are generally found to be in jobs involving more risk taking. Eagly and Crowley (1986) supported this in turn, finding that 66 per cent of many different studies found men to be more helpful than women; probably due to cultural rules concerning gender regulations.

According to Bierhoff (1991), the effect of urbanisation is stopping people following the natural patterns of living together in communities. This is supported by Korte and Kerr (1975), who found that rural inhabitants in Massachusetts were more likely to help (callers who had dialled the wrong number or mail post that was 'lost') than those living in Boston. Milgram's (1970) hypothesis was that emergencies were far more occurrent in cities, and so the inhabitants did not notice them as much, and did not deem most situations as in need of their help. People with small-town backgrounds were far more likely to help, as the emergency situation would be a novelty and attract more attention (Gelfand et al, 1973).

Student work. Reprinted with permission from H. Ling (2007)

The argument

The argument is typically something that undergraduates find difficult to write, but most are quickly able to discern when they're reading someone else's work. You will notice a common 'thread' or 'theme' through the source you're reading; this is the argument: the authors' angle and opinion. You need to consider whether you agree with what is being said or not. You cannot ever state this in the first person in terms of 'I think …'. However, your subsequent reading and writing will show your opinion through how you present the information and evaluate it within the context of other information, all in the third person.

⇒ We explore the topic of writing style in more detail in Chapter 9.

Activity 8.2

Looking at the extract in Activity 8.1, answer the following questions:

- What story is the writer trying to tell?
- Is the argument (story) clear from how they've structured the essay?
  - Give reasons for your answer.

The evidence

Evidence is vitally important when looking at any source—whether it is one you are producing or one you are reading. Scientists, of which you are now one as a psychologist, are much like crime scene investigators: they both have to focus entirely on the evidence to come to conclusions. Opinions are of no value unless they are backed up with evidence, while bias arises from simply being too lazy to look at a wide enough range of sources in the first place—inexcusable for any scientist. During your degree you will soon find that evidence is everything, and your tutors will be looking for you to substantiate every statement with evidence supporting it. Researchers are no less exempt from this, no matter how experienced they are, and all are still required to provide evidence for their theories and ideas.

Any source you read will have a multitude of other sources they refer to as evidence for their results and/or arguments. To evaluate the evidence presented, ask yourself the following questions:

1 Is there enough evidence to support what is being said?

2 Is this evidence from a variety of authors?

- If there are only a few authors cited then the material presented is liable to bias towards a particular point of view.

3 Is the evidence presented relevant or does it appear to be a side-line to the main arguments presented?

4 Have I read any of this evidence?

5 Have I read anything similar?

6 Have I read anything which says something different and disagrees with this author?

....

Activity 8.3: Answer questions 1–5 with regards to the extract in Activity 8.1

There are some final questions to consider when thinking critically about the information you're reading.

1 How consistent is this information in terms of the theory it relates to?

2 Are there any important implications or applications of this work which have (or have not) been considered?

3 How rigorous is the methodology?

4 Are there any inconsistencies or inaccuracies which detract from the results obtained and call the conclusions into question?

5 Can you think of any alternative explanations for the claims that the theory/research makes?

....

Using these questions will help you really get to grips with the difficult task of critical thinking and help make the process a little easier. The method for critical thinking I've outlined will hopefully demystify it a little and help you read and write more objectively in future, leading you to better marks for your assignments.

....

Trying to remain objective

As a student of science, your task now is to remain objective and to put all subjective opinions to one side. This is not easy, even for experienced scientists: everyone has opinions and can often wish to express them. You'll need to be careful to avoid expressing opinions directly in the first person ('I think . . .'), and you'll need to master the ability of doing so in writing using evidence only.

Reading and remaining objective is a bit easier than writing and remaining objective. The trick is to clear your mind of all preconceptions and ideas, reading what is actually written then slotting it into the things you already have read about the topic being covered. Authors typically have a set of ideas that they want to communicate and you have no way of knowing whether or not their writing is laced with a big dose of biased opinion. Your job as an evaluator of evidence is to read things with a large pinch of salt and not take information at face value. If a writer has evidence to back up their assertions, or if their conclusions are based on sound experimental evidence, then you can be fairly confident that there is little bias and it is a valid source of information.

✎ Checklist

Check you've understood the key points covered in this chapter by seeing if you can answer the following questions:

✔ What is evaluation?

✔ What things do you need to think about when you're reading somebody else's work?

✔ How do you evaluate your own work?

✔ What can you do to remain objective?

✔ How do you think critically about paragraphs?

✔ How do you critically evaluate arguments?

✔ What do you have to remember about evidence when critically evaluating written work?

📖 References

Bierhoff, H.W., Klein, R. & Kramp, P. (1991). Evidence for the altruistic personality from data on accident research. *Journal of Personality*, 59, 263–280.

Eagly, A.H. (1987). *Sex Differences in Behaviour: A Social-Role Interpretation*. Hillsdale, NJ: Erlbaum.

Eagly, A.H. & Crowley, M. (1986). Gender and helping behaviour: a meta-analytic review of the social psychological literature. *Psychological Review*, 100, 283–308.

Eisenberg, N., Miller, P.A., Shell, R., McNalley, S. & Shea, C. (1991). Pro-social development in adolescence: a longitudinal study. *Developmental Psychology*, 27, 849–857.

Gelfand, D.M., Hartmann, D.P., Walder, P. & Page, B. (1973). Who reports shoplifters? A field experimental study. *Journal of Personality and Social Psychology*, 25, 276–285.

Korte, C. & Kerr, N. (1975). Response to altruistic opportunities in urban and nonurban settings. *Journal of Social Psychology*, 95, 183–184.

Milgram, S. (1970). The experience of living in cities. *Science*, 167, 1461–1468.

Miller, J.G. (1994). Cultural diversity in the morality of caring: individually oriented versus duty-based interpersonal moral codes. *Cross-Cultural Research*, 28(1), 3–39.

Nadler, A (1986). Help seeking as a cultural phenomenon: differences between city and kibbutz dwellers, *Journal of Personality and Social Psychology*, 51, 976–982.

Piliavin, I., Rodin, J. & Piliavin, J. (1969). Good Samaritanism: an underground phenomenon? *Journal of Personality and Social Psychology*, 13, 289–299.

Tower, R.K., Kelly, C. & Richards, A. (1997). Individualism, collectivism and reward alloca-
tion: a cross-cultural study in Russia and Britain. *British Journal of Social Psychology*, *36*,
331–345.

Yang, M.M. (1994). *Gifts, favors, and banquets: the art of social relationships in China*. Ithaca, NY:
Sage.

Chapter 9

So you think you can write good?

It is quite likely that, before you picked up and started reading this book, you were probably convinced you knew how to write a half-decent essay, or at least write an essay that more or less made sense. You should be able to see what is wrong with this chapter title, 'So you think you can write good?'. Hopefully you spotted that 'good' should be written as 'accurately' or 'properly' (or even just 'well'). If you did, congratulations—but read the chapter anyway. If not, then this chapter is one you should read very carefully!

It's amazing how easy it is to slip into the informal language you use when texting, emailing, or talking to your friends. You may have found you got away with it at school. However, this is not how you should write in your essays and reports at university and beyond. Here, the focus is very much on formal and precisely written prose.

If you're wondering what 'prose' means, it refers simply to the written word—the text, the nuts and bolts of your essay. The phrase 'continuous prose' refers to long sections of writing, such as an essay. If you find you are asked to write in 'more continuous prose' then it means you are breaking your writing up into sections that are too small. This means either that your sentences are short and disjointed so they don't fit together very well, or that you have too many subsections to your paragraphs or sentences, preventing you from developing an argument or point effectively. Of course, it could mean that you have written in bullet points rather than sentences. This is something that you should never do in written work (the one exception being the materials section of your method, as explained in Chapter 11).

There are many different ways to write but here we will focus on how to write formally for your essays and laboratory reports; in other words, the main focus of your work while at university. What will not be included in this chapter is a full breakdown of writing skills and so forth. Instead, there will be information that specifically targets key areas where students at university commonly experience problems.

We discuss the writing of essays in Chapter 10, and the writing of lab reports in Chapter 11.

We are going to break down the task of writing into five building blocks, which can aid your understanding of both English and writing, helping you to create more organized and effective reports and essays. Naturally, you may not need all of the tools below, but there are some important points within the chapter that will be of use to all situations where writing is involved; there are also some specific points to note which relate directly to writing within psychology.

The building blocks of writing: types of words

Most of you will have a fairly healthy grasp of language by this point in your academic life. However, you may not have remembered all that you were taught at school. If you feel that your vocabulary is not a varied as you would like, my suggestion would be to read more in general. You will find that individuals with the largest vocabularies are the ones who read the most books. My English teacher Mrs Davis used to say she could tell which book I'd been reading when she marked my essays as I'd taken on the style of writing of that book and had introduced new words to my vocabulary. So, as I found, reading is a natural and easy way to expand your vocabulary. However it only works if you read books which challenge you in some way. You will be doing a significant amount of reading during your studies; hopefully the technical terminology will sink in the more you read. Box 9.1 contains some common types of words that you will have heard of many times before, but possibly not have a clear understanding of—despite using them instinctively on a daily basis.

The building blocks of writing: what is grammar?

Firstly, try to write down what grammar actually is. What you will have found, unless you remember all of the early teaching from your English classes at school, is that

---

Box 9.1

Adjectives: qualify or group nouns together. They can place the noun (e.g. home, away), time the noun (e.g. sooner, later), or describe the manner of the noun (e.g. slow, quick).

Adverbs: have two forms, adverbials which give information (e.g. here, slowly, already), or sentence adverbials which link the text (e.g. finally) or allow comment (e.g. fortunately).

Conjunctions: are words which join together other words and phrases (e.g. but, because, therefore, since).

Nouns: identify an object, thing, person or place. ('book', 'table', 'man' are all examples of nouns.) They can quantify (e.g. one, several), determine (a, an, the) or be modified by using an adjective (e.g. young or funny).

Proper nouns are words which indicate people or places. These have their first letter capitalized (e.g. Pavlov, England). They also do not necessarily have to be a single word (e.g. *Oxford English Dictionary*).

Prepositions: are smaller words used to join nouns, and so on, into phrases (e.g. as, by, before, until, after).

Pronouns: are used as substitutes for other words, enabling you to refer back to previously defined information (e.g. we, they, mine, theirs, who, that, which, this, themselves).

Verbs: generally referred to as 'doing' words (e.g. to draw, to think, to have), they provide information about the subject (person or thing).

you won't be able to pin down exactly what it is. We all know that we need to write using good grammar in our essays and reports, but actually defining it is rather more difficult.

Grammar describes the way your sentences are constructed, and determines how your sentences 'work' (or not, as the case may be). Grammar can be thought of as a series of building blocks, which are assembled to form an overall structure: your written prose. Most of you will have no problem instinctively writing grammatically correct sentences; but knowing what the building blocks of grammar are will help enormously with your confidence when writing essays and reports. Knowing about grammar will also help you avoid negative comments from your tutor, and help you understand the comments when you do get them!

Sentences are broken up into clauses, each of which can stand on their own as a sentence. A simple sentence is one clause. Multiple sentences are just those with more than one clause. Clauses are joined together in various ways: by using punctuation, rephrasing the two clauses so the join is seamless, or by using 'joining' words such as '*and*'.

The building blocks of writing: structure and organization

Sentences

A sentence should make sense by itself: it must be complete within itself, and end with a full stop. This sounds rather obvious, but it's amazing how many sentences are written by students which are not complete within themselves and don't make sense (see Example 9.1). The first three sentences are simply incomplete and make no sense on their own; you're left with more questions. The last example sentence is the opposite of these; it has far too many ideas in it and should split up into several sentences rather than one. This example shows you how important full stops are.

Example 9.1: Examples (taken from student work with permission)

- I also feel that those who scored highly aggressive on the initial questionnaire.
- After which it declines.
- Clear insight into how a simple misconception can result in a difference between success and failure.
- Reactive depression is quite mild to quite serious whereas endogenous depression is extremely severe, symptoms of depression can occur because of maladaptive thinking for example if you always think negatively about yourself and think that you are unable to accomplish tasks then this can lead to depression also a decrease in the neurotransmitter serotonin can cause depressive symptoms as it plays a large part in emotions. (Cardwell et al., 2004).

....

Exercise 9.1: Correcting sentences

Correct the last sentence in Example 9.1 by placing punctuation in the correct places for it to make sense rather than being one big incorrect sentence. For the answers, see 'Answers to exercises' at the end of the book.

....

Paragraphs

A paragraph is a collection of sentences combined to convey one single, logical point of your argument. It is therefore impossible for a single sentence to qualify as a paragraph. It's important that your paragraphs communicate a single point only. If you find you are splitting a single point in your argument over several paragraphs, you will need to join them together into one larger one. Alongside this, if you find that you are making several points in one paragraph you can chose either to change the emphasis of the points you are making, combining them into a logical cohesive section of your argument, or splitting them into several smaller paragraphs.

Each subsequent paragraph should follow on from the previous one in a logical manner. The idea behind your reports and essays is to tell some form of story, whether it is your argument for a particular essay discussion point, or whether it is the story of your experiment. Using paragraphs effectively can help you make your story more logical, organized and clear. There is no set rule as to how long a paragraph should or should not be. However, as noted above, you should never have a paragraph as short as a single sentence. Figure 9.1 shows you how paragraphs can neatly link into each other, but how each paragraph consists of a single idea.

⇒ We discuss writing essays in more detail in Chapter 10.

The end result for your essay or report should be a sequential and logical provision of information; a little like a story, it should have a start, middle and end. This means that there should be an introductory paragraph and a concluding paragraph.

....

The building blocks of writing: squiggly symbols (aka punctuation)

The easiest way to describe punctuation is to say that it equals written breathing. The best way to check if you've got the punctuation about right in your essays and reports is to read them aloud to yourself. If you have got the punctuation about right you will not be out of breath by the end of the first paragraph. On the other hand, if you find that you have problems breathing, because the words keep coming and there is nowhere to breathe, then you probably need to sort out your punctuation. Now imagine that your tutor is reading your essay or report aloud: punctuation describes the elements of your written prose where the reader gets a chance to breathe. In effect, punctuation does for the written word what dynamics and tempo do for music: it gives the written word some depth and tone.

Visual information processing itself is the transformation of a visual input into a meaningful perceptual experience. As the light from the environment passes through the eye, the lens and iris combine to direct light onto the retina. The cones and rods, which make up the cells in the retina, contain cells which convert light into electrical energy which is sent to the brain through the optic nerve, millions of cell fibres which make up the 'blind spot' and transmit information collected from the eye directly to the brain.

> This paragraph is just briefly describing how light is processed by the eye

As this information flows up the optic nerve, it travels through the optic chiasm and to the lateral geniculate nucleus (LGN) which is a part of the thalamus. Once here, they form optic radiations which lead directly to the primary visual cortex where further processing occurs. The information is processed by the visual cortex and sent on one of two pathways to the rest of the brain: the dorsal pathway to the parietal lobe or the ventral pathway to the temporal lobe.

> This paragraph is briefly describing how information travels to the visual cortex

The parietal lobe deals with information about visual movement in the environment, where something is in the visual field, allowing the observer to detect the direction of moving targets, judge distances of moving objects and to be able to judge distances in order to pick objects up. The temporal lobe deals with what is in the visual field, acting like a giant dictionary of what an object is.

> This paragraph is briefly describing how information is directed to different parts of the brain

Figure 9.1: An example of paragraphs which link and flow into each other (information from Carlson et al., 2010).

Punctuation also has another job: it enables you to change the meaning of sentences. In Example 9.2, there are two sentences with identical words. However, they both have very different meanings.

Example 9.2: How punctuation can change meaning

> All that is different between the two pairs of sentences is two commas, but the meanings are completely different

(a)

1(a) The lecturer said the student was not concentrating.

1(b) The lecturer, said the student, was not concentrating.

> The difference between sentence 1a and 1b is the topic, or subject, of discussion

(b)

2(a) The cat thought the dog ate the chicken.

2(b) The cat, thought the dog, ate the chicken.

> Here, you can see that sentence 2a is speculating on a situation, whereas sentence 2b makes a statement about it.

Types of punctuation

Before reading this section compete Activity 9.1.

Activity 9.1: Defining punctuation

For each of the punctuation symbols listed, write down what they look like and when you think you would use them. If you can't work out how to phrase their use then use examples to explain what you mean.

- Comma
- Parenthesis
- Full Stop
- Colon
- Semi-Colon
- Dash
- Hyphen
- Apostrophe
- Single Inverted Commas
- Double Inverted Commas

Commas

Commas are the written form of taking a 'breath'. Officially this means putting a comma between the different clauses in the sentence, the sections, or to simply make the sentence easier to read. If you want to know if you've got your commas in the correct place, read the text in Exercise 9.2 out loud and work out where there should be commas; then put them where you think they should go. For the answers, see 'Answers to exercises' the end of the book.

Exercise 9.2: Commas confusion

Psychology is the study of everything from biology and neurology to behaviour language and social interactions. Essentially it is the study of what we do and why we do it. In this way psychology is different from the other sciences which look at what and how things happen as we psychologists are looking at why things happen as well.

There are also other uses for commas. For example, they can be used to separate items in a list. If you want to write a list of words a researcher used then you can list them as in Example 9.3.

Example 9.3: Commas in lists

The researcher was interested in replicating the study by Baddeley et al. (1975), but using common animal names such as cat, rat, monkey, and rabbit, and uncommon animal names such as dragon, sloth, and mammoth.

The other major use for commas is to present parenthetical information—that is, 'asides'. Most of you would use brackets to add an 'aside' in a sentence. Actually, you should be using commas either side of the 'aside' statement, but it is acceptable to use brackets. However, the flow of writing is often interrupted when you use them, so in essays and reports it is often better to use commas instead. In Example 9.4, the same phrase has been written with commas and then with brackets.

Example 9.4: Commas or brackets

> Commas help the sentence to flow clearly and logically

(a) *With commas as brackets*: The researcher found that we are more able to remember animal names which are common, such as cat and monkey, than uncommon names, such as sloth and dragon.

(b) *With brackets as parentheses*: The researcher found that we are more able to remember animal names which are common (cat, monkey) than uncommon names (sloth, dragon).

> Brackets disrupt the flow of the sentence and hinder comprehension of the point

Using commas after 'and' can be a tricky subject, and while researching this book I came across various arguments both for and against its use. The general consensus appears to be that having a comma before the last item in a list, before the 'and', can be quite useful in order to avoid ambiguity (see Example 9.5)—for example, 'the flag was red, white, and blue'.

Example 9.5: Comma use to avoid ambiguity

Avoiding ambiguity

Words found in a thesaurus do not always sound more impressive, they can sound ridiculous as the words chosen are not always synonymous with the original word used.

'And' in a list

Gibson's approach to visual perception involves the following concepts: motion parallax, the optic array, optic flow, horizon ratio, texture gradient, and affordance (Carlson et al., 2010).

Inverted commas: single and double

Inverted commas are those punctuation marks which look like commas, but are placed above the words rather than below. Single and double inverted commas are frequently misused and confused in undergraduate essays. If you are one of the many who get confused about which to use when, then read this section carefully.

There is no strict rule about whether to use single or double inverted commas. The main idea is to be consistent within your report or essay; you should never be using them interchangeably in a single piece of work, but you may use them both in different ways. The easiest way to think about it is to use *double inverted commas for quotations* and *single inverted commas for emphasis*, or to highlight that something is not your idea.

Double inverted commas are commonly used as quotation marks. These are used whenever you are taking material direct from another source and using it word for word (that is, you are 'quoting' the material). When providing a quote in this way you must include a reference in the text to indicate where the quote came from; you will need to state the page numbers in brackets after you have written the quotation, as shown in Example 9.6.

We discuss the topic of referencing in more detail in Chapter 13.

Using quotations is a sticky subject in psychology. Some lecturers are happy for you to include them, others prefer you not to. In principle, the use of properly cited quotations is fine. However, a perceived problem with them is that they show no evidence of understanding—and this is generally one of the things we, as lecturers, are looking for in your essays and reports. A better approach is to paraphrase what you want to quote instead of using lots of quotations. By doing this, you can show that you do understand the content—although you still need to provide a reference in the text, as explained in Chapter 13. The difference between paraphrasing and quotation is illustrated in Example 9.6.

➠ We discuss paraphrasing in Chapter 10.

Example 9.6: Quotations versus paraphrasing

(a) Quotation

"Mental muscle will weaken if not exercised, but you don't need to memorise Shakespeare to keep the brain in shape … Acquisition of new skills, be they physical or cognitive, keeps our little grey cells fit—and that can only be a good thing." (Aaen-Stockdale, 2006, p.415)

> Don't forget to include a reference with your quotation–including the page number

(b) Paraphrasing of the quotation

We need to make sure we are always using our brain if we want to keep it functioning well. We will lose our mental agility if we do not use our brains on a regular basis. Any new skill can be beneficial to our brains; it doesn't have to be just reading: it can be learning a new skill or a physical activity (Aaen-Stockdale, 2006).

> Don't forget still to include a reference. This may be how you've phrased it, but it's still the writer's work.

Apostrophes

The apostrophe is misused frequently, in particular when it's used with 'it'. The apostrophe has two main uses: to indicate possession and to show that one or more letters have been missed out. There are, of course, situations where the basic rules are amended slightly, and it is in these situations that the problems occur.

'Possession' refers to the use of the apostrophe to show that something belongs to someone—for example, the *dragon's* lair, or the *school's* uniform policy. Example 9.7 shows that the instruments belong to the musician rather than anyone else.

The exception to the rule is when the word 'it' is involved. Because you shorten 'it is' to 'it's', you cannot use the apostrophe to indicate possession, as it creates two words that are identical. This would lead to excessive confusion. So the simplest way to write them is 'its' to indicate possession and 'it's' in contraction form.

Contraction is the formal term for when words are put together to form a new one, producing an overall, shorted word meaning the same thing. The apostrophe is placed where the missing letters would have been. Example 9.7 shows that 'did not' has been shortened to 'didn't', and 'should not' has been shortened to 'shouldn't'.

Example 9.7: Possession and contraction

(a) *Possession:* A musician's instrument is a very precious item, which other people should not attempt to touch without express permission from the musicians themselves.

(b) *Missing out letters (contractions):* They didn't find it funny at all, but the rest of the musicians thought they shouldn't take it so seriously.

Full stops

Full stops should be fairly easy to use correctly. What you need to bear in mind is that they should be used rather more frequently in science reports than in literature-based work. In science it is generally necessary to write in concise sentences with minimal clauses, or sections (see Example 9.8). In literature-based work it is perfectly acceptable to write in long, multiple-clause sentences.

Example 9.8: Using shorter sentences

Biological rhythms regulate all sorts of parameters in our body. These can be stimulated by internal and external events. Infradian rhythms are rhythms that occur less than once a day. Circadian rhythms are those which occur once every day. Ultradian rhythms are rhythms which occur more than once every day (Cardwell et al., 2004).

Colons and semi-colons

Colons are tricky creatures: we all know what they are but very few people know how to use them properly. There are three uses for a colon (see Example 9.9): the first being to introduce lists; the second being to introduce speech or a quotation; and the third being to separate two parts of a sentence which are linked. You should not need to use a colon to introduce speech during your studies in psychology, but you will need to use the colon in the other two ways mentioned here.

Example 9.9: Uses of colons

(a) *Lists with colons and commas*: Psychology is made up of lots of different topics: cognition, biology, philosophy, mathematics, physics, behaviour and perception.

(b) *Lists with colons and semi-colons*: Students need to consider many things when writing essays: what the question is asking; where to get information about the topic; making sure they produce a clear argument; plus critically examining the subject in an objective manner.

(c) *Separating parts of a sentence*: Humour is tricky subject: we all know what we find funny but not everyone agrees with us.

Semi-colons are also tricky; more people know how to use these, but they don't seem to use them often enough. In your essays and reports there are always plenty of opportunities to use semi-colons, but the vast majority of essays I mark don't contain any. The main use of semi-colons is to indicate a break between two parts of a sentence which are closely linked (see Example 9.10); splitting the information into separate sentences changes the meaning slightly simply through that separation. Semi-colons can also be used in lists where multiple words make up the individual items on the lists.

Example 9.10: Separating linked parts of sentences with semi-colons

There are many things you need to learn at university; along with all the knowledge you will acquire, you need to learn how to look after yourselves on a daily basis without parental involvement.

Punctuation marks you should avoid

You all know when to use question marks. What you should remember now is that you shouldn't use them in your reports and essays. This sounds easier than it is: the nature of psychology lends itself to asking many questions. The way to get round this is to use statements rather than questions. It gives the impression of confidence rather than uncertainty. In Example 9.11 below you can see that the question gives the impression that the writer isn't sure about what they're writing about, whereas the statement implies they do know and are about to provide an explanation.

Example 9.11: Questions versus statements

Question
Can Freud's work really be applied to modern culture in any country?

Statement

It can be speculated that Freud's work is not applicable within modern society.

> A statement makes the reader aware that you have an answer for the question

Exclamation marks should also not be used. They are a part of informal writing styles, and therefore do not belong in formal writing. If you want to make a point that something should be taken extra note of then use adverbs (see Box 9.1) to highlight and comment on how your point needs to be taken (see Example 9.12). Doing something as basic as this will help improve the quality of your writing.

Example 9.12: Avoiding exclamation marks

(a) *With an exclamation mark*: Some people still do not realise that psychology is a science!

(b) *Using an adverb to do the same job*: It is staggering that some people still do not realize that psychology is a science.

> The sentence adverb 'staggering' does the same job as an exclamation mark

Italics are used to emphasize certain words within a sentence. Generally, in psychology you won't need to do this very often. Use of italics isn't exactly banned; rather the advice is to use them with caution and only when it is absolutely necessary.

....

Exercise 9.3: Placing punctuation

Put the punctuation in the correct places in the following list. For the answers, see 'Answers to exercises' at end of the book.

1 One fine day in the middle of the night two dead men got up to fight back to back they faced each other drew their swords and shot each other

2 The dragon was most displeased that he was told to stop eating the small kittens as they were his favourite snack and he couldn't work out what he might find to replace them the townspeople were pleased however as now the rat population could be kept under control

3 Of the many creatures available to join Noah on his ark the tigers were by far the most dangerous of the bunch they have very few predators only the panthers lions and elephants stood much chance against them they were however reluctant to interfere with the alligators and crocodiles the rather large jaws kept most creatures away from them

4 The students were silent in the class as they worked hard on their work the teacher looked on with a sense of satisfaction realizing that the students had finally learned how to work independently without complaint she was reassured that they had actually been listening during the previous lesson

....

The building blocks of writing: expressing yourself

Step one

The first thing you need to think about is which 'voice' you are using; the 'voice' is determined by what is called the *personal pronoun*. This simply means the word you are using to refer to an object, thing, person or idea. Box 9.2 spells out the three categories of personal pronouns. For your formal essays and laboratory reports you will always need to write in the third person. This is because science is an objective field of study; the idea is that you communicate ideas and arguments dispassionately and objectively. Use of first or second personal pronouns implies subjective speculation, and therefore makes your reports unscientific and non-objective. So, remember to use the third person whenever you are writing your essays and laboratory reports.

Box 9.2

First (1st) personal pronoun: *I, me, we, ours, mine*
Second (2nd) personal pronoun: *You, your, yours*
Third (3rd) personal pronoun: *That, this, it, his, him, her, hers*

Use of the third personal pronoun is easier than it sounds. In experimental reports, for example, students frequently write the procedure in the first or second person, rather than the third person as they should. The way to avoid this is to simply imagine that you are looking down on yourself conducting an experiment (see Box 9.3: the examples in the third person will help you do this); you can also provide your opinion quite easily using this particular method.

Step two

The next thing you need to think about is the actual tense you will need to use. Many of you will think that there are three tenses in English: past, present and future. Actually, there are only two tenses in English: past and present. The details behind how the future tense works is rather odd, but as you all know how to do it instinctively I'll not cover it here. If you're interested then please see Seely (2009) for details. You don't need to worry too much about the 'future' tense; the one you need to use in your reports and essays is the PAST tense.

Box 9.3 shows you how to phrase your report in the third person past tense, and also give examples of how to provide your opinion using this tense. These are contrasted with the phrases you may have used but shouldn't be—those in the first or second person.

Box 9.3

3rd person: *It would appear that …*

2nd person: *You can see that …*

1st person: *This shows me that …*

3rd person: *The experiment was conducted …*

1st person: *We conducted an experiment …*

1st person: *I conducted an experiment …*

3rd person: *It is generally believed that …*

2nd person: *As you can see, researchers believe that …*

1st person: *I believe that …*

3rd person: *The current experiment provides more evidence that …*

1st person: *Our experiment provides more evidence that …*

1st person: *My experiment provides more evidence that …*

3rd person: *The evidence indicates that …*

2nd person: *This evidence shows you that …*

1st person: *This evidence shows me that …*

3rd person: *The researchers handed out the questionnaire …*

1st person: *We handed out a questionnaire …*

1st person: *I handed out a questionnaire …*

3rd person: *While it has been shown that … it can also be argued that …*

2nd person: *While you can see that … you could argue that …*

1st person: *While I have shown that … I could also argue that …*

3rd person: *The current experiment does not follow the pattern in the literature; this may be because …*

1st person: *Our experiment does not follow the pattern in the literature; this may be because we …*

1st person: *My experiment does not follow the pattern in the literature; this may be because I …*

Different types of writing style

Generally, you will need to write in a formal manner for your essays and reports: it will largely be frowned upon if you use an informal writing style. The question now becomes: what constitutes formal and informal writing?

The manner in which this book is written is not formal. Rather, it is a mix of informal and formal writing styles. There are easy ways to tell if a piece of text is written informally: it may sound as though the writer is talking to you personally; the first or second personal pronouns are used; or words may be contracted (see below). Formal writing does not contain these, contractions are frowned upon and the third personal pronoun in always used.

Acronyms

An acronym is a shorthand form of a phrase, which is assembled from key letters that appear in that phrase. For example, autoimmune deficiency syndrome is more commonly written as AIDS. The use of acronyms in a formal piece of work is absolutely fine (see Example 9.13). However, you must remember to explain what they stand for the *first* time you use them (for example, writing Second Life *(SL)* the first time it's used and then using *SL* subsequently). If you fail to do this then you run the risk of whoever is reading your essay not realizing you know what you're talking about.

Example 9.13: Acronyms you may use in psychology

- DSM IV—*Diagnostic and Statistical Manual 4th Edition.*
- WMM—Working Memory Model
- PASW—Predictive Analytics Software
  - Formerly called SPSS—Statistical Package for the Social Sciences

Abbreviations

Barring a few exceptions, you should never include abbreviations in formal writing such as essays or reports. It is remarkably common how often 'text' language appears in undergraduate essays, despite the obvious fact that it is not formal language and common sense dictates that it should not be used. The language you use when texting friends or chatting on messaging programs is automatically informal, and should never be used in your essays or reports.

There are some commonly used abbreviations which can be used without explanation, for example AIDS, DNA or BBC. These are known to those outside science and require no explanation. However, there are some commonly used abbreviations among students which *should not be used*, in reports in particular.

These are as follows:

- pp should always be written as 'participant'.
- fig may appear abbreviated in many journal articles, but it should always be written out in full for your essays or reports (figure)—regardless of what you read in journal articles.
- quantity abbreviations such as '2nd' should always be written as words (second).

Contractions

A contraction refers to the combination of two words into one: for example, don't (do not), didn't (did not), won't (will not); or shrinking a single word such as cannot (can't). Occasionally, more than two words get contracted into terms in common use; one of these which you are probably familiar with is *'innit'*, a contraction meaning *isn't it*, or *is it not.* When you think about *innit* like this, it should make rather less sense when it's tacked onto the end of the vast majority of sentences by some.

As a rule, contractions are not used in formal writing. They may be scattered liberally throughout this book, but it's written in an informal manner in order to make it more accessible to those reading it. As a rule, this is not an aim of formal writing; what you need to do is convey your arguments effectively, using technical terminology. This applies to written work in all subjects. If it's a formal essay or report, simply avoid contractions.

Effective writing—how to communicate your thoughts clearly and precisely

Tip one

Plan your essay or report and make sure you know exactly what you want to say. This includes what studies and evaluation points you want to use. Make sure you work out which order you want to put your points in. This way you can make sure the flow of the essay or report is logical and answers the question posed.

Tip two

Define all terms when you first use them, and put the abbreviation or acronym in brackets. After that, you can use the abbreviations or acronyms without further explanation.

Tip three

Avoid ambiguity: make sure your meaning is very clear.

Tip four

Avoid commonly overused words such as also, therefore and finally. These are frequently overused at the start of sentences in undergraduate essays, and there is no need for it.

✎ Checklist

Check you've understood the key points covered in this chapter by seeing if you can answer the following questions:

   ✔ When should you use a comma?

   ✔ Can you write 'and' after a comma?

   ✔ Why should you try to use commas instead of brackets for parenthesis?

✔ What's the difference between a colon and a semi-colon (and when should you use them)?

✔ Why should you try to avoid using quotations?

✔ How do you make a statement with words instead of an exclamation mark?

✔ Which tense do you use when writing essays and reports?

✔ Which personal pronoun should you be using?

✔ What key thing should you do when using acronyms?

📖 References

Aaen-Stockdale, C. (2006). Clowning about in brain scanners. *The Psychologist, 19*(7) 414–415.

Baddeley, A.D., Thomson, N. & Buchanan, M. (1975). Word length and the structure of short-term memory. *Journal of Verbal Learning and Verbal Behaviour, 14*, 575–589.

Cardwell, M., Clark, L. & Meldrum, C. (2004). *Psychology (3rd Edition)*. UK: Harper Collins.

Carlson, N.R., Martin, G.N. & Buskist, W. (2010). *Psychology (4th Edition)*. Hove: Pearson Education.

Seely, J. (2009). *Oxford A–Z of Grammar & Punctuation*. USA: Oxford University Press.

📖 Useful sources of information

Haddon, J. & Hawksley, E. (2006). *Getting the Point: A Panic-Free Guide to English Punctuation for Adults*. Edinburgh: Floris Books.

Seely, J. (2009). *Oxford A–Z of Grammar & Punctuation*. USA: Oxford University Press.

Chapter 10

Writing essays

You are likely to have written many essays in your education so far; now you're studying psychology you have many more to come. Some of you will already have acquired the skills it takes to write a good essay, but there are probably many more of you who could still do with a few pointers. This chapter will focus on the core elements required to write an effective essay specifically in psychology. (For ease of writing and comprehension, the terms 'essay' and 'assignment' have been used throughout this chapter. However, all the information given here is equally important for dissertations and theses as well, so readers of all levels should pay careful attention to this chapter.) Obviously different writing styles are appropriate to different publications, so it is important to remember that the writing style used for this book will not necessarily be the same as that to be used when writing an academic essay.

At a basic level, psychological essays are no different from any other essay you'll ever write. However, at a more specific level you need a lot more reliance on evidence (be that theories and/or experiments other people have done), and less reliance on speculation and personal opinions. In this chapter, I will not be covering the steps you need to produce the perfect essay, those come with practice only. Instead, I have provided a collection of tools which will help you develop your own essay-writing skills, hopefully helping you to achieve better grades on your assignments and improve your writing as a whole.

For those of you who think you already write a perfect essay, well done, but there's really no such thing! There are always new things you can learn and always improvements that can be made, so read on and hopefully you will learn something new to help you improve your essays and assignments. We'll go through how to set up your essay, how to clearly answer the question, how to convey your understanding and clearly present your argument and how to effectively use evidence to make your points.

Structure—the basic essay format

The fundamentals of essays are something you will all be familiar with: essays have a beginning, a middle and an end. However, many of you may not have had specific instruction on how to use this information to your best advantage. Much like an hourglass, essays are broad at the start and the end, but narrow into more detail in the middle.

Hopefully most of you will have covered how to use paragraphs to structure essays. Indeed, many English departments in UK schools teach students to use a particular method to help them learn how to accurately and effectively answer essay questions: the PEE method. The acronym PEE stands for *point, evidence, evaluation* and will be covered in more detail below; it is a useful way to ensure you contain a decent amount of material (enough evidence to support what you want to say), and commentary on that material, sufficient for you to be able to answer the question.

Addressing the question

Both teaching staff and students agree that answering the question is the most important part of an assignment. Unfortunately, it's one of the most difficult aspects of an essay to do, and one that many students struggle with. This is not because they can't, but more that they get so caught up in the essay itself that they get distracted and wander off-topic. Occasionally, when presented with more complex questions, students don't quite understand what is being asked of them, so end up writing about the topic area rather than answering the question being asked.

Common words in essay titles

There are a number of words that appear frequently within essay titles, and they all indicate specific things about what you must do within your essay. However, they are often misinterpreted, so the first thing you need to do in this section is see if you know what they all mean (see Box 10.1 for answers).

1 Analyse

2 Assess

3 Compare and contrast

4 Criticize

5 Define

6 Describe

7 Discuss

8 Examine

9 Illustrate

10 Interpret

11 Justify

12 Outline and evaluate

13 Relate

14 To what extent

Note: The list of words and phrases in Box 10.1 is by no means an exhaustive list, but simply captures some of the more common words or phrases you will find in essay titles.

Box 10.1

Analyse: Look at each element of the topic in great detail.

Assess: Estimate the value of the topic relative to the wider context of the topic area and the question itself.

Compare and contrast: Look for similarities in the topics mentioned, then set them in opposition with each other to highlight their differences

Criticize: Discuss the merits of a study, idea or theory in the light of your opinions, supporting and/or contradictory facts and other evidence from studies or theories. Support your discussion with plenty of evidence.

Define: Precisely state the meaning of a word or phrase.

Describe: Provide a detailed account of the topic without evaluation.

Discuss: Examine a particular argument as given in the essay title. Investigate this topic through use of an objective debate in which the pros and cons are clearly described and evaluated.

Examine: Investigate the nature of the topic.

Explain: Make sure the topic under discussion is made clear, all details are interpreted and any discrepancies accounted for.

Illustrate: Illustrate to provide explanation or clarify what the topic is about. Typically this will mean using plentiful studies and concrete, possibly real-world, examples to illustrate your answer. It can also be used to imply the inclusion of pictorial figures.

Interpret: Expand on and clarify the meaning of a topic; make clear and explicit, using your own judgement.

Justify: Draw conclusions and provide evidence to support those conclusions.

Outline and evaluate: Provide the main features or principles of the topic, emphasising structure and arrangement rather than minor details. Then make an appraisal of the topic, including supporting and contradicting evidence and ideas.

Relate: Explain how ideas or theories are connected to each other, how alike they are and how they affect each other.

To what extent: Describe the scope of the topic and discuss how far it goes to being able to answer the question being asked.

Go to www. oxfordtextbooks. co.uk/orc/parson/

....

Exercise 10.1: What is the question asking?

What is each of the following essay questions asking? What sorts of information would you include? Where would their focus be? For the answers, see 'Answers to exercises' at the end of the book.

_____

Discuss the different perspectives taken on schizophrenia over the course of history.

Describe the aetiology of the different stages of schizophrenia and its relation to how it can be treated.

....

Hints for staying focused when writing essays

Staying focused in your essay is an easy way to ensure your argument stays on track and you don't get _lost_. Use the points below to help you. Some examples of essays are provided online.

1. Work out what the keywords in the essay title are

The key to understanding an essay title lies in the keywords. These tell you what the essay is about and what you need to focus on during the essay. In the essay titles on schizophrenia in Exercise 10.1, the first title contains the keywords _discuss, perspectives,_ and _history_, whereas the second contains the keywords _aetiology, stages_ and _treatment_. It should be immediately obvious that the essays are looking for very different things, and it is also very clear what you need to focus your research on for those essays.

2. Brainstorm the essay title before starting to write or collecting more evidence

Brainstorming or free associating is a really good way to focus your essay and make sure you are answering the question throughout. It will help generate ideas and provide you with a complete answer to the question posed: remember that an essay is a response to a question; the essay is the evidence for the answer provided in the conclusion. Brainstorming will create a plan for your assignment, and will help you decide which material to use, and what not to use. It will also help you work out what the question is asking of you: at this point if you're not quite sure you can ask your tutor to explain it to you.

3. Make an essay plan (see Exercise 10.2)

Essay plans may seem very boring and sensible, but they're recommended for a reason: they're the best way to stay focused in your essay. Make sure you include all the key points you've produced in your brainstorming session. These points need to be listed in a logical order so they can be turned into a coherent narrative which will provide an answer to the essay question at the end of the essay. You need a logical progression from question and introduction to conclusion.

4. Make sure you have a solid starting point to your essay

A solid point generally takes the form of an initial paragraph which gives a brief overview of the essay topic. If you like you can provide a brief explanation of how the question will be addressed in the essay. Try to avoid a blow by blow description; this will render the essay a pointless read, and will annoy whoever is reading it. For example, try not say "I will do X and then I will do Y": you need to use the tactics outlined in Chapter 9, which discusses writing skills, and elevate your writing style now you're at university. These tactics will help you focus on the essay question.

5. Be ruthless with what information you include: only include information which addresses the question

A big problem with many essays is the level of 'waffle' that is included. Psychological essays are science essays. This means they have to be concise and to the point, with lots of evidence to back up any assertions. Deciding what information to include is difficult, but all it takes is a rather ruthless approach: decide before you write your essay, which pieces of evidence you are going to use and stick to that decision. If you absolutely have to get more evidence then do so as soon as possible: writers who change their mind about what to include throughout the writing process produce work that is illogical and lacks fluency. Deciding in advance what to include helps overcome this problem.

6. Don't rely on facts, research and quotations: discuss properly

It's easy enough to provide a list of evidence that supports the question posed in the title of your assignment: you can provide many facts and research studies. However, without a discussion linking these facts and studies together, your essay will look like a list rather than an essay.

7. Make sure each paragraph contains only one point—and refer to the essay question in each

Each paragraph of your essay should only contain one point or idea. This helps to make the essay clear and easy to read, and will improve the overall structure. A sentence at the beginning of each paragraph should be used to alert the reader to the idea or point of that particular paragraph, ideally linking with the previous point in the last paragraph and the keywords taken from the essay title. Referring to the essay title, or keywords, in each paragraph ensures you keep a tight reign on what you are writing, and will hopefully prevent you going off-topic. If you find that you've written a paragraph that makes no reference to the essay title or keywords, and does not relate to the rest of the essay, get rid of it. This may seem rather drastic but if this information is not contributing to your essay then it won't contribute to your marks: it's taking up space where useful information, which will get you marks, should be going. The last paragraph is for rounding up of your essay so you should not introduce new ideas or material at this stage.

8. Don't forget to PEE

PEE, better known as *point, evidence, evaluation*, is a common tool used to help with paragraph formation and structure within your essay. You may well have come across this before at school in your English lessons. The basic idea is to include your point, then provide some evidence, and follow this with evaluation. This whole process takes one paragraph, however long this might be. Don't get caught up in trying to do each part of the PEE. in a single sentence, you will end up with short, disjointed paragraphs.

9. Make sure you have a beginning, a middle and an end to your essay

As we saw at the beginning of the chapter, all essays require structure: you must start, discuss and conclude your essay. All essays have a point to them — to answer the essay question by means of developing ideas and points throughout the essay, to arrive at a conclusion, or answer, at the end.

10. Write at least one draft—never submit your first attempt

Draft essays are essentially practice essays. Drafts are very useful as they help you resolve any problems there might be with organisation and content within the essay. It's also quite helpful for you to see if there are any basic mistakes, such as spelling errors.

....

Exercise 10.2: Essay plans

A useful exercise at this point is to produce an essay plan. Some of you will be familiar with this part of the essay-writing process, but others will not. It is a good skill to learn though, and will help improve the quality of your writing.

Using the essay question provided and go through the steps in the list below. There are no right or wrong answers for this exercise, but an example is provided in the 'Answers to questions' at the end of the book.

Discuss the influence of nature and nurture in the development of behaviour (Essay length: 2000 words)

- Brainstorm the topic area
- Write a plan of your essay
  - If you want to do this at paragraph level then fine, although I'd recommend not doing this as it can be a little restrictive once you begin writing your essay. You need to allow yourself room to develop good points when you come to write your essay later, so don't get bogged down in what you might put in each of the paragraphs.
- Answer the following questions:
  1 Does this plan address the question?
  2 Have I included enough ideas to fill the essay?
  3 How could I improve my plan?

....

Structure—introductions and conclusions

Many students think that an essay needs to be stuffed full of facts and figures, studies and theories. This is not necessary: as we saw when covering staff and student expectations (see Chapters 3 and 5), the most important point of an essay is to provide the reader with enough information to convince them that the question has been answered correctly and effectively. Ideally, you will be able to convince the reader to agree with you in the conclusions you are drawing at the end of the essay through your presentation of evidence and argument.

We covered the basic structure of an essay at the beginning of the chapter, but the introduction and conclusion require special consideration: these two sections wrap your whole essay up in a sensible and logical package that answers the question. In other words, if your introduction and conclusions are strong, you will probably be creating a logical, sequential and strong essay which answers the question you have been set.

A *good introduction* clearly refers to the main points within the essay title, giving an overview of the key concepts on which the essay is based so that detail later on in the essay can be understood. This does not mean stating explicitly what you intend to do in the essay, as you may have been taught prior to university. (However, this is a method you can use until you get more confident.) For example, the essay on nature versus nurture in Exercise 10.2 could have an *intentions* introduction (this is what we don't want you to write, but don't mind so much in early level one essays) that goes a little like this:

In this essay the effect of nature and nurture on behaviour will be investigated. The concepts will be defined and then there will be a discussion of how much of our behaviour is due to nature and how much is due to nurture, or experience. The influence of nature and nurture on each other will also be discussed.

A really good introduction will refer to the essay question's keywords and explain them, while making it clear what the focus of the essay is. For example, the essay on nature versus nurture we covered in the previous section could have an introduction (that we do want you to write) that goes a little like this:

Both nature and nurture influence our behaviour. However, the key issue to be established is how much each contributes to the behaviours we display and what interactions there may be with the opposing force. Nature is all those elements of ourselves which we have inherited from previous generations—that is, the biological aspects of ourselves that we were born with. Nurture is all we have learned through our experiences and observations of others since we came into the world.

This above introduction is focused and clearly outlines the scope of the essay to come and defines the necessary concepts briefly and precisely.

A *good conclusion* answers the question and draws on the keypoints that you would've made throughout the essay. It also shows the reader what you think about the information you've provided. The conclusion is a singularly important part of your essay: it reveals what you think of what you've found out, and it shows your ability to draw logical decisions regarding arguments in your essay. This is why it is so important to include a conclusion and why you will lose marks if you don't include one.

For example, if we go back to the nature–nurture essay, a possible conclusion could be as follows:

> *It is meaningless to speculate that some aspects of our behaviour are purely the result of nature or nurture: it is evident that both nature and nurture play an important role in shaping our behaviour right from the moment we are born.*

Here there is a brief statement which indicates that equal information on both sides of the argument has been presented throughout the essay. A simple statement at the end of an essay that answers the question posed is all that is needed to provide an efficient and explanatory conclusion. It is also evident where the writer's opinion lies—firmly in the realm of nature and nurture having equal influences on human behaviours.

....

Exercise 10.3: Beginnings and endings

Look at the sample introductions and conclusions from various essays below and decide whether they are good or bad, and why. Each of these samples are explained in detail in 'Answers to exercises' at the end of the book.

....

Sample introductions

Example introduction 1

Essay question: What are the implications of research into attachment and day care for childcare practices?

> *Day care refers to non-parental care of children who live with their parents. This means that foster care is not included, nor is residential care. Foster care and residential care are concerned with looking after children who have experienced deprivation or privation, so it is difficult to know whether this or the care itself is the cause of any problems seen. Since day care involves separation from the primary attachment figure, attachment theorists would predict that this separation would adversely affect children's social development.*

Example introduction 2

Essay question: Describe the aetiology of the different stages of schizophrenia and its relation to how it can be treated.

Schizophrenia is a genetic disorder which requires an environmental trigger, usually in the form of significant stress, to be activated. Treatments for schizophrenia typically rely on individuals taking medication to control their symptoms, although these drugs are only useful for those with positive symptom such as hallucinations; they are ineffective in those with negative symptoms such as apathy and catatonia. The problem with medication is that the familiar hallucinations are removed and this can be quite upsetting for the schizophrenic individual, as it is as if their companions have suddenly left them.

Example introduction 3

Essay question: Discuss the reasons why people yield to majority influence.

There are several aspects to majority influence but they all centre on individuals conforming in order to be accepted into social groupings. People, as a whole, like being right and they like being liked. Normative social influence is where people conform in order to be liked and accepted as 'normal', whereas informational social influence means people are conforming in order to be accurate in what they are doing.

Sample conclusions

Example conclusion 1

Essay question: Outline and evaluate studies into psychological explanations of eating disorders.

Twin studies never show 100% concordance so it can't be just genetics: there has to be something else going on such as psychological trauma or family disturbance. It would be wrong to classify all anorexics the same though, so tailor-made rehabilitation programmes need to be used rather than a 'one size fits all' method. There is considerable research evidence into anorexia nervosa, much of which has shown that although there are biological and genetic elements, it is more likely that emotional and psychological factors trigger this particular eating disorder.

Example conclusion 2

Essay question: What are the implications of research into attachment and day care for childcare practices?

Another criticism is that 'aggression', in terms of the study, encompassed a whole range of behaviours that could be construed in a different way: for example, seeking adult attention, clowning around, and talking a lot. Moreover, the average rate of aggressive children in the US (where the study was conducted) is 17%—exactly what was found in another day care sample. It could be argued that children in day care are simply developing earlier than those not receiving day care.

Example conclusion 3

Essay question: Can the effects of privation be reversed? Evaluate with reference to research evidence.

The studies that have been mentioned have shown that privation is more reversible than first thought. The studies have shown us that the longer the period of privation is, the harder it is to reverse the effects of it. Overall, there is evidence to support both that the effects of privation can be reversed and that they cannot. It seems to be that there cannot simply be a generalized rule for recovery, but that the circumstances under how long and why privation has occurred have to be considered carefully in each individual case.

Demonstrating understanding

The most important thing you need to do in your essay is demonstrate you understand what you're writing about. We will establish in Chapter 12 that the inclusion of a large raft of quotations is *not* a method by which understanding is demonstrated. However, although your tutors are looking for evidence that you understand the theory, concept or research area, you are not expected to regurgitate everything you know about the topic in order to impress them and *prove* you understand. If anything, this will show you don't understand and have simply employed the 'carpet bomb' approach: include everything and hope some of it's right. There are a series of ideas here for how you might improve your ability to express what you do understand within your essay.

Chapter 12 discusses plagiarism and how to avoid it.

1. Write in your own words about the information you have gathered

We cover this point in Chapter 12, but it is worth repeating here: by using your own turn of phrase and expressions, rather than copying someone else's from a book, you are revealing that you understood what you have read and can be credited with having learned that material. If you copy or use anther person's turn of phrase, you cannot be credited with having learned the material, and will lose marks accordingly. As we cover in Chapter 12, quotations should be used sparingly or not at all. It is always possible to re-write information into your own words (always remembering to cite the source(s) you are paraphrasing), and unless it is a particularly wonderful way of expressing a vital point, it is probably not worth including a quotation.

2. Indicate why the information is relevant to your essay

Rather than simply stating a research theory or concept, you need to indicate why it is relevant to your essay and the argument you are trying to make. Many undergraduate essays are guilty of simply stating a lot of research evidence and describing concepts, but there is minimal evaluation and explanation to support the arguments they may, or may not, be making. Points are made in the explanations, not in the evidence—the evidence is there to support the point you are making; it is never the point itself.

The easiest way of avoiding this error is to write your essay without evidence, and put the evidence for all your points afterwards. This way, you avoid using research theories and concepts as points, and you use them as evidence *for* your points instead. Note that in the extract below, the experiments of Goodale et al. (1991) and Servos et al. (1992) are not described. Instead, the key findings are used as evidence for the points being made; a description of the studies is not necessary in this instance.

Visual information about an object's structure and location are used to plan the movements of the limbs and hand before the grasping movement even begins (Goodale et al., 1991). In binocular feedback there are several types of cues available, such as stereomotion, diplopia and retinal disparities. Important information about the hand's trajectory could, therefore, be provided by the moving hand. Therefore it is necessary to establish whether binocular vision contributes anything to the online control of prehension or whether monocular vision will do just as well. Previous studies, notably Servos et al. (1992), have found that monocular visual cues are less effective than binocular cues for the on-line control of manual prehension.

---

3. Make sure you look outside the reading lists

In your first year you might want to stick to the reading lists provided, unless you are especially confident. However, from your second year onwards, you should be looking at the reading list as well as *other* texts and journal articles. It may be that during your first year you encounter the problem of everyone taking the same book from the library, and not being able to get hold of it, in which case you are forced into looking for other material. Just remember that most generic psychology textbooks contain roughly the same information so you are *not* at a disadvantage if the one your lecturer recommends is unavailable. The same goes for more specific textbooks: there is a plethora of books available on all subjects within psychology so there will always be one available on your essay topic.

4. Avoid regurgitating your lecture notes

If your lecturer wanted to re-read the lecture notes that they spent time preparing then they'd re-read them themselves. Lectures explain concepts and theories; they are never going to be pre-prepared essay plans. Producing arguments and essays is your job as a student who has to show evidence of learning and understanding; this is never going to be possible if you simply repeat what you heard in a lecture.

5. Avoid excessively detailed descriptions of research studies

A mistake commonly made by undergraduates, particularly those coming from A level psychology, is to describe every tiny section of the research studies they are including in their essays. This is a mistake because all it shows is your ability to read and repeat information; there is no opportunity to explain or relate to the essay question in any way if you simply describe a study in detail. The point being made here is to use the parts of the study that you need, and simply leave the rest. You will be providing a reference, so the reader can always find out the rest of the information if they so wish. However, it is a waste of valuable words if you provide every detail of the study. Use your words carefully in essays: you have a limit and so you must make sure each one counts.

Developing an argument

The concept of arguments in essays is difficult to grasp given the common meaning of the word 'argument'. An argument in the written world does not involve fisticuffs or shouting. Rather, it involves the calm presentation of ideas that lead to a particular end point, with one side of an argument being presented as better than the other. In other words, you're having a debate with yourself.

Arguments in essays are simply the development of ideas in a logical manner, typically aimed at leading the reader towards a particular conclusion that directly relates to the essay question. An argument is an objective presentation of ideas from different perspectives, which supports and validates the conclusion being drawn.

For it to be truly objective, both sides of an argument need to be presented. An objective argument will naturally not involve the personal opinions of the writer (in this case, you). Indeed, no subjective presentation of ideas should occur within your undergraduate essays, unless it is specifically called for by your tutor. A good argument avoids bias by including a lot of theories and research studies to support both sides: you should write fairly about the pros and cons of each standpoint within your essay argument.

Here are some guidelines to help you construct arguments in an objective fashion.

1. Try to avoid being one-sided: look at a variety of perspectives

A one-sided essay will be very biased towards one point of view only: this is against the whole idea of being objective, which is so important within psychology. It doesn't matter what your personal ideas are, or what conclusion you want to work towards; you need to present ideas from every point of view in order to draw an objective conclusion effectively.

2. It's OK to sit on the fence: don't feel you have to decide one set of ideas is better than the other

On many occasions it is not clear who may or may not appear to have the best argument to make about a particular topic. In this case it is perfectly acceptable to end your essay sitting on the fence. Just be sure to word your conclusion carefully, highlighting the fact that there is equal evidence on both sides of the debate, so a firm conclusion can't be drawn.

3. Read a lot of different sources: the more you read, the more ideas and perspectives you'll come into contact with

It's very true that the more you read the more you learn. This does not mean that you'll remember everything you read. Rather, you'll become more familiar with a subject and be able to work out which bits are, and are not, important. You tend to learn (and remember) the general concepts that underpin a subject area rather than all the explicit details about that subject; this makes life far easier when you come to write essays and assignments. If you have got a good overview of a topic area *before* you sit down to write your essay, you stand a much better chance of being able to get the key points and arguments across effectively. If you've read plenty of source material prior to starting writing, you will know which bits are important, how many different sets of ideas there are, and where the key areas of disagreement are. These are all important considerations when presenting an effective argument in your essay.

4. A logical essay order helps make the arguments clear, fluent and logically ordered

There are two basic methods of providing a well-rounded, unbiased, objective argument. In the first method, you go through one side of the argument and present all the evidence for that argument, and then do the same for the other. For example, you could describe and discuss the biological aspects of schizophrenia and all the evidence for that, and then describe and discuss the psychological explanations. Be sure to compare and contrast the two arguments at the end of your essay, before the conclusion. This creates a very basic order to your essay, which naturally ends up a little less integrated, and relies more on description, not discussion, than does the second, and preferable, method.

The second method of ordering your essay argument is to cover each specific point in turn. If we carry on with our example of a schizophrenia essay, you could discuss the origins of schizophrenia and how the two basic explanations differ, followed by symptoms and then treatments. Each major point can be discussed from both perspectives within that sub-section of your essay, so you compare and contrast as you go along. If you use this second method effectively you will end up with more marks, as it creates a better essay format and can lead to a better discussion with less reliance on description than method one.

Developing your argument from the essay title

Activity 10.1: Developing an argument

For this activity you'll need a general psychology textbook. (If you haven't got one to hand, borrow one from a friend.) This is a good exercise for working together if you can, because there is more scope for differences of opinion leading to friendly debate. Pick one of the following questions:

Stanley Milgram (1963) was justified in his controversial experimental method given what we have earned about human behaviour as a result. How far do you agree with this statement? Refer to research evidence in your answer.

How far can the Channel 4 programme *Big Brother* be considered a social experiment?

1 Brainstorm the topic area covered in the statement above then split your information into arguments for and against the statement.

2 Think about what your point of view is and why you might have that point of view. Are there any reasons why you think like this?

3 Consider the alternative points of view and find evidence to back up these different perspectives.

4 Which side has more evidence to support it and which side has the strongest argument?

5 How would you formulate that into an essay?

Formulating an argument in an essay is straightforward enough once you know how to do it. The first thing to remember is the PEE method: if you make a point you must back it up with some evidence and then explain what it means. There is no point including information and then not explaining why you have included it; you still need to explain why it's there, no matter how relevant and useful the information. Producing an argument is a bit like telling a story: it doesn't make sense if the order is all wonky and you forget to explain key elements. Keeping a tight rein on the structure of your essay will help you considerably in producing a logical and fluent essay argument: keep checking your work to ensure it is telling a logical 'story'.

You need to read widely to ensure your argument is as well developed as possible. Knowing what the topic area is all about it makes it far easier to construct your essay: critical points will be easier to pull out and contradictory opinions and evidence will be easier to find. Which set of evidence and ideas you agree with in a topic area is irrelevant when you're writing your essay; you need to provide a balanced and objective overview of the ideas and evidence for all sides of a particular debate, not just the one you agree with. This principle is an important element of scientific enquiry in general: your conclusion should be informed by a careful and objective weighing up of the evidence; you shouldn't allow your opinions to determine what conclusion you draw. The more evidence and discussion of that evidence you can produce in your essay, the more convincing your conclusions are likely to be.

Using and evaluating evidence in your essays

It is not always clear what counts as a good source to reference in your essays and assignments. Nobody expects you to be brilliant at picking source material straight away; you will automatically get better as you go through your degree. (The old adage that 'practice makes perfect' is very true most of the time, and essays are no different.)

Whatever points you are trying to make in your essay you need to back them up with evidence, theories and/or research studies. It may be quite irritating sometimes to have to do this, but it is convention to show your assertions have the backing of evidence. As you know, Psychology is a science, and scientists can state nothing without providing reasons why they are stating it.

You should mainly be focusing on empirical research evidence as supporting or contradicting evidence. Empirical evidence is essentially drawn from research studies rather than theories and other forms of information. The reason for this is simple: all empirical research is published in peer-reviewed journals, meaning that you can be sure that there is a minimum level of quality associated with that research and you can rely on it as a source of information. Generally it is better not to include any anecdotal evidence or information, however interesting it may be. Such evidence is not empirical or scientific and so cannot be useful to support your argument in a scientific essay. Indeed, non-validated anecdotal material should never be used to hinge arguments on in formal essays and assignments.

As I've said, try not to use quotations if possible. Essentially anyone reading your essay needs to be convinced that you understand what you're writing about; if you use quotations this is not necessarily the case, so you are using valuable words *not* communication understanding. Generally the tip is to paraphrase everything unless it is absolutely crucial to the point you are making that you use the original words, that is, if there is something vitally important that you draw attention to in the original phrasing from the researcher or theorist then by all means provide a quotation.

Finally we come to the assertion of your personal opinion. This is the hard part for many undergraduates: you are told to provide your opinion but are then penalised for saying what you think. The reason you may incur penalties may simply lie in the way

▥➤ We discuss the use of quotations in Chapter 12, when we explore plagiarism and how to avoid it.

▥➤ Chapter 9 discusses writing skills.

TABLE 10.1 Example useful phrases written in the third person

The evidence clearly shows that … (instead of *the evidence shows me that …*)	It is clear that … (instead of *it is clear to me that …*)
It has been demonstrated that … (instead of *I have shown that …*)	The possibility remains, however, … (instead of *you could still say that …*)
It can be suggested that … (instead of *I suggest that …*)	Future work should address/look at… (instead of *my future work will investigate …*)
The evidence naturally leads to the conclusion that … (instead of *the evidence I have presented clearly shows me that …*)	In light of the evidence presented it can be concluded … (instead of *I can conclude, based on the evidence I have presented …*)

you've phrased the presentation of your opinion: you may have used the first or second personal pronoun instead of the third personal pronoun. As we saw in Chapter 9, all academic writing should be in the third person, but simply doing this makes it a little more difficult to state what you think. You are suddenly unable to say 'I think', you have to be more creative with your phrasing. To help you, Table 10.1 lists some phrases that you can use to reveal your opinion in your essays.

··

✎ Checklist

Check you've understood the key points covered in this chapter by seeing if you can answer the following questions:

✔ What is the basic essay format?

✔ Do you know what the words in the question are telling you to do?

✔ How can you stay focused on the question when you're writing your essays?

✔ What makes a good introduction?

✔ What makes a good conclusion?

✔ How do you demonstrate you understand what you're writing about?

✔ What is an argument in terms of essay writing?

✔ How do you create a clear, unbiased argument in your essay?

✔ What kinds of information and evidence should you be focusing on in your essays?

✔ After you've found your information for your essay, how do you use it?

📖 References

Goodale, M.A., Milner, A.D., Jakobson, L.S. & Carey, D.P. (1991). A neurological dissociation between perceiving objects and grasping them. *Nature, 349,* 154–156.

Milgram, S. (1963). Behavioural study of obedience. *Journal of Abnormal and Social Psychology, 67,* 371–378.

Servos, P. & Goodale, M.A. (1994). Binocular vision and the on-line control of human prehension. *Experimental Brain Research, 98,* 119–127.

Chapter 11

Writing practical reports: how to write up an experiment

What are psychological reports?

Practical or laboratory reports (lab reports) are written in a particular format, which you will become very familiar with by the end of your studies. All journal articles are also based around the same structure. It's very straightforward, as long as you follow the order step by step. This is a skill you must learn when studying psychology, so it's worth keeping this chapter open when you're writing up your lab reports.

A lab report is written after you have conducted an experiment and want to write it up. Its purpose is to tell the reader what you did and why. Your report will also let the reader know how your results fit in with the wider topic area and other people's research. If the reader wants to replicate your experiment, then your report will tell them how. This ability to replicate is important as it allows other people to check your results and support or contradict them with their own experiments. This is how science moves forward and all scientists learn.

There are two basic types of report, the quantitative report and the qualitative report. Most of this chapter will cover quantitative reports, as the basics are applicable to both styles of report. However, there is a section at the end covering qualitative reports.

Box 11.1 shows you the basic differences between quantitative and qualitative data, and therefore what the two types of report cover.

Quantitative reports are those reports which deal with quantitative data only. By contrast, qualitative reports can deal with both, although the emphasis is obviously on qualitative data. You will be producing a quantitative report whenever you have collected numbers such as reaction times, scores on tests and so on.

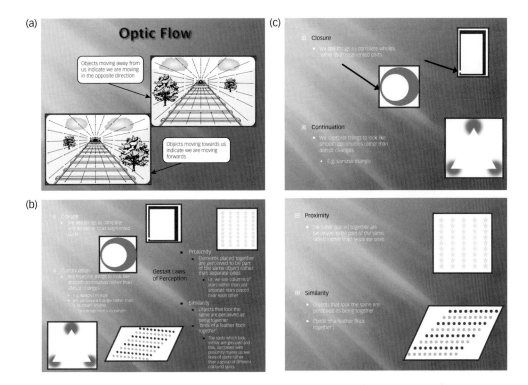

Plate 1: (a) A slide with useful pictures clearly linked to text. (b) A slide with too many pictures and no links to the words. (c) Figure 14.2b over two slides instead.

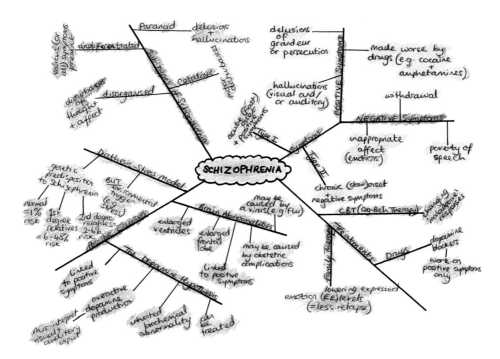

Plate 2: An example of a mind map.

Box 11.1

Quantitative data: Data which has a quantity, i.e. numbers. Analysis involves doing statistics. Any numerical data can be classified as quantitative (unless numbers are being used to classify words—so-called categorical data—in which case your data will be qualitative).

Qualitative data: Data which is richer in quality and contains more information than quantitative data. Analysis involves looking for patterns in written or spoken words (e.g. interviews or questionnaires). This includes any numerical data which represent words.

The basic structure

Your lab report will contain seven sections which I'll go through in turn:

- Abstract (see p.113)
- Introduction (see p.114)
- Methods (see p.118)
- Results (see p.121)
- Discussion (see p.125)
- References (see p.127)
- Appendices (see p.127)

Abstract

The abstract is basically a summary of your entire lab report, which means it's written last as you won't be able to write it until you've finished all the other sections. Ideally you should be able to summarize all the key points of your report so that someone else can read it and understand what you've done. This means you have to write very clearly and concisely, partly to fit everything in, and partly to make sure nobody misunderstands what you have written.

You should aim for the abstract to include one to two sentences related to each section, making the abstract between 150 and 250 words long. This is a maximum word length though, and frequently it helps to keep it to around 150 words. It is important to keep it short as it's a summary, not a re-statement of everything you've written. Also, as most lab reports at university have word limits of between 1500 and 2000 words, you do not want to use too much of this in a summary section; the introduction and discussion will always need more, rather than fewer, words.

The abstract needs to be brief: its purpose is not to tell the reader everything, but to make them want to read the entire report. Remember that the abstract sets the scene for the entire laboratory report and you need to make sure that the person reading (and

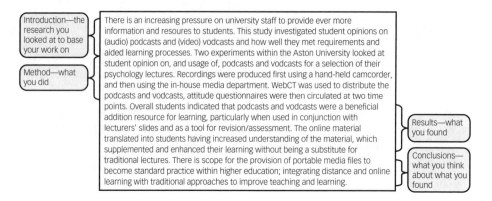

Figure 11.1: Abstract from a published report (Parson et al., 2009).

marking) your report understands the basics of your experiment in this section without having to go any further.

Try not to include too many specific details, but just summarize the key information. Also, try to remember to include your aim and/or experimental hypothesis. That way the abstract and your report are instantly presented in the context of what you've done. In the example in Figure 11.1, the aim rather than the hypothesis is stated as it was an exploratory study rather than a hypothesis-driven experiment and so there was no formal hypothesis. In your practical reports you will normally be expected to produce a hypothesis.

Introduction

The introduction is where you introduce the topic you are studying; you're setting the scene for your experiment. This may sound simple enough, but it's difficult to get right, and is more like an essay than a science report. You essentially have to tell the story of how you decided to do your experiment—how you got the idea and then how you worked out what to do.

Background information is crucial, but you do need to be picky with what you include. You will find that there is an awful lot of information on what you're studying, but not all of it is specifically relevant. You want to make sure you have between two and six studies that directly relate to your experiment, and then discuss these in detail. There are various things you need to consider when you're writing your introduction:

1. There's so much information out there—how do I know what to include?

Choosing what to include from the vast array of information is a difficult choice early on in your studies. There are lots of studies to choose from for all topics in psychology—lots of theories and lots of information. What you have to do is pick the *most appropriate* to what you are specifically writing up. For example, if you're writing up an experiment where you're looking at how the presence of others affects performance in cycling, you'll be delving into the sport and exercise psychology literature. There is a considerable amount here about aggression, tactics and competition; there are also many sports that people can use in their experiments. What you need to focus on in this instance is competition as this is the only element that is relevant to your particular practical. You'll also want to focus in further on the section of the literature that looks specifically at solo performance. All mention of group performance sports (such as football, where a considerable amount of literature is based) is probably not going to be relevant as cycling is typically a solo sport. The main thing to remember is only to include what is directly relevant to your experiment.

2. Is this the best way of illustrating the background to the experiment?

Having picked the information you want to include, the next step is to write it down in a manner which is most appropriate for your experiment. What a lot of undergraduates do is to list everything they've found and describe each study in detail. Unfortunately this is the wrong thing to do. Instead, work out the story you want to tell and use the information you have to illustrate that, not get bogged down in what each study or theory says in its entirety. An introduction is much like an essay in that you need to tell the story of how you came to be doing this experiment in the first place.

> ➡ We discuss the writing of essays in Chapter 10.

You should focus on the concepts rather than the detail from the studies you include. The studies are there as examples; for the most part, you should simply focus on the findings and conclusions from studies you include. When mentioning theories, you only need to focus on the key sections which relate to the experiment *you* are doing.

In short, if you find you are listing everything that you've found rather than using the information to tell a story, you will need to change how you do things. One easy way of doing this is write down the key bits of information from each of the studies you have details of, then use those notes to write your introduction.

3. Is everything clear?

Have you written everything clearly throughout your introduction? If not then you might want to reword some of it. What you want is for the lecturers marking your work to clearly see that you understand. Frequently, students do understand what they've written but get in a bit of a muddle when they write it, or they may choose to use words which they've found in a thesaurus and don't fully understand. In both situations the student then loses marks because they haven't conveyed that they understand very well. The tip here is to write in plain English as much as possible and use the correct technical language. Read through what you've written carefully: are there any bits where you're wondering what you mean? Getting a friend to read your work helps here too as they don't know what you meant to say so they will be able to point out anything that isn't clear.

4. Are there any gaps in the research and how does your experiment tackle them? In other words—why are you doing this experiment?

This is a surprisingly crucial element of an introduction, and it's the one most often forgotten about by undergraduates. This section should allow the reader to make the connection between your research and what has been done before; leading straight into the aim and the hypotheses. This element of the introduction should explain why you're doing your experiment; it's the bridge that links the previous research carried out by others to your own experiment. You need to spell out what has *not* been looked at as well as what has, as chances are your experiment will be targeting one of these gaps. Now is the time to point this out and explain why it's useful to study the gap you've identified.

The aim of your experiment

You need to be able to state what you are going to be looking at in your experiment. This does not require a whole paragraph; you should be able to do this in one sentence (see Example 11.1). The aim goes at the end of your introduction, just after you've explained what you're going to be doing relating to previous research, and just before your hypotheses.

Example 11.1: Aim

This study intends to investigate the claims made by Triplett (1898) and look at how the presence of a competitor influences the effort made, and therefore distance travelled, when cycling.

The hypotheses—your predictions for the results

Your aim should lead neatly into your hypotheses. Your hypothesis is a prediction of what you think will happen in the experiment and is therefore directly linked with the aim and what other researchers have found (what you've written in your introduction). This is not as simple as it first seems. You need to be able to provide reasons for your predictions; you can't just randomly predict something without there being evidence to suggest *why* you're predicting it. Looking at the evidence you've presented in your introduction tells you what other researchers have found, and their results should help you predict how your results will turn out.

There are three main types of hypothesis and you need to be able to state two of them: one experimental hypothesis and the null hypothesis. You should create these before you do your experiment, and they should be firmly based on what you have found in the literature that you have discussed in the main body of your introduction.

You won't always need to spell hypotheses out in a separate section, but it's a good idea when you're first starting out; this way both you and whoever is marking your work will know exactly what you're trying to say. When you get more experienced you will be able to weave them into the end of your introduction.

Experimental hypotheses

The experimental hypothesis is also known as the alternate or alternative hypothesis, and can sometimes be written as H_1. This hypothesis should state the prediction that you will see a significant difference somewhere in your results as a result of a change in your independent variable (IV) (see Box 11.2). Specifically, the experimental hypothesis states that there will be a change in the dependent variable as a result of manipulations in the independent variable (see Box 11.2).

Box 11.2

Repeated measures design/within subjects design: Where everyone does all levels of the IV (everyone does everything)

Independent measures design/between subjects design: Where participants only take part in one level of the IV (participants only do one part of the experiment)

There are two types of experimental hypotheses: directional or non-directional.

Directional hypothesis

The directional hypothesis is also known as the one-tailed hypotheses and states the specific direction the results will change in. (For example: *People will cycle faster (and therefore further) when there is someone else cycling alongside, as indicated by Triplett (1898).*) This hypothesis says there will be a difference and then says where that difference will be. Hence the name 'one-tailed': there is only one option for a significant difference predicted in the results.

Non-directional hypothesis

The non-directional hypothesis is also known as the two-tailed hypothesis and states only that there will be a change in the dependent variable, but not the direction in which that change will be. (For example: *There will be a difference in how fast people will cycle when there is someone else cycling alongside.*) Hence the name 'two-tailed': more than one option is available as a significant result.

Null hypothesis

This is the hypothesis that says there will be no change. (For example: *There will be no significant difference in how fast (and therefore how far) people cycle when there is someone else cycling alongside them.*) In science you have to cover your bases: you need to state it is possible to get no change in the dependent variable as well as predicting that it might change. This is the function of the null hypothesis—to state that there will be no significant difference in the dependent variable as a result of manipulations in the independent variable, and that any differences found are due to chance.

Methods

This section is probably the most important section of your report; it contains everything you did during your experiment, along with the details about what your experiment used and how it was put together. If anyone is going to repeat your experiment, this is the section they need. So it needs to be really detailed: if you're not sure if you've got enough detail, put some more in. In this section more is definitely better than less.

The methods section is split into various sub-sections. These must be included in the order presented below. Make sure each is labelled clearly so that it is obvious to anyone looking that you have included all the sections required.

Design

In this sub-section you need to include details of the type of design you have used, i.e. independent or repeated measures (see Box 11.2), and what your variables are, both independent and dependent (see Example 11.2). You also should specify how many levels there are of your independent variable (see Box 11.3).

> **Box 11.3**
>
> *Independent variable*: What you control, for example word lists or questionnaires
> *Dependent variable*: What you measure, for example number of words correctly recalled

Don't get carried away with describing the detail of your experiment in the design section; that's for another section, the procedure (see later). This section is simply to describe the different parts of your experiment (see Example 11.2).

Example 11.2: Design section from a report

A 2 × 2 mixed design was employed. The between-participants variable was handedness, left-handed (LH) or right-handed (RH); while the within-participants variable was side of presentation of the visual stimulus, left visual field (LVF) or right visual field (RVF).

Participants

While it may sound obvious that this section needs to include details of your participants, it's easy to miss crucial information, without which your study would be impossible to replicate (see Example 11.3 below). For example, you need to say where your participants were from. You also need to mention how you obtained your participants, the sampling method (see Box 11.4).

Box 11.4

Random sampling: All individuals in a population have an equal chance of being selected

Opportunity sampling: Individuals selected are from an easily accessible section of the population, e.g. fellow students

Volunteer sampling: Individuals select themselves for the experiment, through sign-up sheets or response to an advertisement

Stratified sampling: The total population is sampled at strategic points to ensure all sections are represented within the sample.

You also need the following important information about your participants.

- Mean (average) age: preferably in years and months
- Age range: youngest to oldest
- Gender ratio: you will usually find that there are more females than males, a common problem within psychology courses.

You also need to include any other information which you might have used to group participants, for example IQ scores or handedness (see Example 11.3).

Example 11.3: Participants section from a report

There were 19 right-handed participants (RH), 16 females and 3 males, mean age 23.1 years, range 18–44. There were 10 left-handed participants (LH), 9 females and 1 male, mean age 21.2 years, range 18-31. Handedness was assessed using the Edinburgh Handedness Inventory (EHI) (Oldfield, 1971). Mean score for the RH was +86.62, range +62.5 to +100 and the mean score for the LH was –70.34, range –23 to –100. The Participants were taken from an opportunity sample from the Psychology Department in a university in the UK. All participants had normal or corrected-to-normal vision.

Materials

This is where you list everything you used in your experiment. You don't need to go over the top, but you do need to include details of everything you used, right down to pens and papers. This means you need to include details of the type of computer you used, the stimuli you used and any software that was used. If you have just used pen and paper then that is what you write.

This section is important as it shows other researchers what they need to be able to replicate your study (see Example 11.4). If, for example, you've replicated Triplett's experiment (1898) on audience-enhanced performance using bicycles, you would need to include details of the makes and models of bicycles you've used. However, this is one section you can write as a list rather than in sentences.

You will see in Example 11.4 that there is a lot of technical detail. This is important in all experiments where you use a computer. There are differences between types of computer, graphics cards and so on, so to replicate accurately you need to know precisely which hardware (the actual computer components) and software (the programs on the computer) were used.

Example 11.4: Prose materials/apparatus section

Stimuli were produced using a VSG 3/2 graphics card with v.5.021 visual stimulus generator (CRS Ltd.) and displayed on an EIZO T562-T 17" colour monitor. Responses were made on a button box with contact switches, with 0.25 mm throw. Lighting conditions were limited to one overhead spotlight located posterior to the participants and angled so there was no glare on the viewing monitor.

Procedure

This section is possibly the most important sub-section of the method section; it is the section which people look to in order to replicate your experiment. The procedure is also the most detailed section of your report, and includes everything that happened during the experiment. The easiest way to describe what you need to write is as follows: write down everything that happened from when your participant came into the room until they left at the end of the experiment.

As you can see from Example 11.5 there is plenty of detail, and it would be very easy to replicate the exact conditions and order the experiment was carried out in based on the information provided. However, Example 11.6 is less well written. It is a procedure for an identical experiment and, superficially, there is enough information to roughly know what happened. But there is simply not enough detail for somebody to know what happened in the experiment, never mind replicate accurately. Make sure you put enough detail in so that there is no room for doubt about what happened, how it happened, and in what order.

Example 11.5: A well-written procedure looking at audience facilitation (Triplett, 1898)

Participants were seated together in a hall. Volunteers were selected verbally and stayed seated while waiting to be called into the experimental room. The first volunteer came and sat on the cycle machine A. The experimenter instructed the volunteer to cycle as fast as they could for one minute, as timed on the stopwatch. Once this was completed, a second volunteer came down and sat on cycle machine B. The experimenter instructed both participants to cycle as far as they could in one minute, as timed by the same stopwatch. Participants repeated this procedure until all volunteers had cycled alone and in tandem. The participants were then debriefed verbally.

Example 11.6: How not to write a procedure

Volunteers were sat in a hall. A participant cycled on one machine, then another cycled on another machine. They did this for a minute. The experimenter made sure everyone had a go. At the end there was a debrief session.

A quick word about ethics

A-level psychology is guilty of 'over-egging' the ethics debate within psychology. Yes, it is very important to follow ethical guidelines, but it is also crucial to remain objective and not get too carried away. The guidelines set out by the British Psychological Society (BPS) ensure that individual participants are protected from any kind of harm, so as long as these are followed there is no problem.

⫸ The British Psychological Society website is at http://www.bps.org.uk/

What you need to remember is that any experiment you take part in or perform while at university will comply with ethical regulations; you simply wouldn't be allowed to do it otherwise. This means that, unless you are specifically asked to, you should *not* be including an ethics section in your report.

One word which pops up from time to time in reports is the word 'fair'. It is possible to have a very long philosophical debate about fairness, however, the BPS guidelines contain one very important point which covers this aspect of human free will and answers the critics: the right to withdraw at any time. If a participant does not want to do something, they don't have to. This is good, as the whole concept of fairness disappears: participants decide for themselves. You can therefore safely assume that every participant who completed your experiment was happy to do so and did not consider it 'unfair' in any way.

Another topic which students tend to get over-concerned with is deception. It is important firstly to remain objective, and secondly to keep an eye on the context of your experiment. If you have deceived your participants about why they are actually cycling against someone else then it's probably not going to worry anybody very much. If you've not told them that they're not really electrocuting somebody when they think they are (as Milgram did in 1963) then you have a cause for concern. Of course, you can't do Milgram's study now because of the ethical restrictions; so when discussing studies done in the past you need to take into account the ethical regulations, or lack thereof at the time.

Results

Your results are made up of two very important parts: the pictures/tables/number and the words. All students remember to include tables and graphs in their results, and the vast majority remember to include any statistics that were done. However, not all students remember to actually describe what those tables/graphs mean.

Pictures and numbers

This is where you describe the data generated by your experiment. There are two types of statistics you need to include here, and it's very important that you know the difference between them. Descriptive statistics, such as the mean and the standard deviation, tell the reader what the results look like. Inferential statistics, such as t-tests, tell the reader if they are significant or not: in other words did your result occur due to manipulations in your independent variable, or are your data due to chance?

There are several types of descriptive statistics—measures of central tendency and dispersion—but you only need to include the ones which are appropriate for the data you have. Never include all the alternatives (see Box 11.5).

Box 11.5

Measures of central tendency:
   Mean—average score (use with interval/ratio data)
   Median—middle score (use with interval/ordinal data)
   Mode—most common score (use with nominal data)
Measures of dispersion:
   Standard deviation—average distance of each score from the mean (use with mean)
   Inter-quartile range—range of the middle 50% of data (use with median)
   Range—total spread of data (use with mean and median)

➠ We discuss plagiarism in Chapter 12.

For inferential statistics you must report them as shown in your statistics textbooks (see Figure 11.2). Students often get scared about plagiarism and think that the reporting of statistics is included in this. This is a mistake as the reporting of statistics is one area where you must use a very specific format. This is so that the reader knows all the key information such as how many participants you used, what level of significance was reached, and so forth (see Figure 11.2). So make sure you pay close attention to you lecturers and textbooks for how to report each statistic.

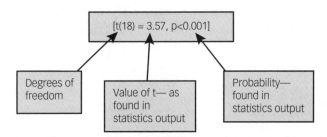

Figure 11.2: Example of how to write out an inferential test (depicted here is a t-test result).

There are specific ways of reporting every statistic and these can be written either between paragraphs or in-line with the text (see Example 11.7). As you progress in your psychology education, you should be aiming to write them in-line with the text.

Example 11.7: How to write out your test results in the text

Slides were still considered to be the media type which supplemented the students' studies best [χ^2 = 6.325; df = 2; p < 0.05]. The least popular media format were podcasts; however, there was only a trend towards significance both in terms of ease of use [χ^2 = 5.002; df = 2; p = 0.082] and ease of understanding [χ^2 = 4.726; df = 2; p = 0.094].

Numbers are good, but pictures are more helpful to most readers. Always include some figures (graphs and other pictures) as well as tables of numbers. Don't double up on information though: use a table *or* a graph to depict your results, but never provide both for the same set of numbers. This is a waste of time and space within your report. If you want to include both, put the graph (figure) in the results section, and the table in the appendix.

In Figure 11.3 there is enough information to make it clear that there was a very different response from the left- and right-handed participants. However, without an explanation, it makes very little sense. For this reason you need to explain it in words too.

Words

The main thing to remember is to use text to explain all the numbers: tables do not explain themselves. You should expect to write at least half a page alongside the

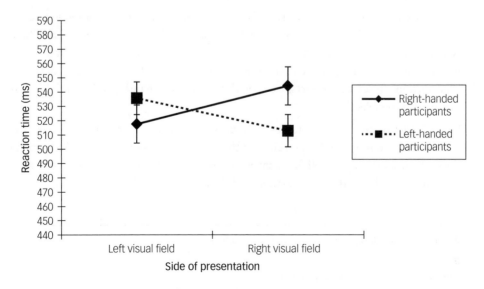

Figure 11.3: An example line graph.

pictures and tables. This is important as you cannot guarantee that the person who is reading your report is going to understand how all the numbers fit together; they may be brilliant at statistics, but it is not their experiment so you need to make sure that your results come across as you want them to. The only way to do this is to write prose.

You should always start your results section by describing your data—and always make sure you specifically refer to all tables and figures by number in the text. (This way, the reader is in no doubt about which figure or table you're talking about at a given point.) Never forget to give all tables and figures titles. Just remember not to produce full-page figures; anything you create should be able to fit on the same page as its explanation. In Example 11.8 you can see that suddenly Figure 11.3 makes a little more sense. It only takes one sentence, but you do need to explain every aspect of your results in words.

Example 11.8: How to explain a graph (see Figure 11.3)

The left-handed participants responded quicker to LVF stimulus presentation than RVF presentation, $[t(79) = 2.51, p < 0.02]$ (see Figure 11.3). The reverse was shown for the right-handed participants (see Figure 11.3), $[t(79) = -3.811, p < 0.001]$.

What not to do or include

There are many common mistakes undergraduates (and some postgraduates!) make in the results section of lab reports. These are easily avoidable and hopefully you won't make them now that they've been pointed out.

- Don't discuss your results! This sounds obvious really when there's a section called 'Discussion', but it's very easy to do when you're actually writing your report. There is a natural tendency to interpret what you have as well as describe it: your years of writing essays have taught you to interpret as you go along. Unfortunately, this is not how it's done in science reports; we spell things out before interpreting and discussing in a different section.

- Don't forget to refer to your tables or figures in the text. A lot of people make the mistake of including a table and thinking that's enough. It's not. You need to explain the table in sentences as well, but as you have probably got more than one table and/ or figure, you will need to refer to them as follows:

As you can see in Table 1, the mean scores show that . . .

or

The mean scores (see Table 1) show that . . .

- Never put any raw data in the results section, i.e. all the individual responses in your experiment. These must always be included it in the appendix, if at all. Your tables and figures are there to *summarize* the raw data.

- Never include statistical output. Most of you are probably using a form of statistical software called PASW (SPSS). This software will give you a lot of information every time you run an analysis. But, as you will have learned from your research methods classes, you don't actually need most of it! The main point here is not to include the output directly. Make your own tables from the data given. The inferential tests should always be written as stated above, so the tables you get those numbers from are never included.

  - The exception to this is the graphs produced in statistical software. These are fine, but make sure you label them correctly and don't leave the automated titles in place. The reader must be able to understand them.

Discussion

The discussion is quite a tricky section, and a common mistake is to quickly summarize everything and then describe in detail what went wrong. While this is not inaccurate, it is not the correct way to do it. The last thing a reader wants to know is that it was pointless reading the previous four or five pages because even you think your experiment is rubbish! This will not put whoever is marking your report in a good mood!

Make sure you follow the steps below and you will avoid this trap (some examples of discussions are available on the book's website).

⇒ See www.oxfordtextbooks.co.uk/orc/parson/

Always remember to stay positive. Whatever may or may not be wrong with your experiment, you have still learned something, and there will always be a reason that things didn't go quite according to plan!

Step one

The first thing you need to do in your discussion is to summarize your results. This does not mean re-stating everything you wrote in the results section. Instead, spend a couple of sentences highlighting your key findings—the findings that relate directly to your hypotheses in the introduction. What you should *not* do here is include any more tables or figures. All you should need to do is to refer to the ones in the results section.

Step two

Do your results support your hypothesis? State clearly whether your experimental or null hypothesis has been accepted, and briefly state why and how you have come to that decision.

Step three

Next, you need to state if there are there any similarities between what you have found and what other people have found. This is where you need to refer back to your introduction and the studies you discussed there. You can bring in other studies briefly at this point of your discussion, but only very briefly, and only if it contributes directly to the explanation of your results—never just add more information for the sake of it.

Step four

Here you need to consider the wider implications of your study. How does what you have done add to the research you discussed in your introduction? How does what you have done contribute to our understanding of the topic you have studied? This section is a positive section, and shows how what you have done fits in and contributes to the research world at large.

Unfortunately it is unlikely that you will be doing any ground-breaking research during your undergraduate degree (unless you are in a department which allows free reign with topic choice for final year dissertations). However, the skill of writing lab reports is one which you will use if you carry on and do such studies, at which time you need to be able to say how your work will affect the research community and the population at large. This does not have to be a long section. If you really haven't found anything interesting then a couple of sentences will do.

Step five

Finally, you get to criticize your experiment! Hopefully you have written at least four paragraphs by now. This section needs to remain positive, despite its critical nature. Constructive criticism is positive and helpful and allows people to see how their existing work can be improved; this is very different from simply pointing out what is wrong with the experiment, as you will have seen in Chapter 8. Focus here on the method section, looking at some of the following: sampling methods, sample population, number of trials, and level of control over the variables.

This step does not need to be exhaustive: the main purpose is to highlight why you may have got results which were not in line with previous research—hence the reason you discuss your results in the context of previous research *after* you've given an overview of this previous research.

Step six

In this step you describe what you could do if you were to carry on with your research in this area. Do your results leave any questions in the area unanswered? If so, here is where you state how you would address these in a further study. In other words, what experiments would you do next? Don't go into great detail though; a quick summary is all that is required.

Step seven

Now we come to the last part of the Discussion section, the summary and the conclusions of your report. It is important to conclude a lab report, much as you would conclude an essay. At the beginning you use the aims and hypotheses to set yourself a question. The conclusion is where you provide the answer to this question.

This is a very brief section; do not get carried away with discussing what you've found. Simply re-state the key points and come to a conclusion.

References

This is a very important section in which, just as in an essay, you need to include a list of material you have referred to in the text so that the reader can easily access it if they so wish. Chapter 13, on referencing, shows you how to format these.

Make sure you check your text in the report; have you put references where you should have? Don't forget, it is equally important to reference information from other sources in lab reports, and that includes statistical books you may have used.

Also, don't forget that you need a reference list here, not a bibliography. If you are a combined honours student you may find you are asked to provide a bibliography with essays for your other subject/s: in psychology there is no variation, we do reference lists always. So, the following rule of thumb applies for psychology: if you've not referred to it in the text of your report, don't include it at the end!

⇒ Read Chapter 10 to learn more about essay writing.

Appendices

This section allows you to put anything that didn't fit into the methods or results sections in your report. Rather helpfully, this section is not included in word limits, so you don't have to worry that you'll go over the standard 1500–2500 word limits set for lab reports.

Here you can include questionnaires, stimuli, statistical output, raw data, and any additional graphs and tables. The most important thing about this section is to refer to it in the text. The same rule applies as for tables and figures in the text: unless you refer to it there's no point including it.

HINT: statistical output can take up a lot of pages so, rather than levelling a rainforest when printing it all out, copy all the tables and put them into a Word document. They will take up less space and you can simply delete the ones you don't need. This saves space and paper when you do print out.

Qualitative versus quantitative reports— what's the difference?

Right at the beginning of this chapter we looked briefly at the differences between quantitative and qualitative reports (see Box 11.1). We have covered quantitative reports in a great deal of detail. Now we need to look at qualitative reports, as there are some very important differences.

The only time you will need to produce a qualitative report is when you have used questionnaires, interviews or focus groups. In these instances you will need to produce a results section which also includes details of the qualitative data analysis techniques you have used, such as thematic or content analysis. There are statistics specifically for qualitative data, which you will learn in your statistics lectures and books; these are reported in much the same manner as quantitative results, so the same rules apply as already stated above.

However, a qualitative report is very much concerned with the quality of the data produced and how it was analysed. For this reason your method section will usually include an *Analysis* section. This is sometimes included in quantitative reports, but this is less common than for qualitative reports due to the clarity of statistical reporting, and is only employed when analyses are very complicated.

Qualitative methodology: analysis section

Here you need to explain exactly how you categorized your words into themes and categories, how you coded these and what you did afterwards (i.e. any qualitative statistics, if that applies). Techniques such as Thematic Analysis and Content Analysis are methods of qualitative analysis, but are highly subjective if you're not careful. The golden rule as a psychologist is to remain objective, which is why qualitative analysis is so difficult to do and so time consuming: it is very difficult to remain objective with words. For this reason it helps to have someone else check your codes and themes to see if they agree.

Qualitative results

A qualitative results section may feature both qualitative and quantitative data, so don't forget to cover both of them. The quantitative data may come from closed questions in a questionnaire or interview, and can be analysed using standard parametric tests. For the qualitative aspect you will need to cover what your content and/or thematic analysis has revealed. Make sure you include plenty of tables here to summarize your results; qualitative data do not really lend themselves to graphical representations so it is unlikely you'll need those. If you can create a graph which makes your data really clear then by all means include one; but generally you may find that tables are a better way of displaying your results.

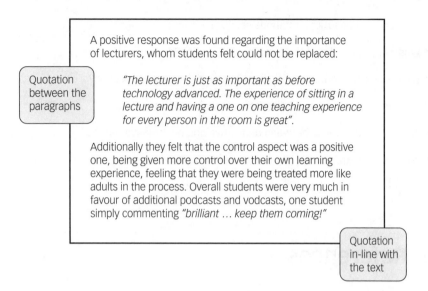

Figure 11.4: How to integrate qualitative data quotations into a results section (Parson et al., 2009, p.224).

In a qualitative report it is important to remember to include quotations in your results and discussion sections. These quotations should be carefully chosen to accurately exemplify your points (see Figure 11.4) and can be included in-line with the text, or separately. This choice depends on the emphasis required rather than explicitly on the writing style used. If you need to make a big point and the quotation is a perfect representation of a key point, putting the quotation between paragraphs is a good idea. Otherwise put the quotation in-line with the text as you would in a traditional essay. Unlike traditional quotations you do not need to include a reference. However, you may want to refer to a particular participant. If so, remember not to refer to them by name, but give them a number instead.

➯ We discuss referencing in more detail in Chapter 13.

✎ Checklist

Check you've understood the key points covered in this chapter by seeing if you can answer the following questions:

✔ What are the different sections of a lab report?

    ✔ And what is the order in which they are presented?

✔ What is included in an abstract?

✔ What information do you need to include in the introduction of a laboratory report?

✔ What is the difference between and aim and hypothesis?

✔ How do you construct a methods section?

✔ What do you need to include in a results section?

✔ What kinds of information do you NOT include in a results section?

✔ How do you create a good discussion of your experiment?

✔ What is the difference between qualitative and quantitative reports?

✔ What is the extra section you need when doing a qualitative report?

✔ What must you not forget at the end of your lab report?

References

Oldfield, R.C. (1971). The assessment and analysis of handedness: the Edinburgh Inventory. *Neuropsychologia, 9,* 97–113.

Parson, V.J., Reddy, P.A., Wood, J. & Senior, C. (2009). Educating an IPod generation: Undergraduate attitudes, experiences and understanding of vodcast and podcast use. *Learning, Media and Technology, 34*(3), 215–228.

Triplett, N. (1898). The dynamogenic factors in pacemaking and competition. *American Journal of Psychology, 9*(4), 507–533.

Useful sources of information

Coolican, H. (2009). *Research methods and statistics in psychology* (5th *Edition*). UK: Hodder Education.

Field, A. (2003). *How to design and report experiments.* UK: Sage Publications.

Field, A. (2009). *Discovering statistics using SPSS.* UK: Sage Publications.

Howell, D.C. (2009). *Statistical methods for psychology (International Edition).* USA: Wadsworth.

Kantowitz, B.H., Roediger, H.L. & Elmes, D.G. (2005). *Research methods in psychology, (International Edition).* USA: Brooks/Cole.

Kinnear, P.R. & Gray, C.D. (2009). *PASW Statistics 17 made simple.* Sussex: Psychology Press.

Robson, C. (2002). *Real world research: a resource for social scientists and practitioner-researchers (2nd Edition).* Oxford: John Wiley & Sons.

Chapter 12

Plagiarism

During your degree you will be told to avoid plagiarism, and will probably find there are fairly serious consequences if you don't. It will probably all sound quite scary to start with, particularly to those of you who've never studied psychology before. However, despite the seeming scare tactics employed by some lecturers, it's very easy to avoid falling into the plagiarism trap.

What is plagiarism?

Plagiarism is the use of someone else's work or ideas without proper reference to their source. This includes copying passages of work, sentences and phrases, and presenting them as your own work. However, and though many students may be unaware, it also includes passing off the ideas and arguments of others as your own, without referencing. This applies even if you paraphrase, use unpublished material or use ideas from a friend's work.

Paraphrasing, or rewording passages so they are not copied, is not a method to avoid plagiarism: the ideas presented are still there (and are still not your own ideas) no matter how they are rephrased. The only sure way to avoid plagiarism is to reference every single piece of information that is not your own.

Collusion

Collusion is a little-known form of plagiarism which is taken as seriously as other forms. Collusion arises when two or more students have worked together to produce a single piece of work, but is presented as individual work by all students. Those students whose work is similar in wording, structure and phrasing will be subject to disciplinary procedures within their department. This is a serious offence: working together might be a good idea for much of your studies, but passing a virtually identical piece of work off as independent writing is a problem. You are the only person responsible for your degree, and while you may feel frequently like you don't know what you're doing and you need help, you must produce your final piece of work by yourself.

When you have your degree, your future employers will expect you to be able to have mastered certain skills—one of them being the ability to write reports. This is a basic transferable skill. So what happens if you've barely written an essay because you got a friend who was much better at writing essays than you to do it for you throughout your degree? You'd be stuck without a basic ability to write a competent and in-depth report for your new boss—and could risk losing your job as a result.

To say that you should write your own assignments might sound obvious, but unfortunately it is not so obvious to all, hence the need to mention it here. The main thing most of you need to take care about is the preparation of lab reports, where you have worked together as a group and have the same data.

⟱ We discuss the writing of lab reports in Chapter 11.

In this instance, make sure you all understand the results and what you've done, then make sure you write up the reports separately. As long as you've clearly written up by yourself, having the same basic format for the method and results sections is absolutely not a problem at all.

Avoiding plagiarism—it's easy when you know how

⟱ We explain how to format references properly in Chapter 13.

It is very easy to avoid plagiarism by referencing properly, paraphrasing effectively and not working too closely with your friends. At the end of your essay or report, there should be a reference list containing all the authors cited in the piece of work you have written. Acknowledging your sources correctly is essential for good grades from level two onwards, the only year we allow some leniency is level one, while you are still learning how to reference.

It's easy enough to avoid plagiarism so there's no need to panic. First, close the book or journal when you're writing. This might sound simple, but it's incredibly effective: if the book is closed then you are not copying. Instead, you're relying on your memory and so will find it much harder to copy verbatim (unless you have a photographic memory).

The major tip for avoiding plagiarism is to make proper use of referencing, as explained in Chapter 13. If you reference all material you have used from other sources you won't have a problem avoiding plagiarism. The difficulty is that most students don't think they need to reference anything other than studies or theories. This is a typical mistake, and one that is easily rectified. As stated above, all the ideas and words you take from someone else can lead to plagiarism, if used without referencing. So, make sure you provide a reference for anything you take from another source—all the ideas, theories and studies you use in your assignments and so on.

Another trap students frequently fall into is to provide a reference the first time they mention information, theories or studies from another source, but then not referencing them after that. Unfortunately, this is not enough to avoid plagiarism. It is fine to reference an idea only once within a paragraph, but the next time you mention the information again you need to provide reference again. This may seem rather irritating, and use up more of your word allowance than you would like, but it's something you have to live with: it's what you have to do.

Chapter 13 contains plenty of tips on how to provide in-text references. However, the way you place this within the sentences is clarified further here. Example 12.1a includes a typical paragraph from an undergraduate essay, with no intentional plagiarism. However, as you can see from Example 12.1b, the second piece of information actually has a separate reference which should be attached to it, but has been forgotten about in Example 12.1a.

Example 12.1: Finding and avoiding plagiarism in your work

(a) *Plagiarism*

Some work has been done on covert orienting within student attentional processes (Grimlock, 1997) which shows that students perform at their best during the mornings, but it has also been found this is only the case after the students involved had eaten a substantial breakfast.

> Note the second part of this sentence makes you wonder where the information came from

(b) *Avoided plagiarism*

> Look how easy it is to remove the query about where the information came from

Some work has been done on covert orienting within student attentional processes which shows that students perform at their best during the mornings (Grimlock, 1997); however Rufus et al. (1999) investigated further and found this was only after the students involved had eaten a substantial breakfast.

In Chapter 9 we looked at writing tips and tools, including how to paraphrase to avoid quotations. In Example 12.2, the contrast between quotations and paraphrasing is exemplified again, although this time the emphasis is on the fact that paraphrasing is preferable to quotations: using paraphrasing can help you work ideas into your essay arguments more clearly than using a series of quotations.

Example 12.2: Quotations versus paraphrasing

(a) *Quotations to exemplify a point*

> Note that each quotation has its own reference, complete with page number

"Movement is relative—something moves by comparison with something else" (Haigh, 2005, p.8). The brain decides what is moving, but it can make mistakes: "the moon (small) seems to race past the clouds (big)" (Haigh, 2005, p.9). Persistence of vision is where an image stays on the retina after the stimulus has disappeared, but there is more than one explanation for these after-images: persistence and "the brain's ability to see movement across gaps" (Haigh, 2005, p.9). One victim of a stroke lost the ability to see movement and lived in a static world: "Water pouring from a kettle looked like a frozen column and people walking about would disappear and then reappear in a new position." (Haigh, 2005, p.9).

> The series of quotations do not make for a linked and 'flowing' paragraph: it is disjointed and reads as though it is a series of separate pieces of information rather than the integrated paragraph it should be

(b) *Paraphrasing: showing understanding of a point*

> Note that each separate point has its own reference—a single reference at the end of the paragraph would not be sufficient as there are multiple separate points being made

The brain sees movement as relative, whereby objects move relative to others. This means that the brain can make mistakes: it sees the moon as moving relative to the clouds rather than the other way around (Haigh, 2005). There are two explanations of why an image can remain on the retina after it has disappeared: a phenomenon called persistence, and the brain's ability to see movement across gaps (Haigh, 2005). People who have had strokes affecting the areas of the brain dealing with movement perception cannot see any form of motion: pouring water appears static, and people seem to appear and reappear in different locations (Haigh, 2005).

> The paraphrased version of this information is far easier to read, the points have been rearranged so that they flow and present an integrated paragraph

---

Activity 12.1: Paraphrasing

In this activity, re-word the following passage from an article by Reddy et al., (2009). This exercise is more difficult than it appears, as none of the content relates to the study itself, but rather is taken from the introduction. This means you will have to use secondary referencing throughout your paraphrasing of this passage. If you're not sure how to do this, read Chapter 13 before attempting it.

Rogers and Freiberg (1994) suggest that the student has in abundance all that is required for learning, so that what needs to be provided to facilitate learning is opportunity, space and encouragement. Cranton (2001) and Brockbank and McGill (2007) suggest that a supportive classroom atmosphere in which students can feel safe to ask questions, make relationships, and be open to learning is important. Kift and Nelson (2005) argue that creating environments for active learning helps students to manage transition. Maslow's (1970) work on motivation suggests that more basic safety, security and belongingness needs must be satisfied before higher level needs. It follows that engaging in learning and reflection requires that students first feel safe, relaxed, and involved, and Cartney and Rouse (2006) showed that awareness and understanding of emotional aspects of learning helped to create an environment where students could achieve their potential.

(Taken from Reddy et al., 2009, pp. 38–39)

Can you plagiarise from yourself?

Surprisingly, it is possible to plagiarise from yourself. This section is more important for postgraduates who may have already published articles or posters in journals or at conferences, in which case the poster abstract will have been published in the conference proceedings. However, the message is an important one to remember for all. If you use material from published sources it needs to be referenced, whether you wrote it or not. So it may look and sound a little strange when you're referencing yourself, but it is necessary.

Exercise 12.1: Spot the plagiarism

For this exercise, read the passage below and then look carefully at the paraphrased excerpts that follow it. Make a note of where each excerpt is guilty of plagiarism. For the answers, see 'Answers to exercises' at the end of the book.

> Second Life is an immersive, online-simulated environment, with 3-D graphics that allows users to interact in a manner mimicking real-life interactions. These immersive virtual environments are being use in many applications: gaming, social networking, marketing and commerce. However, one of the ways in which they hold the most potential is in the field of technology-enhanced learning in education. Immersive and collaborative communities of practice, such as are possible in these structured virtual environments, can engage students in innovative and creative ways. Student-centred immersive virtual environments hold the potential to unlock creative problem solving and offer a deeper level of collaborative learning. Highly motivated students produce richer and higher quality work than those who are not (Pajares & Johnson, 1994). This method of learning engages students of all levels and teaches them to be creative with their learning and to think 'outside the box'. It is a method that keeps students working far longer on educational tasks than they would normally, time appearing to go faster because it was an enjoyable experience (Sanchez, 2007).
>
> Excerpt from: Bignell, S. & Parson, V. (2010). *Best Practices Guide for PBL and Second Life*. Higher Education Academy Psychology Network, pp.17–18.

Paraphrased excerpts

1 Second Life is an online environment with 3-D graphics. Users can interact in a way that mimics real life. Immersive virtual environments have a lot of potential in enhancing learning in education. The environment can engage students in an innovative way, with the potential to unlock problem-solving abilities and provide more collaborative learning. It engages students and helps them work

longer as they are enjoying learning more. Pajares and Johnson said that students who are highly motivated produce richer and higher quality work than those who are not.

2 "Second Life is an immersive, online-simulated environment, with 3-D graphics that allows users to interact in a manner mimicking real-life interactions." Environments like this are being used by many to enhance technology within education: "immersive and collaborative communities of practice can engage students in innovative and creative ways." The environments have the potential to help students reach a deeper understanding and allow them to solve problems more creatively. "Highly motivated students produce richer and higher quality work than those who are not" (Pajares & Johnson, 1994). Students keep working "far longer on educational tasks than they would normally because it was an enjoyable experience" (Sanchez, 2007). (Bignell & Parson, 2010).

3 Students are more highly motivated when they enjoy their work and tend to do more of it. Second Life offers the potential, as an immersive environment with 3-D graphics, to enhance learning through technology (Bignell and Parson). Immersive technological environments are being used in many internet social applications, aiming to engage students in innovative ways. Collaboration skills and a deeper learning are enhanced through use of Second Life; while student creativity is enhanced, allowing them to think "outside the box" (Bignell & Parson, 2010), leading to a more enjoyable learning experience (Bignell & Parson).

....

✎ Checklist

Check you've understood the key points covered in this chapter by seeing if you can answer the following questions:

✔ What is plagiarism?

✔ What is collusion?

✔ For what main reason is plagiarism a bad idea?

✔ Why do tutors and lecturers get so cross about plagiarism?

✔ What are the key ways to avoid plagiarism?

✔ How can you avoid plagiarism?

....

📖 References

Bignell, S. & Parson, V. (2010). *Best practices guide for PBL and Second Life.* Higher Education Academy Psychology Network.

Brockbank, A. & McGill, I. (2007). *Facilitating reflective learning in higher education (2nd Edition).* Maidenhead, UK: Society for Research into Higher Education/McGraw Hill.

Cartney, P. & Rouse, A. (2006). The emotional impact of learning in small groups: Highlighting the impact on student progression and retention. *Teaching in Higher Education, 11,* 79–91.

Cranton, P. (2001). *Becoming an authentic teacher in higher education.* Malabar, US: Krieger.

Haigh, G. (2005). The inside story: visual perception. *TES Teacher,* pp. 8–11.

Kift, S., & Nelson, K. (2005). Beyond curriculum reform: embedding the transition experience. In A. Brew & C. Asmar (Eds.), *Proceedings of the 28th Annual Higher Education Research and Development Society of Australasia Conference* (pp. 225–235). Sydney, Australia: University of Sydney.

Maslow, A.H. (1970). *Motivation and personality (2nd Edition).* New York: Harper and Row.

Pajares, F. & Johnson, M. J. (1994). Confidence and competence in writing: the role of self-efficacy, outcome expectancy and apprehension. *Research in the Teaching of English, 28,* 316–334.

Reddy, P.A., Greasley, A., Parson, V.J., Talcott, J., Harrington, K. & Elander, J. (2009). Becoming a psychology undergraduate; integrating study skills and integrating students, *Psychology of Learning and Teaching, 7*(2), 38–41.

Rogers, C. R. & Freiberg, H.J. (1994). *Freedom to learn (3rd Edition).* Upper Saddle River, NJ: Prentice Hall.

Sanchez, J. (2007). Second Life: an interactive qualitative analysis. In Crawford, C. (Ed.) *Proceedings of Society for Information Technology and Teacher Education International Conference 2007* (pp. 1240–1243). Chesapeake, VA: AACE.

Chapter 13

What is referencing?

As you have seen in the previous chapter on plagiarism, the body of theories and evidence that make up the field of psychology comprises ideas from lots of different people. These ideas, from books, journals and other sources, are the intellectual property of the writer—something you need to make clear whenever you make use of any ideas other people have had. We do this through referencing: writing a small note in the text about where the idea or experiment came from (that is, who did the experiment or who came up with the idea). Referencing follows a strict code of practice, which we explore in this chapter. Many references in this chapter are fictional; where real references have been used their details are given at the end of the chapter.

Referencing is simply a straightforward method to help you identify which information you thought of yourself, and which information you found from someone, or somewhere, else. In other words, it is a system for you to *refer* to your source of information. It's like an index for the sources you used to help you create your report or essay.

A reference list is not the same as a bibliography:

- Reference list—contains everything that you have cited (referred to) in the text

- Bibliography—contains everything you have read or looked at during the preparation of your work, as well as the materials you have specifically cited in the text.

No doubt your essays and reports will involve you reading a lot of books and journals that you don't refer to in the text because you haven't directly needed the information in them; these materials only appear in your Bibliography. By contrast, the reference list only includes sources that you've specifically referred to in the text, and not anything else you may have looked at but haven't actually cited. The format of reference lists and bibliographies is identical, though; the rules given below apply to both situations.

A word you will see from time to time is 'cited'. A citation is simply another word for reference:

- Cite = refer to

- Citation = a reference

- Cited = referred to

The decision to use a reference list or a bibliography will be decided for you by your lecturers. However, there will be occasions when you are not told which to include, and in these instances you should always use a reference list. In psychology, we are more concerned with what you have used than with what you may have read, because of the issue of plagiarism. So all your reports and essays are probably going to demand that you include 'References'. You should never include a bibliography if you have been asked for 'references'; a request for 'references' will always mean a reference list.

How to reference

There are different types of referencing system, and they go into great detail about what order things appear in and where you should put commas, full stops and so on. It's very specific. However, as you will have seen in Chapter 11 (lab reports), it's a bit like following a recipe: as long as you put everything in the right place you can't go wrong!

The British Psychological Society (BPS) and the American Psychological Association (APA) use the same system for referencing called the APA format; this is the one you are about to learn. There is another format which is sometimes used within psychology departments, the Harvard referencing system. This will be covered later in the chapter. However, the basic format and referencing requirements apply to all styles of referencing you will ever use: you always need to reference what you did not personally write, and you need to do this in the text and at the end of your essay or report. The references throughout this book, apart from those in the section on Harvard referencing style, are in APA format.

The process of referencing has two components: (1) citing the reference in the text (to indicate that an idea you've just presented is from another source, and not your own); (2) presenting full details of that reference. As such, every source cited in the body of your report or essay should be listed in full in the reference list at the end of your work, as you will be shown below. There are a couple of hints you should also keep in mind (see Box 13.1).

Box 13.1

HINT: The reference list is in alphabetical order always!

HINT: Make sure you check that you have included everything before submitting your work

---

Referencing in the text

You should only put the authors' surnames and the year of publication in your actual essay or report (rather than providing full details of the reference source). This so-called citation is enough information for the reader to look at the reference list at the end to find out any other information they need to get hold of that particular piece of work. You need to provide such a citation *every* time you use a piece of information which is not something you thought of yourself. It may appear as though you are including a citation every few sentences; but don't worry, this is correct (see Example 13.1). In your first year in particular, you will find that very little of your work contains much original work, so you should expect to reference all the pieces of information you put into your essay. In this case, more is definitely better than less.

Example 13.1: Including references each time you refer to somebody else's work

Milgram (1963) studied how far people will obey an authority figure. He wanted to find out how it was possible for people to carry out the atrocities during World War II. Milgram (1963) found that people do obey those in authority far more than they had realised. But this study by Milgram was criticized by Orne and Holland (1968), who stated it lacked ecological validity. This was addressed in a study looking at nurses and their willingness to follow incorrect orders from a doctor (Hofling et al., 1966).

There is generally confusion among students about where to put references in the text. There are two ways to do this: in line with the text, or in parentheses (brackets; see Example 13.2) after the specific piece of information (Example 13.3).

Example 13.2: A reference in line with the text

As Milgram (1963) found, people obey orders from someone in authority, even when these orders contradict their own moral views.

Example 13.3: A reference in parenthesis (brackets)

People tend to obey someone in authority, even though their orders may contradict their own moral views (Milgram, 1963).

➠ For various writing hints and tips, see Chapter 9.

The only variation on the information required in the text is for quotations. Generally, your lecturers don't like to see quotations in your reports at all as they don't show evidence of understanding. You may understand perfectly—but if you've just copied something from a book or article, we have no way of verifying this. For this reason, paraphrasing what other people have written is preferred: there is direct evidence you understand what you're writing about.

However, there are occasions when you won't be able to think of a better way to say something, in which case a few quotations are fine. The additional piece of information you need here is a page number (see Examples 13.4 and 13.5). This will tell the reader which page to look on should they want to check that the author really did say that.

Example 13.4: Referencing quotations in the text

Tomlinson (1977) reported that "given the prevalence of cravings and associated stereotypical withdrawal behaviours, there is no doubt that the case for chocolate to be classified as a drug is a strong one" (p.557).

Example 13.5: Referencing quotations in parenthesis

Teachers report that children in classrooms can ask the strangest questions, typically those questions which have nothing to do with the subject you are trying to teach: "on one occasion the question 'What happens when you cross a squirrel with a hedgehog?' caused the lesson to be temporarily abandoned while an answer, 'squidgehog', was sought." (George, 2007, p.125).

In your essay or report, when an article has three or more authors, write the full list the first time you use it and then subsequently write (first author, et al.) (see Example 13.6).

Example 13.6: Referencing multiple authors in the text

The use of podcasting was investigated by Parson, Reddy, Wood and Senior (2009) to see if it was a viable tool to enhance the student learning experience. Parson et al. (2009) found that there was a very positive response to podcasts from the student population.

The most common mistake students make when referencing is not the format of referencing in the text, or when to reference. Instead, they get confused about *what* to reference. I've just stated that you need to reference all material you didn't personally think of yourself, but this is a rather vague statement. Many students reference every study they use (studies and experiments are typically fairly well referenced from level one onwards) but then forget to reference the theoretical and general statements they make about topic areas they're discussing. The general non-experimental information needs references too as you didn't think of it, the researchers in the field did. All the information you get from textbooks, not just the experiments, needs a reference (both in the text as a citation and at the end in the reference list).

Referencing at the end of your report

Now you need to learn how to format your references at the end of the essay or report. There is a special format to references: every comma and full stop needs to be in the correct place, and the main titles should always be in italics, or underlined if you're writing by hand. The basic order for references is as shown in Figure 13.1.

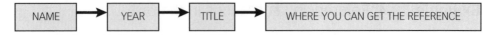

Figure 13.1: The basic order of reference format.

Obviously it's a little bit more complicated than this, but this basic format holds true for all types of reference. As you continue to read about how to write each of the references, make sure you pay close attention to where the punctuation goes.

Referencing books

> Author surname, Initials. (year). *Title*. Place of publication: Publisher.

Example 13.7: A book

Bryant, A. (2006). *How to dance when playing the saxophone*. USA: Leamington Press.

If the book is a revised edition, meaning that the author has updated it, then the reference looks like this:

> Author, Initials. (year). *Title (Edition)*. Place of publication: Publisher.

Example 13.8: A revised and re-published book

Donnelly, L. (2009). *Parapsychology: fact or fiction? (2nd Edition)*. UK: Gorman & Norse.

Referencing books with two authors

> Author, Initials. & Author, Initials. (year). *Title*. Place of publication: Publisher.

Example 13.9: A two-author book

Davis, L.S. & Walters, D. S. (1998). *Surviving University on a Student Budget (3rd Edition)*. UK: Northern Press

Referencing books with more than two authors

Author, Initials., Author, Initials. & Author, Initials. (year). *Title*. Place of publication: publisher.

Example 13.10: A multiple author book

Boon, G., Fisher. A.J. & Boon, J. (2008). *Rectory life in the 21ˢᵗ century*. UK: Theology Press.

It is worth noting how this reference format differs in the text from in the reference list at the end. The first time you use the reference, you have to list all the authors, but thereafter you can write Boon et al. (2008)—that is, you name the first author only. But you cannot put 'et al.' at the end in the reference section; you must write out all the authors in full.

Referencing an edited book

> Used to denote that these individuals were editors, not authors

Author, Initials. (Ed.) (year). *Title*. Place of publication: publisher.

Example 13.11: An edited book

Muse, C. (Ed.) (2009). *Musical Influence: reflections from musicians*, UK: Rock Press.

Referencing a chapter in a book

Chapter Author, Initials. (year). Title of chapter. In Editor Initials. Editor Author (Ed.), *Book title* (pages). Place of publication: publisher.

Example 13.12: A chapter in a book

Reddy, P. (2010). Tricks to avoid students. In J.G. Giant (Ed.), *The teacher's and lecturer's unofficial handbook* (pp. 24–45). UK: Academic Press.

You will notice that it is only the title of the original book that is in italics, not the chapter title.

How to reference a journal article

> Author, Initials. (year). Title of article. *Title of Journal, Volume number* (issue number), page numbers.

Example 13.13: A journal article

Hewlett, R. (2009). An existential investigation of being a psychologist. *Psychological Reports, 49*(10), 345–351.

You will also see a group of numbers at the end of journal references; each one has a specific meaning. When you are looking for these they can usually be found at the top or bottom of pages on the article itself.

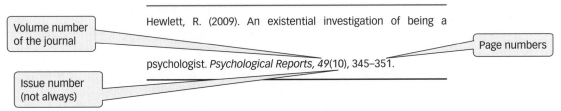

You will notice that only the title of the journal itself is in italics, not the article title—it is the journal name that is considered to be the main title, not the article title. However, notice that it's not just the journal title in italics in this type of reference: the issue number is also in italics.

The rules for two or more authors are just the same as for books. For really long lists of authors (more than six) it is acceptable to write 'et al.'. Et al. simply means 'and others', or 'and more'. This is the only circumstance where you can get away with putting 'et al.' in the reference list. You'll need to write them all out for six authors or fewer.

Example 13.14: A journal article with multiple authors

Ling, H., Culloty, H., Johnson, M., Hewlett, R., Torabi, J., Simmonds, J., et al. (2008). Cognitive bias in hamsters: a study of wheel usage. *Psychological Reports, 37* (2), 89–45.

Referencing an article in a newspaper/magazine

> Author, Initials. (year, day month). Title. *Newspaper or Magazine Title*, p.page number.

Example 13.15: A magazine or newspaper article

Goldman, C. (2009, 7 November). Tips on overcoming stage fright. *The Strictly Gazette*, p.11.

How to reference from the Internet

Generally you will find that your tutors don't like you using Internet pages and websites; there may even be a ban on using Wikipedia™ as I have implemented for my own students. It's not that your tutors have a particular grudge against this website; it is more that it is accessible for editing by all and subject to information additions which are not always accurate. For this reason it is not a reliable source of information, and ideally should not be used in your essays or reports (see Box 13.2). In addition, we want you to look at the large supply of books and journals in the library rather than take the lazy and quick route of searching the web. All the topic information you'll need for your assignments is typically going to be in the library, and we want you to use this resource as it is the best source of information you have during your studies. As a general point, at university you should be focusing on academic materials such as journals, books and formal reports as sources to get your information from. We are generally not impressed when students look online for something which is present in a core textbook, or use an Internet dictionary. These are not acceptable uses of the Internet: you should use your recommended books for core information.

You can get a wealth of material on the Internet which we *do* approve of; most journal articles are available online these days as are many books, newspaper articles, formal reports and so on. All of these are appropriate sources which you *can* get off the Internet. What you need to focus on with material you use in assignments is the quality of the information rather than its mode of delivery.

We discuss different information sources in Chapter 6.

Once you start recognizing higher quality sources of information you'll find it much easier to search through the contents of the Internet for suitable material. The hint in Box 13.2 shows you what you need to focus on first and foremost when looking at web pages.

When referencing information you have obtained from the Internet, you will find that most of it is logical and follows the patterns you have already seen in references. The main

---

Box 13.2

HINT

If you cannot find all of the components for an APA-style Internet reference then this means only one thing...

the reference is not suitable for academic use

So don't use it! If you cannot find an author or date then you should look elsewhere for material. All suitable sources will have all the components you need for a reference!

difference is that you need to put in the date and time you have accessed the information. This is important as many internet sites are not permanent repositories of information, and may disappear at some point in the future. And of course, you need to put the html link, web address, in as well.

For online information the date is always written in the American format, with the month coming before the day. So if you accessed a journal article on 12 November 2009 you would write 11/12/09 rather than 12/11/09. Don't forget to write the time you accessed the journal article down when you actually access it! It's very easy to get caught up in searching for material online, but unless you write down the date and time you will have problems with your reference later on. If you forget, don't worry, simply go back online and access the information again, then use that date and time. Of course, if you can no longer access the information, you'll probably want to find another source anyway!

Online journal article (also available in print)

Author, Initials. (year). Title of article [Electronic version]. *Title of Journal, Volume Number*(issue number), page numbers.

Example 13.16: An electronic version of a printed journal article

Differ, L. & Meadows, J. (1999). A systematic investigation of the link between conductor hand gestures and personality [Electronic version]. *Journal of the National Conductors Association, 6*(1), 149–156.

Online only journal article (not available in print)

GMT = Greenwich Mean Time, so typically the time in the UK. In between mid-April and mid-October you'll need to subtract an hour to account for BST (British Summer Time)

Author, Initials. (year). Title of article. *Title of Journal, Volume Number* (issue number), page numbers. Retrieved month/day/year, 24-hour time GMT, from web address

Example 13.17: An online journal article

Tomlinson, J.H. (1997). Chocolate: food or drug? *Welsh Journal of Food Addiction, 5*(3), 351–359. Retrieved 06/18/09, 18.00 GMT, from http://www.wjfai.co.uk/dessert/query.cfod?cmd=Retrieve&db=PubMed&list_uids=1977&jht=Citation

Online reports/documents

> Author, Initials. (year). *Title of report*. Retrieved on month/day/year, 24 hour time GMT, from web address

Example 13.18: An online report

Bignell, S.J. (2010). *Internet surfing triggers library decline*. Retrieved 06/10/10, 16.24 GMT from http://www.cyberlife.org/Template.cfm?Section=PRB&template=/ContentManagement/ContentDisplay.cfm&ContentID=200407

You will find that some online formal reports do not have authors and yet are valid forms of information. These are absolutely fine to use as long as you are sure they are from a reputable source. In the text you would put the report source in place of an author. Examples of this would be the National Health Service (NHS) or Home Office Reports. In this case the following rules apply.

> Report source (year). *Title of report*. Retrieved on month/day/year, 24 hour time GMT, from web address

Example 13.19: An online report where no author is listed.

Office of National Statistics (2009). *Trends in alcoholism*. Retrieved 04/12/09, 13.54 GMT from http://www.ons.co.uk/reports/alcohol/trends=9845

Primary versus secondary referencing

The styles of reference you have just seen are all primary references. However, what you will find, especially during your first and second years as an undergraduate, is that most of your information will come from textbooks. You can reference the textbook, but it does look a bit odd when you discuss Milgram's (1963) study but reference the textbook you got it from. Instead, there is a way of telling the reader that you read about the study in a more indirect way—not from the original source, but from a second source that discusses it. The process of citing this second source is called secondary referencing.

- Primary reference
    - You have directly read the original document (for example a journal article).
- Secondary reference
    - You have not read the original but the author of the source you are consulting (for example, a textbook) did read the original, and is presenting the original idea in their words.

Secondary referencing

You will find that the majority of your references will be secondary references until you begin to make use of primary journal sources. All textbooks should have a list of the sources they have used to create the textbook at the end of the book, or at the end of each chapter.

When compiling a secondary reference you should cite both the book you yourself are consulting, and the original material that the book author consulted. All you have to do is find the reference in your textbook for the particular experiment or idea you are citing, and put it in front of the reference for the book itself. So it's a bit like gluing the two primary references together. The rules for multiple authors you have seen above also apply for secondary references.

> Author, Initials. (year). Title of article. *Title of Journal, Volume Number*(issue number), page numbers, cited in Author, Initials. (year). Title of article. *Title of Journal, Volume Number*(issue number), page numbers.

Example 13.20: An article found inside another article

George, E. (2007). Are squirrels a logical choice for discussion? *Language*, *5*, 124–129, cited in Calton, S. & Thorpe, R. (2001). Bizarre questions from children. *Psychology Today*, *13*(9), 472–477.

You will notice that all the journal titles in this example are in italics. Main titles are always in italics, and this applies when you are referencing a piece of work from a book as well. The only exception is the title of a chapter in a book. The chapter title is not the main title, the book is. Consequently, the chapter title is *not* in italics.

In-text secondary referencing

Secondary references should be cited in the text in the same way that primary references are (and the full reference then given in the reference list). As you saw above, you need to include a name and year every time you cite somebody's work. Don't forget that 'cited in' means 'referenced in' (see Box 13.2).

(Author, year, cited in, author, year)

Example 13.21: In-text secondary referencing

It has been reported that chocoholics exhibit the same activity at a neurological level as those who are addicted to caffeine (Tomlinson, 1997, cited in Donnelly, 1999).

The Harvard system

As was mentioned earlier there is another style of referencing used within the psychology education system, Harvard referencing. This style is not used as frequently as the APA format, but it is used enough to warrant some understanding of the differences. Most of the differences between APA and Harvard formats lie in the punctuation used within the references themselves. With the formats below look carefully at the full stops, how the names are laid out, and which bits are no longer in italics. The main differences can be found in Box 13.3. I won't give examples for all the different types of publication, just where there are major differences between APA and Harvard formatting.

Box 13.3

1 When there are multiple authors, 'and' instead of '&' is used.
2 Full names are used when known
3 There is no full stop after the year
4 There is a full stop instead of a colon between the place of publication and publisher
5 The edition is not in either italics or parenthesis (brackets)

Referencing books

Author, Initials. (year) *Title*. Place of publication. Publisher.

Author, Initials. (year) *Title*, Edition. Place of publication. Publisher.

Referencing books with two authors

Author, Initials. and Author, Initials. (year) *Title*. Place of publication. Publisher.

Referencing books with more than two authors

Author, Initials., et al. (year) *Title*. Place of publication. Publisher.

Referencing an edited book

Author, Initials. (ed.) (year) *Title*. Place of publication. Publisher.

Referencing a chapter in a book

Chapter Author, Initials. (year) Title of chapter. In: Editor Author. Editor Initials (ed.) *Book Title*. Place of publication. Publisher. p. page numbers.

How to reference a journal article

Author, Initials. and Author, Initials. (year) Title of article. *Title of Journal. Volume Number* (issue number), page numbers.

Referencing an article in a newspaper

Author, Initials. (year) Title. *Newspaper*, Day Month Year, p. page number.

Example 13.22: A newspaper or magazine article

Bennett, M. (2006) Advertising the seemingly impossible. *Landover Press*, Friday 23 October 2007, p. 2.

Online materials

There is no standardized layout for online references in the Harvard style, so the following formats are informed by the conventions being used in most UK universities. However you should check the referencing style guides provided by your department to see if there are any variations you should be following during your degree.

Online journal articles

Author, Initials. and Author, Initials. (year). Title of article. *Title of Journal, Volume Number* (issue number), page numbers. [WWW] Available from: web address [accessed day/month/year].

Example 13.23: An online journal article

Inver, N. and Land, H. (2001). The Loch Ness Monster: theories and evidence. *Journal of Extraordinary Life Forms*, 9(9), 76–80. [WWW] Available from: http://www.onlinejournals.com/tjoelf/2001/9/9/article=997680.pdf [accessed 24 August 2002].

Online reports/documents:

> Author, Initials. (year). *Title of Report*. [WWW] Title of web page. Available from: web address [accessed day/month/year].

> Report Source (year). *Title of Report*. [WWW] Title of Web Page. Available from: web address [accessed day/month/year].

Example 13.24: An online report

Turner, C. (2003) *How to Support Wildlife in the City*. [WWW] Available from: http://www.gardeningworld.co.uk/SWFC/template.cfm&contentID=305445/report [accessed 23 November 2003].

....

Exercise 13.1: Referencing: spot the mistakes!

Spot the mistakes in this list of references and correct them in accordance with the APA format for referencing. Then go through them again, but this time correcting them in accordance with the Harvard system of referencing. For the answers, see 'Answers to exercises' at the end of the book.

There are a couple of additional reference types hidden here, but you have already seen all the information you need to correct them, so be brave and have a go!

1 Carter, P.R., Reddy, W and Martin, F.M. (2004) Students. Beer monsters or future prime ministers?.
   (*Albert Publishing UK*)

2 B R. Russell. (2000) Learning to fly, 9th Edition, Newcastle. UK. Anderson Publishing.

3 Bowen, L.L. (1995) Perspectives *on Tie Choice: is there a link with personality?* Décor and Personality, pages 766-777, 34(3).

4 A. Ferdin and A. Tash (1997) 'Musical taste in Cats. In Groves, R. J. and Forsyth, B. C. (Eds.) '*Variations in Taste Between Species'* (1997), (pp. 161-187), UK: Diggory Press

5 Ollivander, D. (1982) *The Mystery of Wand Choice* (1st Ed.) (Ed.) Hobgoblin Press: UK

6 Rawlings, E. (2004) *Secrets of the Classroom*. (4th). Smith House, UK

7 P.J. Fforde. How To Get Lost in A Good Book. In *Reading and Language Theories*. Bennett, E. and Rochester, E. (Eds.) Bath, UK, Sensibility Press (2002) (pp. 415-430)

8 Edwards, H. *What Really Happens Before Broadcasts*. (1999), retrieved 17.59 GMT. 10/12/04, http://www.newsreports.co.uk/NRaC/template.cfm&contentID= 3051955/report.pdf

9 Coleman, C. and Skelton, F. (2009). *Summer Schools: the inside story.* The University Journal, 7 (5) 45-52

10 Sparrow, J. (2002) *The Difficulty in Finding Rum*, in, (Ed) Turner, E. *Pirates and Their Idiosyncrasies*. Portland: Caribbean Press (pp187-214)

11 http://www.randomhousepublications.co.uk/was/query.rwod?cmd=Retrieve&d=Publist_uids=195423&jht=Citation. A Review of Post-Modern Social Observations. Writing and Society, 9 (2), 453-459, retrieved 05/12/09, 16.32 GMT, Coupland, P. (2008)

✎ Checklist

Check you've understood the key points covered in this chapter by seeing if you can answer the following questions:

✔ What should you reference in your essay or report?

✔ What is the difference between a reference list and a bibliography?

✔ What are the two styles of referencing covered in this chapter?

✔ What are the two ways of referencing information in the text?

✔ When is it acceptable to use quotations?

✔ What order does your list of references go in at the end of your report or essay?

✔ What is the basic order of a reference?

✔ Can you correctly write a reference for all the items listed in this chapter?

📖 References

Hofling, C.K., Brotman, E., Dalrymple, S., Graves, N. & Pierce, C.M. (1966). An experimental study in nurse-physician relationships. *Journal of Nerves and Mental Disease, 143,* 171–180.

Milgram, S. (1963). Behavioural study of obedience. *Journal of Abnormal and Social Psychology, 67,* 371–378.

Orne, M.T. & Holland, C.C. (1968). On the ecological validity of laboratory deceptions. *International Journal of Psychiatry, 6*(4), 282–293.

Parson, V.J., Reddy, P.A., Wood, J. & Senior, C. (2009). Educating an IPod generation: Undergraduate attitudes, experiences and understanding of vodcast and podcast use. *Learning, Media and Technology, 34*(3), 215–228.

📖 Useful sources of information

BPS Reference Guide (APA Format)

- The British Psychological Society (2004). *Style guide* [Electronic version]. Leicester, UK: Author.

APA Reference Guide

- American Psychological Association (2009). *Publication manual of the American Psychological Association (6th Edition)*.Washington, DC: Author.

Harvard Reference Guide

- British Standards Institution (1998). *BS recommendations for references to published materials*. BS.5605:1998. London, UK: BSI.

Chapter 14

Presentations and posters

There are a couple of assumptions associated with presentations and posters. Students tend to see presentations as terrifying occasions, where they have to stand in front of what feels like hundreds of pairs of eyes, talking about something they only half understand, only for it to be criticized when they've finished. Then, students go to the other end of the spectrum with posters, making the assumption that they are done by hand, generally with the aid of coloured felt tip pens and badly drawn pictures. They see them as an exercise their 10-year-old nephew would turn their nose up at, a childish practice which is not to be taken seriously—after all, how professional is a poster? The answer? Very professional—and a key part of formal academic conferences, as we'll see in more detail later on.

Both of the assumptions set out above are inaccurate. Presentations are done, at least at undergraduate level, in a supportive atmosphere on things you have already been taught, whereas posters are done on computers with preformatted templates.

⫸ Some exemplar templates are given on the book's website at www. oxfordtextbooks. co.uk/orc/parson/

This chapter will go through the reality of presentations and posters, hopefully enabling you to be more confident when you have to do both for real during your studies. Both are often a core part of undergraduate courses; you will probably have to do them in the real world once you leave university too. Most of you will probably end up preferring posters to presentations—after all, they do appear a less intimidating prospect. But presentations are straightforward enough; just remember that even your lecturers get nervous before a big lecture!

Presentations—standing up in front of people and talking to them intelligently

Presentations are generally the bane of every students' existence at university. You will typically get grouped together with people you may or may not like, then have to stand up in front of your peers and sound vaguely intelligent for around 15 minutes or so. This is the case at undergraduate level; as a postgraduate you're on your own, which makes the whole experience even more terrifying for most of us. Most students regard this as a form of legalized torture, but it's actually an incredibly useful skill to learn. In almost every job you can think of that will require your degree you will have to have the following skills:

- Working with people you like
- Working with people you *don't* like (you won't be able to work with your friends throughout your working lives I'm sorry to report, and there will always be someone in a group you have a problem getting along well with)
- Talking clearly and intelligently about work-related issues
- Talking in front of colleagues
- Standing up and giving presentations to other colleagues from outside the company/department.

You may even end up in teaching, at which point you will need all of the above skills every day of your working life.

Giving presentations is a crucial skill to learn, and there is no better place to do so than in a supportive environment with people who can actually help you learn this skill directly.

The most common mistake people tend to make in presentations is to include every tiny detail about the given topic. While this may lead to an incredibly accurate presentation, it is likely to leave your audience asleep. Make sure you include the basic information on the slide, but plan to present the majority of information verbally, either as part of your presentation, or in response to questions posed by your audience if they're interested. What you are talking about might seem like the most fascinating subject in the world to you, but everyone has different interests and it is wise to leave some scope for questions. Other reasons apart, questions are perceived by the audience to be daunting for the presenter, so if there are gaps in your presentation that you know a lot about you can wait for questions at the end and dazzle your audience with your knowledge!

Slides

Use as many slides as you need to complete your presentation, unless there is a set limit you've been given. Don't be afraid you have too many: as long as you stick to the time limit you've been given you'll be fine. You want to include headings and general ideas, not explicit details of what you're going to say. This way you avoid giving a blow-by-blow account of everything and allow your audience to listen to you rather than to sit reading while you talk in the background. Not having everything on the slide in front of you can feel very intimidating—like walking a tightrope without a safety net—but it makes for a better presentation so take a deep breath and go for it.

Also, don't squish information onto slides: spread it out. If information is crammed together it's hard to read and you won't be able to work out where you are, never mind the audience. As I said at the beginning of this paragraph—spread it out and move some information onto subsequent slides.

The two slides in Figure 14.1 show what a good, clear slide should look like, and what a highly detailed slide looks like. Figure 14.1a is a pretty good slide: there is a clear

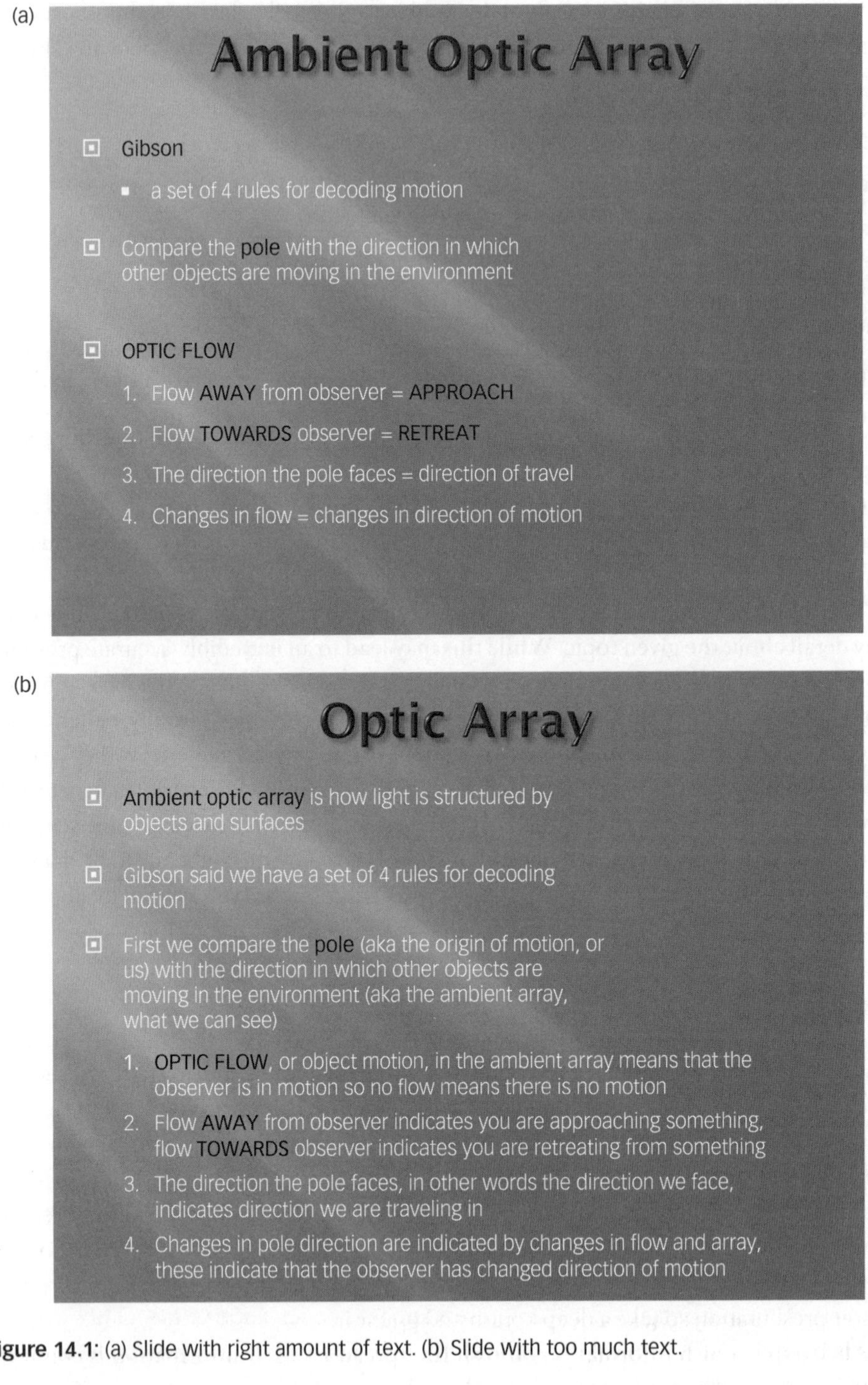

(a)

Ambient Optic Array

- Gibson
  - a set of 4 rules for decoding motion

- Compare the pole with the direction in which other objects are moving in the environment

- OPTIC FLOW
  1. Flow AWAY from observer = APPROACH
  2. Flow TOWARDS observer = RETREAT
  3. The direction the pole faces = direction of travel
  4. Changes in flow = changes in direction of motion

(b)

Optic Array

- Ambient optic array is how light is structured by objects and surfaces

- Gibson said we have a set of 4 rules for decoding motion

- First we compare the pole (aka the origin of motion, or us) with the direction in which other objects are moving in the environment (aka the ambient array, what we can see)
  1. OPTIC FLOW, or object motion, in the ambient array means that the observer is in motion so no flow means there is no motion
  2. Flow AWAY from observer indicates you are approaching something, flow TOWARDS observer indicates you are retreating from something
  3. The direction the pole faces, in other words the direction we face, indicates direction we are traveling in
  4. Changes in pole direction are indicated by changes in flow and array, these indicate that the observer has changed direction of motion

Figure 14.1: (a) Slide with right amount of text. (b) Slide with too much text.

heading with a couple of pieces of information below it. There is minimal information on this slide because the detail of the content is described verbally. The slide simply indicates the important aspects of the topic so that any one who needs further clarification can later on look up the appropriate information. Figure 14.1b on the other hand contains far too much detail. The slide should just contain a brief indication of the content; the rest can be spoken during the presentation. Figure 14.1a is clear and easy to digest whereas Figure 14.1b contains so much information that anybody reading it will miss everything the person speaking is saying—they'll be too busy reading the slide. It is a case of less being more—a fine balance between clarity and provision of enough information for clarity to lead to understanding.

⯈ The PowerPoint slides shown in Figures 14.1 and 14.2 are available on the book's website. Go to www.oxfordtextbooks.co.uk/orc/parson/

Pictures

There are two key points to bear in mind when incorporating pictures into slides.

1 Include lots of pictures if you can. Colourful slides mean people are looking at them rather than you—something many people find helps their confidence when speaking to large groups of people. This method certainly helps me: I put as many pictures in as I can without distracting from the material being presented. While pictures can be very helpful, however, make sure you don't end up presenting a bunch of pictures with no text; this is not helpful to anyone and means you have lots of talking to do as you have to have plenty of verbal description to go with the images you present.

   In Figure 14.2 you can see that Figure 14.2a has two pictures that are a good size and have brief captions clearly linked with them. Figure 14.2b, on the other hand, has a number of pictures which are vaguely linked with the captions, but the captions are excessively long and detailed. This slide is far too busy and muddled. It would be far better to split this information over two slides (as in Figure 14.2c) than to cram it onto one single one (as in Figure 14.2b).

2 Make the slides colourful. There are many themes available in PowerPoint, and they are all there to make your presentation look as professional and interesting as possible. Try to use a sensible theme though: this is science and you don't want a patterned background distracting the listener from the content. (This would have the same effect as having an excessive number of pictures.) Stick to less 'busy' themes that have solid colours and possibly patterns on the sides and in the corners.

Additional materials

Sound recordings can sometimes be useful in a presentation. Try to incorporate the files into PowerPoint slides if you can. It is far more professional to click on a button in PowerPoint than having to exit your presentation and open another file. Don't worry if this is beyond your technical capabilities, though; just make sure that you have everything set up ready to go so you're not faffing around to find a file when you've come out of your presentation. The same goes for videos: either incorporate them or make sure they are all set up and ready to go. Make sure any videos you use don't last longer than a few minutes unless they are absolutely vital. Even then they should be as short as possible. Remember this is a presentation, not a movie session!

(a)

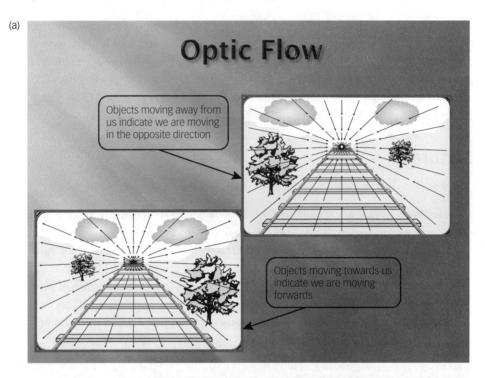

(b)

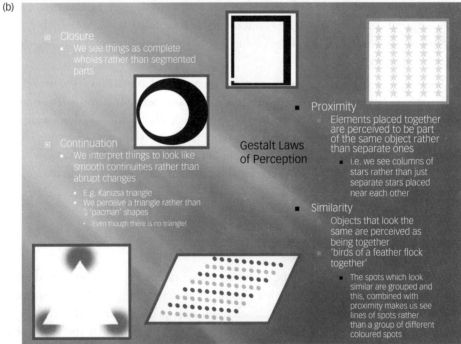

Figure 14.2: (a) A slide with useful pictures clearly linked to text. (b) A slide with too many pictures and no links to the words.

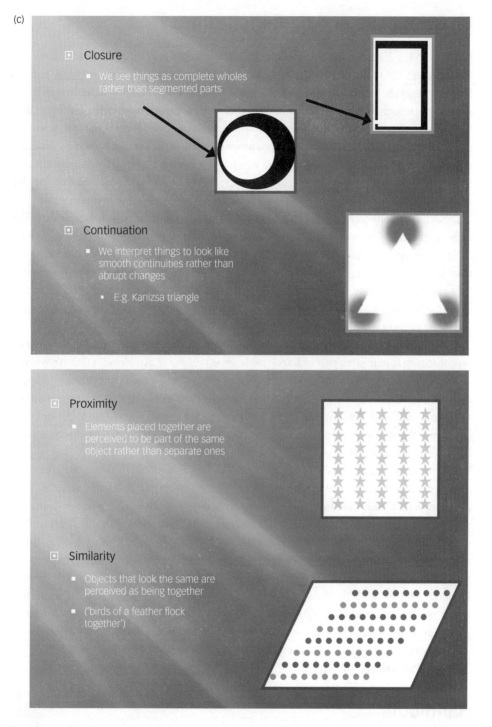

Figure 14.2: (c) Figure 14.2b over two slides instead. (See Plate 1 for a full colour version of all these slides.)

Internet links and demonstrations

All links to the Internet should be embedded in your PowerPoint slides—and make sure you're connected to the Internet beforehand. Creating a link to the Internet is easy enough. Firstly you get the web address of the site you want to link to, then you write that into your slide. If you select this internet link and right click you are given an option called 'hyperlink'. Select this and type in your Internet link to the *address* option it gives you. Now, when you run your presentation, all you have to do is move the mouse over this link and you should be able to click on this and go straight to the web page you want to show. You should check all links before you start your presentation however; there is nothing more embarrassing than a key piece of information being unavailable because you typed a link in incorrectly.

Demonstrations can be good fun, particularly if you want to demonstrate something more practical. However, try to avoid asking for volunteers; very few people ever put their hands up to volunteer, and you don't want a delay while you try to persuade people they want to take part. You also run the risk of picking someone who unfortunately isn't taking it seriously and doesn't really make any effort to do anything. You want your demonstration to go smoothly so, instead, ask a friend to be your co-demonstrator; this way your presentation will go the way *you* want it to go.

With demonstrations, make sure you have everything you need beforehand: there is no substitute for an extra pair of hands and careful preparation. However, don't worry if it doesn't go to plan, simply make sure your notes include what is supposed to happen and tell the audience as you go along. Make sure your running commentary matches what you are doing. Presentations can be daunting for those new to them, but once you have gained confidence with speaking in front of people they can be good fun, and can help to relax both you and your audience if done well.

The trick is to use any laughter that may occur as a positive thing, whatever the reason for it (even if it's because the demonstration is going fantastically wrong). Treat it as a sign that your audience is listening and is engaged with what you are doing and saying. Even if people are laughing because the demonstration is going spectacularly wrong, at least they've listened to what you've said and *know* it's going wrong, which means they also have a fair idea of what is *supposed* to happen—something that you successfully communicated to them. The tip here is not to get embarrassed: laugh with the audience and 'go with the flow' of that particular moment. The concept of something going wrong and people laughing is generally mortifying for first time presenters. However, it is something that you learn to use positively as you get more experienced. The view I tend to take now is that at least if people are laughing, they are listening and haven't fallen asleep—in which case I must be doing something right!

Hand-outs

The advice you will get on presentation hand-outs depends on the person you speak to: some people like them and always provide them, while others cannot abide them and prefer people to make their own notes. Realistically, the choice to give hand-outs or not depends on type of presentation you are giving and of course whether you want to or not!

Hand-outs can be useful if there's a lot of complicated information to get across: people can make their own notes based on what you are saying, rather than trying simply to understand the slides in isolation. If your presentation is short you probably don't need hand-outs, but if it is longer than about 10 minutes it might be a good idea.

Generally hand-outs take the form of PowerPoint slides; printed three or four to a page (see Figure 14.3). If you want to print out all the notes about your presentation

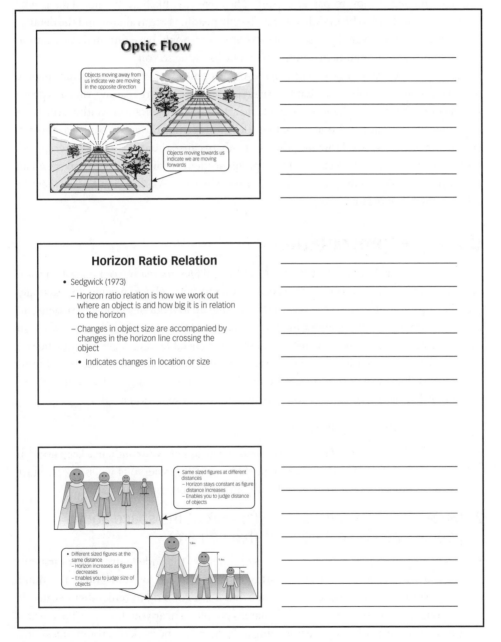

Figure 14.3: Example of a page of notes provided at a lecture or presentation. The three-slide option allows for your audience to take notes relating to a particular slide.

which you've typed into the notes section in PowerPoint, by all means do so, but be prepared for everyone to fall asleep, or simply read them and not pay attention. Before you get offended with the idea that someone might fall asleep in your talk, how many lectures have you nodded off in (or become so distracted in that you realized you're no longer listening to what's being said)? Think of it this way: if you were given a hand-out that contained every word that was going to be said at the *start* of a presentation, would you have any motivation to pay attention? The answer is likely to be 'no'. This is why most hand-outs tend to be in slide format, as only headings are available and the detail is provided in what you say. This is also why your slides should have minimal information on: too much and your audience simply won't be listening to you.

The choice of when to give people hand-outs is up to you. If you don't want people miss what's on the screen and what you're saying because they're reading, then it's probably a good idea to make hand-outs available after your presentation. With lectures we now typically provide hand-outs prior to the lecture starting, though in some cases you'll get the notes afterwards. However, this is mainly because there is a lot of material presented in a relatively long lecture and we prefer students to listen rather than spend all their time scribbling down the information we're saying. We also don't want them to miss anything important.

Giving the presentation

So you've got your slides ready, your audio and visual files are ready, your demonstration and friend are ready, and you've sorted out your hand-outs. All you need to do is actually give the presentation. This is the scary bit. Standing up in front of a crowd of people and making sense while talking about intelligent things is fairly daunting for most of us: all the preparation is easy in comparison. Even experienced lecturers get nervous before big lectures or presentations. However, their nerves are likely to surface about 20 minutes before talking rather than a week before, like the average student. There are a number of tips that you can take with you to help with the presentation itself.

1. Speak clearly and slowly

- This will help you to stay calm and focused, as well as help your audience keep up with what you're saying. If you speak too quickly you will get nervous when people start looking confused. Slow down and those confused looks should go away.

2. Make eye contact if possible (or look at the space above people's heads so it appears that you are)

- This helps you engage with your audience, and it has the added advantage of making sure you are speaking to the room rather than to your feet or your notes. You don't have to stare at your audience all the time, but it is a good tip to remember because it lifts your head out of your notes and enables people to hear you. If you're like me and have a fairly quiet voice, you're not going to be heard at the back of a room unless you both lift your head up and project your voice (or you have a microphone).

3. Don't read off a sheet of notes

- This tip links with the last one: you want people to hear what you are saying. Even the shyest people will be offended once the presentation is over if they get marked down solely because people couldn't hear that they did, in fact, know what they were talking about.

- Learn what you want to say beforehand, but make sure you use a highlighter on your notes so you can quickly find sections of your presentation in them. You'll find that if you've learned what you want to say, the slides end up being enough to trigger your memory for everything you want to say. Your notes then become a little like a security blanket: you probably won't need them but knowing that most of your talk is in front of you is very reassuring.

4. Don't waffle. Try to stick roughly to the topic at hand and what you want to say about it

- If you waffle while you're talking and include lots of information you've not planned to say, you'll end up going off on a tangent and then getting lost (at which point you will be that person at the front of the room rummaging desperately through their notes trying to work out what they should have been saying, and crucially what they should say next).

- You will find that you may be able to get away with significant tangents as you get more experienced at presenting. However, this is not a hard and fast rule: some experienced presenters are still capable of getting lost in their own tangents.

5. Don't be afraid of questions

- The reason you should not be afraid is that you have put your presentation together and have done the research. Therefore, you are perfectly capable of answering the questions that are likely to arise. The questions at a student level are unlikely to be unrelated or tangentially related to your presentation so you should already know the information you need to answer them: it is simply a matter of finding the information amid the mass of terrified neurons in your brain! If you do think the questions are unrelated or outside the scope of your talk then say so and move on. If you are a postgraduate reading this then you should prepare for tough methodological and hypothetical questions, just make sure you know your experiment inside out and concentrate well during the question so you know what is being asked.

- Don't be afraid of saying 'I don't know'. There is absolutely no shame in saying this, though many people think that, if they're standing at the front of a room, they should know everything. This is not the case: until you're an expert in your field it is perfectly fine to say you're not sure or you don't know.

- Many lecturers and presenters dislike questions as they interrupt the flow of their presentation, and for this reason they request all questions to be left to the end. This is a good tactic if you're nervous, as you won't be distracted while you're giving the presentation itself. Hopefully by the time you get to the end you'll be a little calmer and more able to answer questions accurately.

- Questions during a presentation can be daunting for anyone who has never taught in a school or presented to large groups of relative strangers before. In a school you get used to it and adapt your presentation style to fit, but this takes practice and plenty of concentration, so the advice for anyone new to presenting, or in any way nervous about doing so, would be to request that all questions are saved until the end of your presentation.

- If you're feeling brave and think you can cope with questions during your presentation, ask people to put their hand up when they want to ask a question; this way you can finish your sentence or point before answering their question. Make sure you acknowledge their question though. You will probably find that most questions are related to information you are about to present anyway, so you can answer them by carrying on with your presentation.

Posters—presenting your work with minimal talking to people!

Posters are a popular method among academics for presenting a short study or idea quickly and easily, in a format which allows for discussion of concepts rather than a simple presentation of material. Posters tend to be used in the early stages of research as they are easier and less intimidating than full blown research talks for new researchers and students. They are also used when a project has been completed and you simply want to disseminate findings at a conference. At conferences, as well as the workshops and research talks, you generally get several poster sessions where people stand next to their poster and chat about it to anyone who's interested. It's much less stressful for those new to the field or who are not overly fond of giving research talks.

What you should include

The vast majority of poster templates you will find on the Internet are designed around business users. While these can be helpful, they are not particularly suitable for the formats you need to be familiar with for psychology posters. You will find that your department has a series of templates that it uses for posters. You don't need any specialist software to create a poster. Instead, the vast majority of templates are in PowerPoint, so can be opened on any computer.

In psychology, the purpose of a poster is typically to show what we have been doing in our experiments. Consequently, the traditional format for experimental reports needs following fairly closely. This means that you need sections that mirror those presented in a full report, but with the content far more summarized. You also need to make sure that your results are the most clearly displayed item, so important graphs (figures) and tables of data need to be prominent, as do the conclusions you have drawn.

While the basic layout of a poster revolves around the clear presentation of information, in any way you like, there are things on psychology posters that need to be included, and for which space needs to be made available. You can see an example template which explains the content you should include in Figure 14.4.

➠ A copy of this template is also available on the book's website at www.oxfordtextbooks.co.uk/orc/parson/

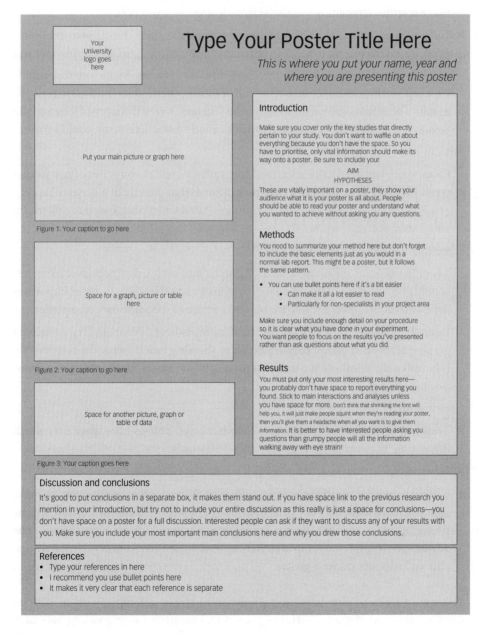

Figure 14.4: Poster template and what to include in the poster.

The key elements to include are:

1   A title

- This needs to be clear and preferably positioned at the top of the page. It must be the first thing people read when viewing your poster.

2   Your name

- You need to take ownership of your poster: state your name clearly underneath your title, and say where you are presenting your poster. This dates it and turns it into a reference, meaning you can refer to it later on if you need to.

3   Introduction

- Make this brief. You don't have space to write a huge amount (between 100 and 200 words is fine) so stick to describing the key area and studies. Make sure you include your aim and hypothesis clearly at the end of this short introduction. This may not be as long a section as you might like, but you still need to tell the story of why you did your experiment, what you wanted to achieve and what you thought would happen.

4   Results

- Once again, you need to be selective. Hopefully you will have a series of results that you want to present, but you need to pick the ones that directly fit with your hypothesis and aims. Anything else can be communicated when people stop to talk to you about your poster.

5   Clear figures showing key results

We discuss the use of figures and tables in Chapter 11.

- There is no point including a load of graphs and tables that nobody can understand. The rule for not doubling up on figures and tables is even more important here: you should never include a table and a figure of the same data on a poster.

- Instead, pick the one which shows the data to its best advantage. Try to include graphs rather than tables: they are better at showing exactly what the relationship is between the numbers you are presenting, and are easier for people reading your poster to digest.

6   Conclusions

- You need to make your conclusions clear but brief. You do have space for a small discussion, but only in the region of 100–150 words.

7   References

- These are just as crucial for posters as they are in every other assignment, so make sure you include them. They can either be in a separate box at the bottom of your poster or integrated into the box containing the discussion and conclusions. The advantage with references is that you can make the font considerably smaller to take up less space on your poster.

Go to www. oxfordtextbooks. co.uk/orc/parson/

There are a series of templates on the website for you to use, along with an exercise where you are asked to mark a series of posters and determine how good, or bad, each one is (also see Exercise 14.1, later in this chapter). My comments on the posters will be available, and you will be able to compare your comments with the marks the posters would actually have got.

Level of detail to include

A poster does not contain much space so you have to be very selective about what to include, particularly when dealing with introduction and discussion sections. Try to make sure you only include key pieces of information that relate directly to the study you are reporting. A lot of information may be related to your study, but this is for people to ask you about rather than for your poster to include: your focus should be *your* experiment, not other people's experiments. Figure 14.5 shows you some examples of good and bad introductory content. Figure 14.5a shows you an example of well-presented and clear introduction. The background material is clearly presented and the aim and hypothesis are clearly stated. Figure 14.5b is an example of poorly presented and unclear introduction. The background material is poorly presented with no attempt made to link to the experiment; the aim is just about present but no hypothesis has been provided.

Two things you should always remember to put in at the end of this section are your **aim** and **hypotheses**. It is also good to arrange the poster around the aim and hypotheses; they are the questions you have hopefully answered with your experiment, and so they should be easy to identify. They tell people exactly what you were trying to do and what you wanted to find, so are a central part of a poster.

(a)

> **Introduction**
> Immersive and collaborative communities of practice are possible in structured virtual environments such as Second Life. They can engage students in innovative and creative ways, holding the potential to unlock creative problem solving, increase motivation, and offer a deeper level of collaborative learning. Highly motivated students produce richer and higher quality work than those who are not (Pajares & Johnson, 1994). Virtual worlds have been used successfully as teaching resources in medical education and training (Kamel Boulos et al, 2007), psychiatry education (Yellowless et al, 2006) and more traditional e-learning courses (Hemmi et al, 2008).
>   AIM: to investigate student motivational levels while learning within Second Life
>   HYPOTHESES: that learning in SL will increase motivation and perceived learning

(b)

> **Introduction**
> • Stroop (1935) looked at whether congruent or incongruent information was processed faster
> • Aim is to look at the effect of hypnosis and gender on the stroop task

Figure 14.5: (a) A good introductory section. (b) A poor introductory section.

In the method and results sections you need to be able to get across exactly what you did and found as concisely as possible. Don't skimp on details here: the methods and results are almost more important than the introduction on a poster. They do, after all, contain the information you are actually presenting—the details of how you have answered the questions set by the aim and hypotheses. Some examples of good and bad content are provided in Figure 14.6. Figure 14.6a gives you an example of well-constructed and clear method and results section; the data collection and results are clearly visible. Figure 14.6b on the other hand is an example of a very poorly constructed and unclear method and results section. The data collection and results are lacking in detail, and it is not possible to know what happened or what was found in this experiment.

You do need some graphs and other figures on a poster: a picture can display your results clearly and concisely, saving you the need to describe them in words. Make sure you make some really clear graphs, and include a decent caption explaining to the reader what they actually mean. Of course, you need to label and title all graphs, figures and

(a)

Methods
- Participants: 54 (males: females = 21:33) on a 1st year undergraduate psychology course at a UK University, selected via opportunity sampling. Mean age was 19 years.
- Materials: a list of tasks to accomplish within SL, the university computing laboratory, the follow-up questionnaire
- Procedure: students took part as part of the Study Skills Module in their 1st year. They learned how to use SL then were asked to complete a list of tasks in groups. A questionnaire was circulated at the end of the session, containing questions relating to their experiences.

Results
The majority of participants had no problems using SL at all. The enthusiasm of the experimenters was evident and participants found SL to be a fun and entertaining way to learn. The whole immersive experience was very popular and individuals saw how to SL could be used to support their own courses and work. Some participants had problems using SL itself, although these were mainly technical unfamiliarity issues and orienting within SL itself. All issues experienced were easy to resolve with practice and not related in any way to the content presented within SL. Participants typically spent around 50% longer immersed in academic activity than they normally would.

(b)

Methods
- Split people into groups
- Each group administered the stroop test to each other
- Recorded times on paper

Results
- Males were slower than females on congruent but there was no difference for incongruent
- Hypnosis had more of an effect on males than females

Figure 14.6: (a) A well-constructed method and results section. (b) A poorly constructed method and results section.

tables you include. Figure 14.7 shows you some examples of figures from posters. You can see from Figure 14.7a that this is a well-constructed and clear figure; it is easy to work out what students were asked and how they responded. Figure 14.7b, however, has a multitude of problems. There are no titles on the axes and it is unclear what is actually being depicted. It would be very difficult to work out what the experiment was about, never mind working out what was actually found. In addition the person doing this has used a totally inappropriate (and inconsistent) graph format which only distracts from the content. Three-dimensional effects look fun but they detract from the content and make it harder for people to work out what was actually found—something you should be making as obvious as possible.

Discussions and conclusions should be clear and contain only information that directly ties your results with the previous literature you cited in the introduction, and with your aims and hypotheses. If there is room for some discussion of future avenues that could be followed by all means do so, but focus on your data and how it links to the field of study. Figure 14.8a shows you an example of a well-presented and clear discussion section; there is plenty of content and the results are clearly linked to both previous

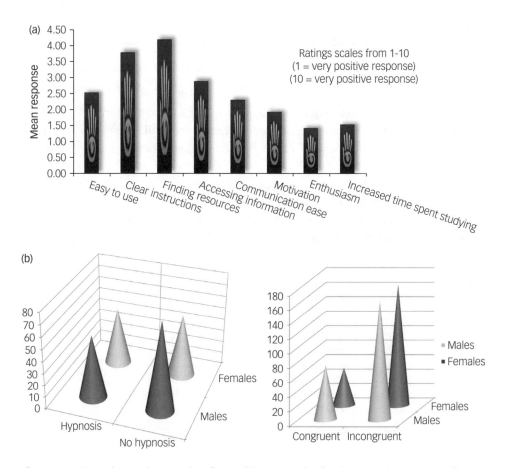

Figure 14.7: (a) A clear and appropriate figure. (b) An example of an inappropriate and poor figure.

(a)

Discussion and Conclusions

Opinion regarding use of virtual worlds in education is generally very positive from those involved in education (Hemmi et al, 2009; Kamel Boulos et al, 2007). Most participants had no problems using SL at all. The enthusiasm of the experimenters was evident and individuals found SL to be a fun and entertaining way to learn; the whole experience was very popular. The general consensus was that the experience was more immersive than traditional methods of learning: providing an increased level of learning for those taking part. In SL students have to hunt for information themselves and integrate it correctly before it makes sense. It is a more thorough method of learning, as it promotes motivation and self-directed learning as well as critical thinking and better problem-solving skills. This study supports the view that increasing motivation through use of innovative teaching methods can facilitate learning and increase the uptake of information in a student population.

(b)

Discussion and Conclusions

- Gender has an effect on the stroop task
- Hypnosis only appears to have an effect on males
- The congruent task is easier than the incongruent one
- This supports previous literature
- Further research could include looking at a wider population rather than just students
- Data analysis was completed and the statistics showed that all the differences provided were significant
- In conclusion the results support the hypothesis

Figure 14.8: (a) A good discussion and conclusion section. (b) A poorly constructed discussion and conclusion section.

research and the hypothesis. Figure 14.8b on the other hand is an example of a poorly constructed discussion and conclusion section; there is no detail, statements are generic and sweeping, plus the student refers to a hypothesis that does not exist on the poster (see Figure 14.5b).

....

Exercise 14.1: Good or bad poster?

➠ Go to www. oxfordtextbooks. co.uk/orc/parson/

In this exercise I want you to go online to look at the two posters provided on the book's website and assess each of them. Use the criteria listed below and decide which grade you would give each poster and why.

Marking Criteria

Excellent	A	1st
Good	B	2–1
OK, not bad	C	2–2
Not very good	D	3rd
Rubbish	E	FAIL

....

✎ Checklist

Check you've understood the key points covered in this chapter by seeing if you can answer the following questions:

✔ What should you remember about the content of slides?

✔ What should you remember about pictures and slides?

✔ How many slides should you use?

✔ What should you not be afraid of with demonstrations?

✔ What should you do when you're giving the presentation?

✔ What should you *not* do when giving the presentation?

✔ Do you know how you plan to deal with interruptions and questions?

✔ Will you provide hand-outs, if so when will you provide them?

✔ Do you know where to get a template for your poster?

✔ What should you *not* do when making a poster?

✔ Do you know how much detail you should and should not include?

Chapter 15

Your dissertation and thesis: what you need to know

In your final year at university as an undergraduate you will do a dissertation, which is essentially an extended laboratory report. At a higher level of study, postgraduates will do either a master's dissertation/thesis or a full doctoral (PhD) thesis, both of which are significantly larger than anything you will do at undergraduate level. A dissertation on a taught master's is simply a longer version of the undergraduate dissertation, and as such the section on undergraduate dissertations is applicable. Both master's research dissertations and doctoral theses are covered in the section on theses. What this chapter will *not* do, however, is tell you in detail how to structure your dissertation: as explained below, undergraduate dissertations follow the same structure as a laboratory report, so Chapter 11, on laboratory reports, gives you all the information you need. The differences between undergraduate dissertations and postgraduate dissertations and theses will be highlighted later in this chapter.

Final year dissertations—your empirical project

Your undergraduate project is a crucial part of you final year at university as an undergraduate. However, it can be difficult to find guidance on completing these projects, not least because different universities refer to them in different ways (so you can never be sure what topic to look for in books and other resources). Your final year project can be called your *dissertation*, your *empirical project*, or simply your *final year project*. Whatever your institution calls it, it's an important part of your overall study—and contributes to a significant proportion of your overall marks—so it's worth putting a lot of effort into.

You usually have most of the final year to work on your dissertation and there is no exam to worry about for this module, plus you'll get loads of help with every aspect. Make the most of this and you can really boost your overall grades.

Writing an undergraduate dissertation is basically like writing an extended laboratory report. However, there is one key difference: you are the one who decides what to do and how to do it. This can be quite a heady concept for undergraduates: after two years of study you are finally told to conduct a piece of research by yourself, either on a topic of your choice guided by staff research interests, or on a topic provided for you by your department.

At some point in the second year you will be asked to choose a supervisor, and it is best to do this with two things in mind:

- Do you like the member of staff?
  - This is important as you will be having a lot of meetings with them and you will need to feel confident discussing your project with them and seeking their guidance. If you don't like your supervisor, this will hinder the process of getting your project done.
- What am I interested in studying?
  - If your department lets you choose you own project ideas you will be spending quite a bit of time during your second year preparing proposals (either formally as an assessed piece of work or informally proposing an idea to a potential supervisor), then around eight months of your final year carrying out and writing up your project. So it goes without saying that you need to like (and be interested in) what you're doing. If your department provides a list of projects, you should pick the supervisor whose interests most closely align with your own.

This empirical project is *your* experiment and *your* responsibility, so it's up to *you* to get it done and finished on time. Having said this, your supervisor will give you plenty of help along the way. But they won't be doing the work for you: if they end up doing too much for you then *you* will be penalized by way of the marks you are awarded being reduced. It is therefore up to you to take the initiative and get on with your project.

Structuring your time and getting organized

Like for so much of your study, the best tip for the undergraduate dissertation is not to leave it until the last minute. Indeed, it is simply too big a task *not* to plan carefully in advance. Reading Chapter 2, on time management, will help considerably. However, you do need to make sure you organize a time schedule with your supervisor. Each individual project will have different requirements, and therefore different deadlines, but your supervisor will be able to help you work out when you should complete each section. Remember, though: it's up to you to meet these deadlines. Your supervisor will check in with you, but you are the one responsible for your project and it's up to you to get it finished.

It's a good idea to write a timetable and plan your time between the start of your final year and the date you need to hand in your dissertation. Set yourself deadlines and make sure you stick to them. If you fall behind and have to rush your dissertation write-up then you won't produce as good a piece of work as you are able. This will lower your mark and may mean you drop a degree classification overall: as we note above, the dissertation counts for a significant proportion of your overall mark.

How much bigger is a dissertation than a laboratory report?

It's all very well saying that a dissertation is an extended laboratory report. But just how extended is it? Unfortunately word limits for dissertations are set by your institution so it's not possible to give exact word limits here. However, what I can do is provide some guidelines.

A standard laboratory report is around 1500–2000 words long. The size of your dissertation will be between 6000 and 12 000 words—so your undergraduate dissertation will be between three and eight times longer. This may sound a lot, but try to remember that you will be spending a long time on this, and you will have plenty of time to produce the project. Most universities state word limits in the following way: 2000 ± 10%. This tells you that you have a target of 2000 words, but with a 10% margin of error—that is, you can write 10% more or 10% less than 2000 words. So, for example, if you write 2200 words you won't be penalized for it. An example of how to split up your dissertation can be found in Table 15.1. If you are one of the minority of students whose methods and results sections will take up far more space than expected talk to your supervisor. If they think that the additional words are justified for clarity then you probably won't be penalized for going over the word limit.

Where to get help

Your supervisor is your first port of call for help regarding all aspects of your empirical project. From literature searches to analysis and writing up, you should talk to your supervisor first and foremost, via email or in face-to-face meetings.

You will probably feel like you're coming to your supervisor with seemingly endless questions, but this is normal so you shouldn't feel worried about it. (In fact, your supervisor will worry more if you never ask questions and never come to ask for help.) Most supervisors will ensure they have plenty of time available for project students, and you will find you don't need to wait until your supervisor's office hours to go and see them. You can simply make an appointment.

Many departments like you to have free reign with which topic you pick for your dissertation, but this comes with a drawback: staff supervising you may not be experts in the field and you'll need to be rather more independent. Some departments simply give a list of projects available from each staff member, in which case your supervisor will be an expert in the field and you'll be able to draw on their expertise. All staff will obviously be able to help with all aspects of methodology and analysis, but unless your supervisor is a specialist in the area you are researching they won't be able to help you as much with the literature review itself. They will pick up enough to know if it's well written and

TABLE 15.1 Word estimations for dissertations

Section	Word guidance		Notes
	Laboratory report	Dissertation	
Abstract	200	250	Abstract length remains roughly the same for all types of experimental report
Introduction	750	2550	This appears a big increase, but you need to include far more detail in you dissertation so you're more likely to find it's not enough space to cover all that you want to in enough detail
Method	200	850	Both your method and results may well end up longer than this, depending on the content and style of your project. Remember that when you add in additional words in one section, you need to take them from elsewhere to keep within the word limit
Results	250	850	
Discussion	600	2500	Your discussion will probably cause you the most headaches, but you shouldn't feel daunted by its length. Once you've properly discussed your results in the context of previous literature you will probably find that you have used a good chunk of your word limit
References	Not included	Not included	Neither the reference list nor the appendices are typically included in word limits, but make sure you check with your supervisor
Appendices	Not included	Not included	
Total	**2000**	**7000**	

where you need more/less information, but the technicalities may not be known to them. It's for this reason that departments like you to pick a supervisor based on their specialities rather than if you like them or not!

If you are in a situation where you're doing a dissertation on a topic which your supervisor is not at all familiar with (for example, if your institution is fairly relaxed about the topics that can be chosen, or if there is a new member of staff who has been assigned students who were allocated to previous members of staff) the important thing to do is discuss your options with your supervisor. In these situations your supervisor will probably advise you that you should amend your ideas to fit with their areas of specialism. Otherwise you will not get as much specialist help. However, if you want to stick with your dissertation ideas, you will probably be able to, but you'll be advised if there are other members of staff who are specialists in the area you are researching in, who you can ask for advice (your supervisor will probably be asking them too!). But remember to check with your supervisor first as they will probably have to check with the other member of staff first before you go bounding in with endless questions. You will find, however, that your supervisor will pick up enough about your topic to be able to help you with most things during your dissertation.

The problem with getting a lot of help

Your dissertation is a semi-independent research project. This means that the more help you get from your supervisor and elsewhere, the more marks may be taken away from you. Your supervisor will be keeping a note of what help they have given you throughout the project period, in particular how much help you needed with methodology, preparation of materials, data collection and analysis. If you needed significant help in many of these areas, then you will lose marks as a result. This may seem a bit unfair. However, remember that your dissertation is an expression of your accumulated knowledge from your degree: if you need a lot of help to complete it, you're demonstrating that you've not learned as much as you should have done, and so marks cannot be awarded.

Despite what I've said here, don't think you mustn't ask for help at all! It really is a question of balance. We don't expect you to be able to do it all yourselves, we are expecting lots of questions. As long as we can see you are in charge of your project, know what you want to be doing and have thought about what you've found then we are quite happy to answer all manner of questions and help you as much as we can.

A quick word on finding information to include

In Chapter 11 (laboratory reports), Chapter 10 (writing an essay) and Chapter 13 (referencing) we noted how lecturers generally do not like to see information taken from the Internet. In your dissertation this is even more important. The material you use in your background reading should come directly from journal articles in preference to any other source. You will be doing a piece of research and, as such, need to be informed by the most up-to-date information available. The information you find in books is incredibly useful as background material to help you understand the contents of the journal articles, but you should focus on papers rather than chapters for the information you cite in your work. Equally, the Internet is a wonderful invention; however, for the purposes of your dissertation please use it as a tool to search for journal articles and the like, rather than using it as a source of information in itself.

What is a thesis and how is it different from a dissertation?

Let's now move beyond undergraduate study into the world of postgraduates, and consider theses. A thesis is drastically different from a dissertation. For one thing it is considerably bigger. Word limits vary but you should expect to write upwards of 20 000 words for a master's research dissertation/thesis, and around 50 000–80 000 words for a PhD thesis. In addition to this you should expect to present information within a series of individual chapters, and not merely a series of sections as you would do for an extended laboratory report. You can probably already see that a thesis is far more involved than your undergraduate dissertation or the master's dissertation, and needs a significant amount of background material to go along with it. Your PhD thesis will be an exercise in determination as much as it is a showcase for your academic and intellectual abilities.

In contrast with undergraduate projects, it is up to you how much you write in your thesis. You're usually just given a vague guideline as to the upper limit. However, it is important to aim for this guideline as it has been set for a reason: it reflects the amount a good student should expect to write in order to produce a thorough and well-written piece of work.

The increase in size is not the only difference between a dissertation and a thesis: a thesis is produced largely independently. You will have a supervisor with whom you will have regular meetings and with whom you can discuss all manner of things relating to your work, but the bulk of your work will be done alone. There are likely to be other postgraduate students around and chances are you will form a close and supportive bond with others in the same position as you.

Chapters and what to do with them

Another key distinction between a dissertation and a thesis is that a thesis is broken down into chapters rather than being one continuous report. Typically you should have several chapters on background literature reviews (structured like long essays with subsections), several chapters on experiments you've done (structured like long laboratory reports of journal articles), and then a discussion chapter and your summary.

As an example here I'll use my PhD thesis to give you an idea of what you should do: when you've read the title you'll probably be very grateful this is the only chapter I refer to it in!

- Title: *Investigations of Attentional Processing in Parietal and Occipital Human Cortical Regions with Magnetoencephalography (MEG)*
  - *53 273 words (including contents, references and titles)*
- Synopsis
  - *304 words*

- Contents list
- Chapter 1: Review Chapter 1—Attention
  - *8345 words*
- Chapter 2: Review Chapter 2—Attention and the primary visual cortex
  - *5455 words*
- Chapter 3: Methodology Review Chapter—Magnetoencephalography
  - *3984 words*
- Chapter 4: General Methods Chapter
  - *2529 words*
- Chapter 5: Experimental Chapter 1—Response of the parietal lobes to a dual attention task
  - *9532 words*
- Chapter 6: Experimental Chapter 2—Handedness and a cued attentional task
  - *6741 words*
- Chapter 7: Experimental Chapter 3—Response of the parietal lobes to a cued attentional task
  - *7902 words*
- Summary
  - *2153 words*
- References
- Appendices

As you can see there are three review chapters, a methodology chapter and three experimental chapters; the word counts show that each of them represents a considerable amount of work. Each experimental chapter contains a separate extensive experiment, written up as a self-contained report complete with all sections required in a standard laboratory report.

⟹ You can find out more about writing lab reports in Chapter 11.

The idea is that each experimental chapter is equivalent to a journal article in terms of style only (though you may not be lucky enough to get it published in that form). Indeed, it is possible to actually submit a thesis that is simply a collection of papers you've published during your time as a PhD student, although this will not be possible for master's dissertations.

When writing a thesis, make sure you adhere to the following guidelines:

- Be clear about what you are writing about
- Include exhaustive detail about the topic matter involved
- Be explicit in how each aspect of your review of the literature relates to the topic

- Thoroughly cover every aspect of your experimentation
- Explain your results in a very high level of detail with enough tables and figures to make it very clear to the examiner that you completely understand your results
- Discuss your findings in relation to your entire literature search and review.

Additional sections you need to think about

In a thesis there are also some additional sections you need to think about, which don't feature within the structure of an undergraduate laboratory report. These are a *synopsis* and a *summary*. The *synopsis* goes at the very start of your thesis and is a short summary of the entire thesis material, covering the key ideas and findings. It's a bit like a very long abstract. The *summary* goes right at the end and is a detailed summary—around two to three pages—describing the key and interesting findings of your work; it should also describe how your work fits into the existing literature, and any implications your work carries.

Both of these sections are distinct to the thesis structure and are straight forward enough. A synopsis is like a really long abstract and the summary is just that, a summary of your thesis covering all the major points and findings. Your supervisor will be able to give you guidance in the event you need it.

▥▶ Examples of both synopsis and summaries are available on the book's website at www. oxfordtextbooks. co.uk/orc/parson/

Structuring your time and getting organized

When you're doing a thesis it is even more important that you learn to structure your time well. With a dissertation you'll get regular contact with your supervisor over the few months that you're doing it. But with a thesis there is far less contact between you and your supervisor and the onus is on you to get everything done. It is also increasingly common to do a PhD part-time alongside working as a teaching assistant in the department, so you have to schedule your research work around your timetabled teaching hours and the huge piles of marking you'll get to go along with this. For those of you who are doing your PhD part-time while working outside the university, you will have to schedule research around your contracted work hours; getting enough sleep is likely to be your biggest challenge here, particularly if you have children. Just remember to talk to your supervisor if there are any problems at all. Chapter 2, on time management, will help considerably.

Where to get help

According to the head of department when I did my PhD, the student–supervisor relationship is like a parent–child relationship. At the start you need your supervisor to give a considerable amount of help. By the end, however, the student is standing on their own two feet and is finding their own way in the academic world.

The advice for where to get help is the same as that for dissertations: your supervisor will be your first port of call, especially at the start of the thesis. However, the onus is on you to organize and run the experiments, produce the literature reviews, and to analyse and interpret your results—and you should expect to look for answers yourself in the first instance rather than running straight to your supervisor: they will not be impressed if you run straight to them with a question without even trying to find an answer for yourself first. Around halfway through your PhD you will start noticing that you can answer questions before your supervisor can, that you can discuss topics more confidently and that you have your own ideas about how things might work out in your results. By the end of your PhD you—and not your supervisor—will be the expert in what you have done; their role in the interim is to guide you and facilitate you reaching this point as best they can.

Throughout a master's dissertation/thesis you will find that your supervisor is the best person to ask for help, whether that be academic or practical. However, with a PhD, you should be able to ask other members of the department to help with methodological and analysis issues as well; after all you are surrounded by lecturers who have been through the same process and will have encountered many of the same issues during their PhDs.

There is also likely to be help somewhere in the department if you're drowning in marking, are struggling to find suitable participants, or are stuck with childcare issues when you've got experimental participants waiting. The important thing to remember is to ask for help should you need it; chances are it will be available. Doing a postgraduate dissertation may well be a tool to teach independent research skills, but you're learning these skills so it's completely okay to ask when you're really stuck—nobody expects you to do everything perfectly the first time round.

✎ Checklist

Check you've understood the key points covered in this chapter by seeing if you can answer the following questions:

Dissertations

- ✔ Are you doing something you're interested in?
- ✔ Do you know your word limit and how much more you need to include?
- ✔ Have you worked out a timetable for getting your dissertation finished?
- ✔ Do you know who to ask for help?

Theses

It is difficult to do a checklist for a thesis as they are individual and determined by the topic and the person writing them. However, there are some things that you can check.

- ✔ Are you doing something you're interested in?
- ✔ Do you understand the volume of work required of you?
- ✔ Do you know what you should concentrate on throughout your thesis?
- ✔ Do you have a good working relationship with your supervisor?
- ✔ Do you know which other members of the department you can ask for help?

Chapter 16

Revision and exam tips

In Chapter 2 we looked at time management, including the subject of revision and exam times. This chapter goes into more detail about your revision and exam periods and provides tools which you can use to help you revise, remember more and therefore improve your exam performance. While this chapter contains many tips and pieces of advice, it is important to remember that not every technique described is useful for everyone. Try each technique out, but then stick to the ones that work for you. Some of you will work best in a quiet room just reading from books, while some of you may work best surrounded by friends quizzing you from the book/notes. It is very important to realize that there is no 'right' way to revise: everyone is different and you should always do what works best for you, not for other people.

Tips for helping you remember course material

Where to study

Finding the perfect revision spot can be problematic, although being in the middle of a crowded pub or club is unlikely to be at the top of anyone's lists. Choosing where to study comes down to individual preference, although most students like using their bedroom as the primary revision area, as it is easily personalized and controlled to suit the individual—and cups of tea (or other beverages of your choice) are readily available throughout the revision process.

The general tip cited most often is to minimize noise and distractions. The point about distractions is correct: you *do* need to minimize distractions while you are revising. However, working with noise is a personal choice: some people need absolute silence, while others find this in itself is distracting and require noise of some description, as we mention below.

Equally, you will frequently find that people suggest finding just one location to revise. This is practical but not always sensible psychologically. Many of you will become familiar with the concept of context-dependent retrieval (Martin et al., 2010). This is a concept whereby we remember things more easily in the location we learned them. However, remembering things most effectively when you're in your specific area for revision is not actually that helpful as you don't sit the exam in your revision spot. Revising in more than one location will help you learn the information independently of this phenomenon, by removing contextual cues of location, and help you remember information more easily when in the exam itself.

Wherever you chose to revise, make sure you can control the level of distraction. Some people like revising in the library as it is generally a very quiet location with almost no disruptions. For others, this feels excessively quiet and they need music on (and not just via headphones), or the option of making noise at regular intervals. The garden is a popular revision location during summer exam seasons. However, this is not always effective as a location as it is possible to get too hot and sleepy then fall asleep. Revising outside as a group is generally better: if you do nod off there is someone to wake you up!

Make sure your revision location has everything you need for your revision: books, articles, notes, pens, note cards, blank paper and exam details. Having to get up and find things can take time out of your revision schedule, and moving around can be distracting in itself. The point about revision is you need to spend good chunks of time focusing on the information while in one location, be that at your desk or in the library or garden.

Reward systems

It is very important to give yourself a reward system during your revision. A small reward can go a long way towards making you feel like you're making progress. However, make the rewards based on length of time revised rather than whether you can remember a set amount of information. If you *do* want to reward yourself according to the amount of information remembered, have it as an additional reward system.

Rewards can be anything that you yourself will like, be that 15 minutes of TV time for every hour revised, chocolate biscuits, a walk with the dog or an afternoon/evening off at the weekend to spend with family or friends. But make sure you are consistent and don't change the goalposts halfway through revision: if you start off by rewarding yourself for every hour of revision and then change it to every 30 minutes you will make the reward seem less of a reward and more an expectation—reducing the motivation while you are revising.

When to study

The time of day you choose to revise certain subjects depends on the time of day you are most awake. Some of you will be 'night owls' and work better in the late afternoons and evenings, while some will be 'morning larks' and work best early in the morning. While you can all revise at any time of day, you should schedule in your most difficult subjects at the times when you are most alert, and those you find easiest as the times when you are less alert.

Some of you will have time of study decided for you: if you have a job or have family, there may be certain times of day where you simply cannot study. The only tip here is to ensure that you do have certain periods of time free and that you don't allow family or work life to encroach on this, if at all possible. The previous paragraph about time of day still applies though: if you work better in the morning, spend a few hours revising before you have to go to work or get the children up. Similarly, if you work better in the evenings, make sure you have a few hours free then to work.

Travelling time is good for revising. If you get about by the bus/underground/metro systems then you can take books with you to read. If you drive, you might want to think about recording yourself reading either your notes or sections from books. If you save these audio files as mp3 files they can be put on any portable device capable of playing music. You can then listen to these files however you travel. If your lecturers have recorded any of your lectures as audio or video files, download those and listen to them while you are out and about. This should enable you to revise on the move as well as in your allotted time at home.

Active revision versus passive revision

Revision can be an active process or a passive one. Up to this point, many of you will have used mostly passive revision with a little bit of active revision. However, active revision is far more effective than passive and is something that should make up the majority of revision time.

Passive revision is essentially quietly reading through your notes and books. This can be effective, but it is not a method which tests your knowledge and lets you see how much you actually know. Passive revision simply requires that you absorb knowledge, rather than requiring you to learn. Active revision, on the other hand, requires that you seek out information and actively try to learn it through testing, applying the knowledge and answering questions. This involves group work, going through exam papers and actively checking for the correct answers.

Different revision methods

There are many different methods which are known to aid recall of information. A few of the most useful are presented here.

Mind maps

Many students already know about mind maps as a revision tool and will already be firm proponents of the method. Some of you may have tried them and discarded them as a method of revision. This is not a problem. Try again if you like, or look to the other tips and tools in this section for more revision ideas.

For those of you not familiar with mind maps, they are single page diagrams which are essentially a 'road-map' of a particular topic. Information is organized around a central idea via lines, symbols, colours and words. The lines radiating off the central idea are grouped into key aspects of that central idea and information relating to those key aspects is placed together on those lines. It essentially turns a long list of information into a colourful and organized diagram, providing you with more cues for recall than just a list of information.

Creating mind maps is a really easy process: it develops as your revision develops. You can refine and amend your mind map, in much the same way as flash cards, until you have one that represents as much of a topic as you can manage on one piece of paper. There are many images online of mind maps people have created; some are fantastically colourful and some are simplistic and minimal. A combination of these styles is probably best.

In terms of colour, you want enough in key areas to draw your attention to particularly important concepts, but you don't want to spend all your time creating a work of art. After all, the more time you spend learning the information, the better you will remember it.

You probably want to opt for more rather than less content, but stick to key words and bullet points, using enough for you to remember an aspect of the topic. For example writing 'Miller 7 ± 2' should be enough to remind most students (from AS level upwards) that Miller is commonly associated with the concept that we can remember 7 plus or minus 2 chunks of information at any one time.

Creating your mind map

There is a set method of creating your mind map; just follow the basic tips given below. An example of a mind map is given in Figure 16.1.

- The main idea/topic is in the centre of the page (idea circle)
- Main themes of the idea branch off this central idea (theme branches)
- Aspects of these themes are represented as 'twigs' off the theme branches (detail twigs)
- Use colour: make the theme branches bright and colourful, highlight key words and ideas but make sure common areas are in the same colours.

Flash cards

Putting your notes onto cards is a staple of revision for many students. File cards are best, and there is a wide range available from most stationery retailers. The use of flash cards is good for condensing a topic into its key points. If you can condense your notes into a single flash card for each particular topic, and then write several pages based on that flash card, then you are probably ready for your exam.

So, how do you compile a flash card? First go through your notes and highlight key areas of a topic. Then, put the headings of these key areas, along with any keywords associated with that heading, onto a file card. Avoid writing in full sentences; like mindmaps, stick to bullet points and key words. An example of what you might put on a flash card is given in Figure 16.2.

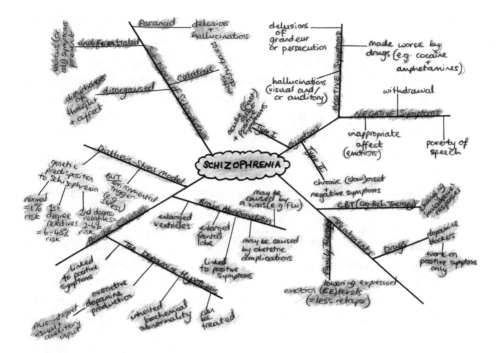

Figure 16.1: An example of a mind map. (See Plate 2 for a full colour version.)

Quiz each other

A really good trick for revising is to work in groups and quiz each other. You can do this in various ways, although the key is that all answers must be given without referring to books, notes or friends.

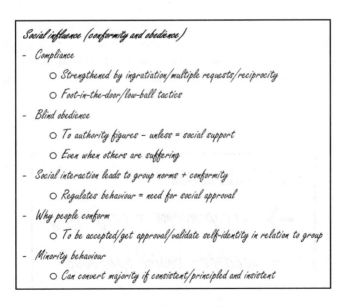

Figure 16.2: An example flash card used to revise social influence.

- Option one: everyone grab a book and pick a section. You each take it in turn to ask the others questions about that section. You can split this method by section.

- Option two: split the topics between you and focus on what you've been given—then teach the others. Teaching a topic is always the best way to learn it. (Statistics made very little sense to me until I had to teach it. Now I can't work out what I was worried about!) This option is a good idea, but you need to make sure you all cover all the topics. It's a bit like running your own seminars.

- Option three: this one is probably the most fun, but slightly less practical than the other two. You each create some questions and then split into teams. You take it in turns to be the quizmaster and turn revision into a competition, with fun/edible prizes if you wish. If you make your learning process fun then it is surprising how much information you can retain about complex topics. This option is probably best earlier in the revision process or when you have multiple-choice (MCQ) or short-answer question exams coming up. You probably don't want to use this option later in the revision process for essay-based exams as you'll need to make sure you can remember lots of integrated detail rather than individual pieces of fact in an essay exam. So testing yourselves using MCQs won't be very helpful in this instance.

The sticky note revision technique

This is an informal technique that's been utilized by a large number of people, myself included. Leaving notes for yourself around the house with keywords/theories or studies is a really good method of learning information independently of location. Post-its or sticky notes are brilliant for this: simply condense information to fit on the note about a theory, study or key aspect of a topic, and then stick them up all over the house in locations you frequent on a regular basis, such as the fridge or the bathroom mirror (see Figure 16.3). Learning information independently of context and location will help enormously when you're in the exam, as you won't be relying on cues you have seen in your room, or the order in which you initially learnt the information.

Figure 16.3: Example of a revision post-it note.

Doing past papers is like doing practice exams: practice makes perfect!

The most useful resource, after books and your notes, are past exam papers. There are always past papers floating around the department. If there are no easy links to any for your particular course, ask your tutor if they can be made available. In the case of MCQs (see below) practice questions should typically be made available for you.

Finding past papers

Past papers are available in various locations, either in the course location on the university virtual learning environment (VLE), in the library or on tutors' computers.

We discuss VLEs in Chapter 4.

In the latter case you have to ask your tutor if you can have a look at them. However, if papers are available on the VLE or in the library, all you have to do is find them and print or photocopy them.

Doing past papers

The most important thing to remember when doing past papers is to put your books and notes out of reach, away from the temptation of looking at them. If you look at books and notes while you are doing past papers then you are defeating one of the main points of doing them in the first place—to test your knowledge. You won't get to look at your books in exams at university so get used to not relying on them. The benefit of this is that you will see how much you are progressing in your revision: as you learn more so you will get more marks on each question on the past papers.

Another key tip with past papers is to time yourself when you are doing them. If you know how long it should take to complete a question, then only allow yourself this much time when you are doing it. After that point stop and make a line underneath what you have written. Then, carry on with the question and try to answer it as best you can. When you go through the answers compare how many marks you got in timed conditions and for the completed answer.

A frequent complaint during exams is that individuals ran out of time to write everything down. This is more to do with exam technique than knowing so much you can't fit it on the page in time. In exams, you need to learn how to plan your time effectively in order to have enough time to answer questions. Many students spend too much time planning and thinking, or staring into space; this is why they run out of time. Past papers can help you learn to plan your time so you don't run into problems with timing.

Where to get the answers

Answers to past papers are found either in the same place you got the papers themselves from or in your books and notes. If the answers aren't kept with the papers, then you will be finding the answers yourself from your notes. This is probably the best way to go through past papers: going over the same topics again after you have spent a portion of time really concentrating on them is a brilliant way of revising. The more ways and times you go through information, the better you will remember it.

Tackling different question types

Various types of question can appear on your exam papers. Typically, your lecturers and tutors will let you know what to expect in each exam. We will go through strategies for each question in this section, along with a brief explanation of the types of question and what they demand.

Multiple-choice questions (aka MCQs)

When you have MCQs in an exam you will have one question and should pick a single answer from the selection provided. While you will have doubtless have seen these before, it is still common for students to answer these questions incorrectly—frequently by selecting more than one answer. You need to select just one answer or you will get zero marks for that question.

*How **NOT** to answer an MCQ: any of these options will result in zero marks.*

06 ⸢A⸥ ⸢B⸥ ⸢C⸥ ⸢D⸥ ⸢E⸥
07 ⸢A⸥ ⸢B⸥ ⸢C⸥ ⸢D⸥ ⸢E⸥
08 ⸢A⸥ ⸢B⸥ ⸢C⸥ ⸢D⸥ ⸢E⸥
09 ⸢A⸥ ⸢B⸥ ⸢C⸥ ⸢D⸥ ⸢E⸥

*How to **CORRECTLY** answer an MCQ*

06 ⸢A⸥ ⸢B⸥ ⸢C⸥ ⸢D⸥ ⸢E⸥
07 ⸢A⸥ ⸢B⸥ ⸢C⸥ ⸢D⸥ ⸢E⸥
08 ⸢A⸥ ⸢B⸥ ⸢C⸥ ⸢D⸥ ⸢E⸥
09 ⸢A⸥ ⸢B⸥ ⸢C⸥ ⸢D⸥ ⸢E⸥

MCQs are typically done with a list of questions, the answers to which you fill in on another piece of paper which is then electronically marked. This piece of paper will have instructions explaining how it should be filled in: read these carefully, as mistakes cannot be rectified later. The trick to MCQs is to realize that half of the given answers *should* be easy to dismiss if you've done some revision. We'll use the question in Example 16.1 on the working memory model as an example.

Example 16.1: Question: The three components of the working memory model are:

(a) The executor, the worker and the watcher

(b) The phonological loop, the executor and the listener

(c) The central executive, the phonological loop and the visuo-spatial scratchpad

(d) The central executive, the visuo-spatial scratchpad and the inner eye.

In this example you should be able to see that the first two answers are obviously wrong: there are no such things as the watcher or listener in any memory models taught on psychology courses. That leaves you with answers (c) and (d). If you have worked out the correct answer, circle it now. The difficulty with the remaining answers is they all incorporate words that are used in the working memory model of memory. However, only one of the answers has the components listed: one contains just an *element* of one of the components. This is a standard trick in MCQs: they're not designed to be easy, and you will find that some require you to really concentrate on what you're reading. The answer to this particular question is (c). In answer (d) the inner eye is an element of the phonological loop (along with the inner ear), but not a component in itself.

Timing is an important thing to remember in MCQ exams: generally you should look at how much time you have been given, then divide it by the number of questions. For example, it is typical to find 60 questions in an hour-long exam. (If you get extra time then factor that in too.) This means you have to answer one question per minute. This can sound quite frightening, but it is actually a large portion of time. What you should remember is that you will answer some questions more quickly than this, leaving a little more time for the more difficult questions.

However, as speed is of the essence here, don't dwell on questions you think you should know the answer to but can't quite remember. The 'tip of the tongue' phenomenon comes into play for a significant number of students in MCQ exams: they know the answer, but they can't quite make it materialize in their head. The tip here is to move on to the next question and come back to the missed question later on. You need to answer as many questions as possible: if finding the answer to one question means you don't have time to answer six you easily knew at the end then it isn't worth spending all that time on just one question. Plus, reading other information and answering other questions can jog your memory, helping you to fill in the gaps in your answers—if you really do know the answer, you'll find you are able to answer more it easily later on.

Short-answer questions

Short-answer questions are written responses to questions, but with a maximum of half a page allocated for your answer. You will typically be allocated between 2 and 10 marks for a shorter-answer question: look at the number of marks allocated and make sure you tailor your answer appropriately. You don't need to write half a page for a 2 mark question; equally, writing a few lines for an 8 mark question is also inappropriate. The trick with short-answer questions is to work out what you need to say before writing. This can be by making notes or simply sitting and thinking about it for a moment, whichever works for you. I'd recommend writing notes however, as this way you won't run the risk of forgetting what you want to write later on. If you start writing as you're thinking, you'll end up turning your half a page into several and wasting time on one question that you could be spending on others.

Waffle doesn't get marks; answers that go straight to the point and directly answer the question do. Keep in mind that a short-answer question is directly tackling what you can remember about the topic. It rarely wants you to explain things in context as that is what an essay is for. If you want a guide for how much to write for a question—one sentence per mark is usually reasonable as long as you stay on the point and don't waffle!

Generally, the rule of thumb for timing in short-answer questions is 'a mark a minute'. If you have a 4 mark question you should be able to answer it in 4 minutes. A number of you may well be wondering if this is asking the impossible. But actually you can write a considerable amount in just a few minutes, and certainly enough to answer a short question. During your revision see how much you can write in a minute, you'll be surprised how much you can get down, and hopefully this will set your mind at ease a little for the exam. Remember that you can go back and add more to a question if you have time left at the end of the exam. Sticking to a set time helps you focus on answering the question and prevents you getting off track and including more detail than you need.

....

Exercise 16.1: Example questions—where have they got marks?

In this exercise read the example question answers and take on the role of the examiner—how many marks would you give each answer? (And what would you give the marks for?) For my version of marking these questions, see 'Answers to exercises' at the end of the book.

Question: What is the difference between classical and operant conditioning (6 marks).

Answer A:

Classical conditioning is association and operant conditioning is reward and punishment. Pavlov did an experiment with dogs to see if they learned to link the bell with the food while Skinner did an experiment with rats and gave them electric shocks or food.

Answer B:

Classical conditioning was studied by Pavlov and states that two unrelated stimuli can become associated together if they are presented at the same time repeatedly. Pavlov rang a bell every time he gave dogs some food and found that the dogs started salivating when they heard a bell rather than when they were presented with food. Operant conditioning was studied by Skinner and states that stimuli are learned through reward and punishment. Skinner gave rats 2 levers to choose from, one gave an electric shock and one gave food. The rats quickly learned to avoid the electric shock lever and only push the food lever.

Answer C:

Classical conditioning states that learning occurs when 2 previously unrelated stimuli are associated together though frequent appearance at the same time. The unconditioned stimulus (such as appearance of food) produces an unconditioned reflexive behaviour (such as salivation), while the neutral stimulus (for example ringing a bell) is presented at the same time. This neutral stimulus (the bell) eventually produces the same reflexive behaviour (salivation) and becomes known as the conditioned stimulus (the bell). The reflexive behaviour is now known as the conditioned response (salivation). In contrast to this slower method of learning, operant conditioning is a much quicker method of learning in that it relies on the immediate effects conferred by rewards and punishments. If an action is followed immediately by a negative event (such as an electric shock) then the action is no longer produced. However, if the action is immediately followed by a favourable event (such as the production of food) then it is repeated.

Essays

By now you will be fairly familiar with essays; they are straightforward enough to produce in exams. While we cover how to write a good essay in Chapter 10, you don't need to remember the finer points of essay writing in an exam. The main focus in an exam setting should be to answer the question posed. The major challenge people face with essays in exams is answering the question that has actually been set with sufficient evidence to convince the person marking the exam they do really understand the concepts and area being discussed. This is key to getting good marks so make sure you focus on what the question is actually asking—answering a question you can answer (but isn't on the question paper) won't get you any marks at all, no matter how well it's written!

A key tip for writing essays in exams is to take five minutes from your allotted time to plan your essay. In most circumstances, five minutes doesn't seem like very long, but in an exam it can feel like you're wasting precious hours planning when you should be writing. Brain storm for a few minutes on the subject of the essay: write down notes (in pencil, in the margins or on a spare piece of paper) about everything you can remember about that topic, theories, names, points, evaluation points and studies. If you do this then you already have a road map for your essay and the structure will sort itself out. You will also then have a list of things to refer back to, thus enabling you to maximise your essay content.

▸ We discuss essay planning in Chapter 10.

Try not to waffle in your exam essay. (You shouldn't anyway, but the consequences are more serious in exams.) If you waffle you spend precious minutes writing sentences that do not translate into marks. Make a point, link it to evidence, discuss it concisely then move onto the next point you want to make. Making the same point several times won't get you more marks; it just means the examiner will get a sense of déjà vu!

Students tend to waffle when they're not sure about what to write and they feel they can't remember much about a topic. This can have beneficial effects: by 'waffling' the student is essentially free-writing, a process that will produce memory triggers that link to important information they need at some point in the process. This is not an efficient method of writing in exams though: time constraints mean that you run out of time before you've amassed enough marks to justify using it. (That said, if you're really stuck, some marks are better than none.) If you find yourself on the verge of waffling, brainstorm for a few minutes instead. Notes take less time to write than sentences, and you will find that you do remember something you can write sensibly about.

Timing is absolutely crucial when you're writing essays in an exam setting. Essays may appear on your exam paper in two scenarios. Firstly, they can be on a paper which is purely essay-based. You then have to pick a certain number to do in an allotted time. Secondly, they can be present on a mixed-question paper and may there may or may not be a choice of question. Whichever format you have, you need to work out how long you have for each essay and stick to it, otherwise other questions will then be impacted on and you won't have time to answer them as well as you might like.

Coping with stress during exam periods

Stress is a big part of the exam experience; there are very few students who do not get incredibly stressed around exam time. However, there are ways of reducing that stress dramatically.

- Find out all the information you need for each exam. This means establishing the time, date, location of exam, and what is required in terms of topics covered in that exam and so forth.

⇒ We discuss reminder systems in Chapter 2, on time management.

- Make sure you set up a reminders system that works for you, be that post-it notes on the fridge and bathroom mirror or reminders programmed into your smartphone.

- Read the time management chapter: organize your time so that you have enough space to revise for each of your exams.

- Don't lose touch with your friends:
  - Friends can offer moral support when you start feeling overwhelmed. It is a strong person who never wonders, at some point during the exam period, if it's all worth it. Friends can help keep you on the right track and help keep your spirits up when they flag.
  - Friends are a source of information: if you have forgotten something regarding an exam or topic, friends doing the same exams as you should be able to provide the answer. Two heads (or more) are always better than one.
  - Friends enable you to stay in touch with reality during exam time. Many students get 'lost' in revision and end up in a daze. Staying in touch with other people socially as well as academically helps keep you grounded in reality and stops you feeling like the exams are the be-all and end-all. This enables you to do better in those exams as you are less stressed about them.

Relaxation and taking time out

Making time to have a break and relax is as important as the time spent revising. Many students forget to rest and finish the exam period exhausted, which is problematic after winter exams when the next semester starts within days of the last exams.

Going back to the rewards system mentioned earlier in this chapter, one good method of providing a reward for all your hard work is to give yourself a set amount of time off per hour of study. It you store all these minutes up you can end up with a couple of hours which you can use to relax and de-stress. Some of you might use that time to sleep, or watch a favourite TV programme. The important thing to remember with this system is to stick to the time you have allotted yourself. The idea of time off will not work if you ignore the time you have allocated to relax and end up spending all night watching TV.

Active relaxation techniques also work very well during revision time: you don't have to practise meditative techniques to benefit from the basic philosophy. All you need to do is to find somewhere where you won't be disturbed, then sit comfortably, close your eyes and listen to yourself breathe for 10–15 minutes. This may sound bizarre to anyone who is not used to meditative techniques: active relaxation sounds like a paradox and listening to yourself breathe is not what most people do. But active relaxation simply means to deliberately relax and the technique described works; it can't hurt to try it. This method helps to calm you down and effectively de-stress (rather dramatically sometimes), leaving you able to focus far better in subsequent revision sessions.

The general idea of meditative techniques is to quieten the mind, which is a good idea during exam time. You want to focus on the topics at hand, not everything else in your head. Those of you who already do yoga, Pilates or practise meditation will already understand the benefits of active relaxation. During exam time, you may want to make sure you fit in each day a session of whichever discipline you follow.

What to do *after* the exam

Some people like to dissect their exam performance, going over how they answered each and every question. If you are not one of these people, you may want to leave as soon as the exam is over. Make your apologies to friends; explain you don't want to go over the exam and you'll catch up with them later on. If friends are dissecting what they wrote, you may become stressed if you hear that the answers other people gave were different from yours. At this point people always assume they are wrong and that they've lost marks, leading to increased stress and lower motivation for subsequent exams. It is entirely possible that the reverse is true. Indeed, it is sometimes more likely that the minority are correct and the majority are wrong. After all, those who get the top marks are in the minority; to do so they will have answered some questions differently from the majority (i.e. correctly rather than incorrectly). If situations like this create stress and panic in you, try not to be part of the conversation in the first place. At the end of the day you won't be the only student who is stressed and wondering if they've done well.

Try also to avoid rushing home to check all the answers: it does no good at this stage as there is nothing you can do about your performance in the exam. It is better to remain calm and controlled than head towards panic because you might have lost marks on a question.

Get some fresh air, some food and spend some time relaxing before you dive into revision again. You need a break before re-starting revision for a number of reasons: reducing stress levels, getting out of the mind-set of one topic, and allowing space for your nerves and brain to recover before revising a different topic. Exams are intense situations which we all need some recovery time from. Tension rarely enhances revision performance. While some people may find switching between topics easy, the vast majority do not, and will probably need a period of relaxation between subjects. Just as you need the space to assimilate what you have learnt on a topic before moving onto another one during revision, you need time to assimilate your personal performance on an exam before moving onto the next one.

And finally—common sense tips

You'll find you get advice from all sources during revision time, including from family and friends. Some of it will be helpful to you, but much of it will relate to their perceptions as individuals rather than being directly useful to you. Everyone revises differently, so try only to retain what is useful to you and use that: do not feel that you have to use the same revision techniques as siblings, friends and tutors. If you are really stuck and want to try another method, maybe because you feel the way you revised in the past didn't work as effectively as you would like, then do so. Whatever method of revision you use, you will be revisiting the information you need to learn. This is the entire point of revision; hence there is no wrong way to revise.

Common sense tips

Not everything during revision is about techniques, relaxation and methods. There are a number of common sense things that people tend not to consider, particularly in relation to sleeping, eating, smoking and dieting.

• **Don't forget to sleep**

    Many students forget their normal sleep routine during revision: they end up working late into the night, sleeping for a good portion of the day and end up drinking excessive amounts of caffeine just to get through the exams. This leads to jittery students who are definitely not thinking at their best. Here are some tips for avoiding the jitters and helping you think more clearly and logically.

    – Make sure you get 6–8 hours sleep a night. If you work until 2 a.m., go to bed about 2.30 a.m. and get up at around 10 a.m. Don't worry about late nights during revision time, but make sure you don't do all-nighters. Working all night will wipe out the entirety of the following day and reduce your revision time. Try to vaguely stick to your typical sleep/wake patterns: you don't want to get your body clock out of sync with the real world within which all your exams are based!

- Go to bed before midnight the night before an exam, and stop working by 10 p.m. There is no point spending all night cramming: you will end up exhausted, wired on caffeine and unable to think properly. The way to approach the night before an exam is to realize that if you don't know it then, you can get up early and go through it the following morning. Waking up an hour earlier than normal is far more beneficial to mental agility than scrambling to get to the exam because you've been awake all night (for no other reason than you have had time to wake up and eat some food).

- **Don't forget to eat**

  This may sound simple; proportionally few people ever forget to eat. However, a significant number of students do forget to eat regular meals when revising, even those who normally make a point of finding time for meals. This sudden change in eating habits is very bad news for the brain. Your brain uses a significant amount of your energy—it needs plenty of glucose and nutrients to work properly. Food is more important when you are revising than at any other time during your studies.

  – Eat a proper meal at least once a day.

  – Don't diet. Revision time is not the time to worry about staying on, or going on, a diet. You should not be restricting carbohydrates in particular during revision time: you may well be eating more chocolate, crisps, and biscuits than you should but a few weeks don't matter in the grand scheme of things. If you are particularly stressed about what you eat make sure you stock up on food such as pretzels and bananas. These contain the carbohydrates you need to fuel your brain but have less fat in them than biscuits and crisps.

    o The caveat here is if you are on a diet for medical reasons you should obviously stick to this, and refrain from excessive consumption of anything not listed on your diet plan.

- **Don't try to quit smoking during revision time (quit before or afterwards)**

  This may sound controversial, but it needs to be stated categorically. Smoking is both a physiological and psychological addiction. The physiological withdrawal is minimal; the main withdrawal symptoms you experience are psychological. Unnecessary psychological stress is not something any student should have during revision periods, so you should not try to put extra pressure on yourself when you don't need to. If you do want to quit smoking, do so once your exams are finished—or several months before they have even started. If you do quit before the exams, make sure you have nicotine patches or chewing gum handy in case you can feel your willpower fading.

  – The only caveat to this advice is if you have been told to stop smoking by your doctor. This is obviously something you should continue to do. You will probably have been prescribed nicotine supplements, such as patches or chewing gum, if this is the case. Make sure you use them exactly as prescribed and follow your doctor's advice.

✎ Checklist

Check you've understood the key points covered in this chapter by seeing if you can answer the following questions:

- ✔ Do you know where you are going to do the majority of your revision?
- ✔ What reward system will you set up for yourself?
- ✔ What time of day are you going to be able to do your best revision?
- ✔ Do you know the difference between passive and active revision?
  - ✔ And which works best for you?
- ✔ Do you know how to do mind maps, use flash cards and how to jog your memory around your home?
- ✔ Where are the past papers and answers kept?
  - ✔ And how should you do them?
- ✔ Are you clear on how to tackle the different types of question you will be getting in the exam?
- ✔ What should you not do during revision periods?

📖 References

Martin, G.N., Carlson, N.R. & Buskist, W. (2010). *Psychology (4th Edition)*. Hove: Pearson Education.

Answers to exercises

Chapter 5

Exercise 5.1: what the standard criteria mean

Standard criterion	What it means
Answering the question	Clearly answering the question that has been given, and focusing throughout on this question
Structure	A clearly defined, logical and clear structure; with a clear introduction, middle and conclusion. The conclusion pulls together important points and answers the initial question set
Evidence of understanding	There is consistent understanding throughout, which is displayed clearly and logically. There is clear evidence of wider reading
A clear argument	There is a logical, well-reasoned argument with supporting evidence. The arguments are based on evidence which is easily available and appropriate
Use of evidence	There are relevent and logical examples from the reading to illustrate the argument. A wide variety of sources have been used
Critical thinking	The material presented is objective and critical, not biased towards a particular viewpoint. There is a conceptual and a methodological critique of the issues, as well as evidence and appreciation of alternative perspectives
Appropriate use of language and writing style	The work is clear, legible and well presented. The text is easy to read and there is correct use of spelling, grammar and punctuation

Adapted from Elander et al. (2006)

Exercise 5.2: how the standard criteria rate

Standard criteria	Student rankings	Tutor rankings
Addressing the question	1 =	1
Structure	5	7 =
A clear argument	8 =	5 =
Use of evidence	7	3 =
Evidence of understanding	8 =	5 =
Critical thinking	3 =	7 =
Referencing	6	9
Spelling	1 =	3 =
Appropriate use of language and writing style	3 =	2

Adapted from Norton et al. (2002)

....

Chapter 7

Exercise 7.1: aim and hypothesis extraction

Individuals are subject to reconstructive errors in the recall of events (Bartlett, 1932), especially when presented with misleading information. Loftus and Palmer (1974) wanted to discover whether the memory of events actually changes as a result of misleading questions or if the existing memory is merely supplemented. They showed their participants a film clip of a car accident and then asked them a series of questions, and found that a simple word change affected the answers given by participants; leading them to conclude that leading/misleading questions can manipulate recollection of an event. This study reproduces this classic study by Loftus and Palmer, with the intention of repeating this result on a modern-day selection of participants. It was hypothesised that changes in adjective will elicit changes in responses given. Forty individuals, aged 16–35, from a school in Birmingham were tested in five different groups in an empty classroom. Participants watched a film clip of a car crash taken from a movie, followed by six questions. Each group were given identical questions apart from the critical question, where the strength of an adjective varied. The results showed that the stronger adjectives produced higher speed estimates. Leading questions can manipulate and affect the accuracy of recall of events.

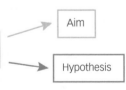

Aim

Hypothesis

Exercise 7.2: understanding the method

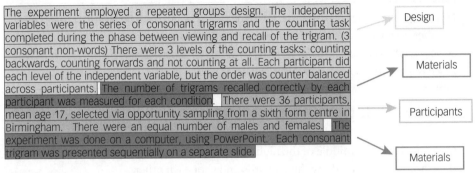

The experiment employed a repeated groups design. The independent variables were the series of consonant trigrams and the counting task completed during the phase between viewing and recall of the trigram. (3 consonant non-words) There were 3 levels of the counting tasks: counting backwards, counting forwards and not counting at all. Each participant did each level of the independent variable, but the order was counter balanced across participants. The number of trigrams recalled correctly by each participant was measured for each condition. There were 36 participants, mean age 17, selected via opportunity sampling from a sixth form centre in Birmingham. There were an equal number of males and females. The experiment was done on a computer, using PowerPoint. Each consonant trigram was presented sequentially on a separate slide.

Design

Materials

Participants

Materials

Procedure:
The experiment was conducted within a secure, isolated room away from any distractions. Participants were shown the trigrams 3 times, to incorporate the three distraction tasks, over seven stages, using PowerPoint. Each stage had an increase in time of 3 seconds, beginning at an instant recall for the first round, 3 second delay for the second round, followed by rounds of 6, 9, 12, 15 and 18 seconds. The three counting techniques employed were counting backwards in 3's, counting forwards in 3's and not counting at all. Different trigrams shall be used each round to prevent potential recall being formed from repetitive use of the same trigram. The experimenter recorded the answers.

What they did in the experiment

They showed people trigrams (three consonant non-words) on a computer and asked them to do one of three things during recall—count forwards or backwards in threes or not to count at all. They asked them to recall at seven different times. Everyone did every style of recall.

What's not clear

There is no indication of how the counterbalancing was organized, and the description of the conditions needs more information so it is absolutely clear what participants did in each condition. The procedure overall needed a little more detail to avoid potential ambiguity.

Chapter 9

Exercise 9.1: correcting sentences

Corrected version of example sentence 4:

Reactive depression is quite mild to quite serious whereas endogenous depression is extremely severe. Symptoms of depression can occur because of maladaptive thinking, for example if you always think negatively about yourself and think that you are unable to accomplish tasks then this can lead to depression. Also a decrease in the neurotransmitter serotonin can cause depressive symptoms as it plays a large part in emotions.

Exercise 9.2: comma confusion

Psychology is the study of everything, from biology and neurology to behaviour, language and social interactions. Essentially it is the study of what we do and why we do it. In this way psychology is different from the other sciences, which look at what and how things happen, as we psychologists are looking at why things happen as well.

Exercise 9.3: placing punctuation

1 One fine day in the middle of the night, two dead men got up to fight; back to back they faced each other, drew their swords and shot each other.

2 The dragon was most displeased that he was told to stop eating the small kittens, as they were his favourite snack, and he couldn't work out what he might find to replace them. The townspeople were pleased, however, as now the rat population could be kept under control.

3 Of the many creatures available to join Noah on his ark the tigers were by far the most dangerous of the bunch; they have very few predators, only the panthers, lions and elephants stood much chance against them. They were, however, reluctant to interfere with the alligators and crocodiles; their rather large jaws kept most creatures away from them.

4 The students were silent in the class as they worked hard on their work. The teacher looked on with a sense of satisfaction, realizing that the students had finally learned how to work independently without complaint; she was reassured that they had actually been listening during the previous lesson.

Chapter 10

Exercise 10.1: what is the question asking?

Discuss the different perspectives taken on schizophrenia over the course of history

The focus in this first essay is the history of schizophrenia, and how it has been viewed, rather than the symptoms. Any essay which got distracted and started describing

- History of schizophrenia:
  - Where the name came from
  - How it was viewed pre-categorization as a mental disorder
  - How it came to be categorized as a mental disorder and treated accordingly
- How schizophrenia is viewed now and how it's different

schizophrenia in too much detail would lose marks simply because you wouldn't have the room in the essay word limit to fully discuss the topic.

Describe the aetiology of the different stages of schizophrenia and it's relation to how it can be treated

- Describe symptoms and stages of schizophrenia:
  - Include the links between types and symptoms
- Describe treatments for schizophrenia:
  - Biological and psychological
  - That is, drugs and cognitive behavioural therapy (CBT)
  - Don't forget to discuss combined therapy.
- Explain how different methods of treatment target particular types of schizophrenia:
  - For example, drugs only target positive symptoms.

This second essay focus is on schizophrenia itself, the details of how it can to be called schizophrenia and so forth are not relevant here, the focus is purely descriptive.

Exercise 10.2: essay plans—an example essay plan

Discuss the influence of nature and nurture in the development of behaviour

Introduction—explain what nature and nurture mean
- Nature—born with
- Nurture—experiences and learning

Nature with nurture influence—evolution model
- Development of eyesight
  - Carpentered world hypothesis
    - Developed versus developing countries
      - Müller-Lyer illusion
  - Blakemoor and Cooper's kittens
  - Visual cliff experiment
    - Depth and learning
- Schizophrenia
  - Genetic predisposition but environmental trigger
  - MZ (monozygotic) twins not 100% concordance

Nurture with nature influence—behavioural model
- Eating disorders:
  - Mother–daughter link
  - MZ twins not 100% concordance

> - Social learning (observation—vicarious):
>   - Bobo doll experiment—Bandura
> - Harlow's monkeys:
>   - Formation of love
> Conclusions
> - Nature provides basis for nurture to develop

Exercise 10.3: beginnings and endings

Sample introductions:

Example introduction 1

The writer here has tried to address the essay question right at the start, although they're a little off-track in the first sentence. From the essay question's point of view it doesn't really matter where the data comes from—you simply need to focus on what it says. So this is a rather redundant comment. The problem with this introduction is the redundant comment then leads the writer off-track and talking about two things that are not a factor in day care—deprivation and privation, which are separate issues and are not relevant to this essay topic. The second section of the introduction starts to get a little bit more to the point, and hopefully it indicates that the essay is going to answer the question set. Remember, if you go off-track in the introduction it is less likely that you'll end up answering the question you have been set.

Example introduction 2

In this example the writer has gone way off topic already: they have ignored the actual title and got sidetracked by the word 'treatment' and decided to discuss the benefits of types of treatment available. This is not going to end well for the writer: despite the essay looking like it will be a good discussion of treatments, it will not be in the context of the stages of schizophrenia which is the crucial element of this essay—the relationship between stages and treatment, not the treatment issues themselves. This essay will not get a good mark. When writing your essays remember to work out what the essay is asking you to do *before* you start writing, otherwise you may end up with a good essay that gets a low mark—all because you didn't focus on the actual question being asked.

Example introduction 3

This introduction is bang on topic; the writer has directly explained what the essay topic is about and what the key aspects of majority influence are. There is every indication that this essay will directly address the question and gain good marks. In your introductions you should always start with explaining what the title is asking you to do: this does not mean write in a school manner of "this essay will start by … then will cover …" and so on. Rather, start your essay straight away but with reference to the topic and cover any definitions you need to in order to fully discuss the topic area later on.

Sample conclusions

Example conclusion 1

This conclusion is OK, but the first section of the paragraph is linked with the bulk of the essay. The last section is the conclusion, and the waffle earlier in the paragraph detracts from the concise nature of the conclusion presented. It is also likely that this writer got a bit distracted earlier in the essay: they mention treatments and reasons for development of anorexia, which was not mentioned in the essay title. When writing your conclusions, remember you don't need to have reams of words and sentences to round up what you've written about, a short paragraph is absolutely fine as long as it related directly back to the essay question provided.

Example conclusion 2

Here the writer hasn't really finished the essay at all. There are no discernable conclusions and it seems that they have simply stopped writing because they wrote all they wanted. It is not unreasonable to assume that a few of you at least are guilty of doing this for whatever reason. In future you should try to make sure you have a proper conclusion, and make sure that you answer the essay question being set, as has been shown in the main body of this chapter (see p. 000).

Example conclusion 3

This conclusion is good: there is reference to the main content and information, plus the writer answers the question directly and clearly. This conclusion also gives you an example of how it is perfectly acceptable to conclude with no direct answer the question set. Sitting on the fence in your opinion is fine if that is what the evidence suggests to you, which it appears to be in this example.

Chapter 12

Exercise 12.1: spotting the plagiarism

Note: [REF]—this indicates that a reference, or part of a reference is missing. If there is already a partial reference in place, then part of that reference is missing, be it the page number for a quotation or the citation for the original article—in other words, the secondary in-text reference.

Italic text—this indicates that the portion of the text has been copied, or so poorly paraphrased it may as well have been copied (i.e. a few words have been taken out so that it appears paraphrased but in fact is not). The more italic text there is, the less credit can be given to the student for comprehension of the original material.

1 *Second Life is an online environment with 3-D graphics. Users can interact in a way that mimics real life. Immersive virtual environments* have a lot of potential in enhancing learning in education [REF]. The environment *can engage students* in an *innovative way*, with *the potential to unlock problem-solving* abilities and provide more collaborative learning. It *engages students* and helps them work longer as they are enjoying learning more [REF]. Pajares and Johnson [REF] said that *students who are highly motivated produce richer and higher quality work than those who are not.*

> There is no reference for the original article anywhere in this paraphrased text

> A reference has been remembered for Pajares & Johnson, but the year has been forgotten!

> The paraphrasing itself is very poor. There is too much similarity with the original text—and the order things are written is virtually identical

2 "*Second Life is an immersive, online-simulated environment, with 3-D graphics that allows users to interact in a manner mimicking real-life interactions.*" [REF] Environments like this are being used by many to enhance technology within education: "*immersive and collaborative communities of practice can engage students in innovative and creative ways.*" [REF] The environments have the potential to help students reach a deeper understanding and allow them to solve problems more creatively. "*Highly motivated students produce richer and higher quality work than those who are not*" (Pajares & Johnson, 1994 [REF]). Students keep working "*far longer on educational tasks than they would normally because it was an enjoyable experience*" (Sanchez, 2007 [REF]).(Bignell & Parson, 2010).

> Using lots of quotations does not show understanding—it is always better to paraphrase than quote.

> The writer has used quotations instead of paraphrasing. However, there are no references for each quotation: name, year AND page number are required for each quotation.

> The references that are provided are incorrect: the quotation is from the paraphrasing in the original extract, not the articles by Pajares and Sanchez.

> While there is a reference to the original article, it is in the wrong place—it should be after every quotation instead.

3 Students are more highly motivated when they enjoy their work [REF] and tend to do more of it. Second Life offers the potential, as an immersive environment with 3-D graphics, to enhance learning through technology (Bignell and Parson, 2010). Immersive technological environments are being used in many internet social applications, aiming to engage students in innovative ways. Collaboration skills and a deeper learning are enhanced through use of Second Life; while student creativity is enhanced, allowing them to think "outside the box" (Bignell & Parson, 2010), leading to a more enjoyable learning experience (Bignell & Parson [REF]).

> This reference is in the right place, it's just the wrong reference—the point is from Pajares & Johnson (1994)

> This reference is in the correct place, but the page number is missing, something you always have to have with a quotation

> This reference is in the right place, it's just the wrong reference—the point about an enjoyable experience is from Sanchez (2007)

Comment on answers

1 The first paragraph is clear plagiarism: substantial sections are not referenced and are directly taken from the original text. This is generally the worst case out of the three. If this type of work was consistently produced by the student, they would, most likely, be warned and then subjected to disciplinary procedures.

2 The second paragraph has so many quotations that, while the plagiarism aspect may not be too severe, there is no evidence of understanding and the student has clearly

taken a lot of information directly from someone else. Even if there is acknowledgement that it is not the student's own work, there is no proper referencing evident so plagiarism is still a factor.

3 Out of the three options, the third is the best in terms of avoiding plagiarism. While the referencing isn't perfect, there is clear evidence of understanding, the referencing problems are easy to fix, and would not be flagged up as plagiarism. There is no evidence that the student is trying to pass off another's work as their own.

Chapter 13

Exercise 13.1: referencing: spot the mistakes

APA format: correct answers

1 Carter, P.R., Reddy, W. & Martin, F.M. (2004). *Students: beer monsters or future prime ministers?* UK: Albert Publishing.

2 Russell, B.R. (2000). *Learning to fly (9th Edition)*. Newcastle, UK: Anderson Publishing.

3 Bowen, L.L. (1995). Perspectives on tie choice: is there a link with personality? *Décor and Personality, 34*(3), 766–777.

4 Ferdin, A . & Tash, A. (1997). Musical taste in cats. In R.J. Groves & B.C. Forsyth (Eds.) *Variations in taste between species* (pp. 161–187). UK: Diggory Press

5 Ollivander, D. (Ed.) (2002). *The Mystery of Wand Choice (1ˢᵗ Edition)*. UK: Hobgoblin Press

6 Rawlings, E. (2004). *Secrets of the Classroom (4ᵗʰ Edition)*. UK: Smith House

7 Fforde, P. J. (2002). How to get lost in a good book. In E. Bennett & E. Rochester (Eds.) *Reading and Language Theories* (pp. 415–430). Bath, UK: Sensibility Press.

8 Edwards, H. (1999). *What really happens before broadcasts*. Retrieved 10/12/04, 17.59 GMT from http://www.newsreports.co.uk/NRaC/template.cfm&contentID=3051955/report.pdf

9 Coleman, C. & Skelton, F. (2009). Summer schools: the inside story. *The University Journal, 7*(5), 45–52.

10 Sparrow, J. (2002). The difficulty in finding rum. In E. Turner (Ed.) *Pirates and their idiosyncrasies* (pp.187–214). Portland: Caribbean Press.

11 Coupland, P. (2008). A review of post-modern social observations. *Writing and Society, 9*(2), 453–459. Retrieved 05/12/09, 16.32 GMT from http://www.randomhousepublications.co.uk/was/query.rwod?cmd=Retrieve&db=Publist_uids=195423&jht=Citation

Harvard format: correct answers

1 Carter, P.R. Reddy, W. and Martin, F.M. (2004) *Students: beer monsters or future prime ministers?* UK. Albert Publishing.

2 Russell, B.R. (2000) *Learning to Fly*, 9th edn. Newcastle, UK. Anderson Publishing.

3 Bowen, L.L. (1995) Perspectives on tie choice: is there a link with personality? *Décor and Personality*, 34(3), 766–777.

4 Ferdin, A . and Tash, A. (1997). Musical taste in cats. In Groves, R.J. and Forsyth, B.C. (eds) *Variations in Taste Between Species*. UK. Diggory Press. pp.161–187.

5 Ollivander, D. (Ed.) (2002) *The Mystery of Wand Choice*, 1st edn. UK. Hobgoblin Press.

6 Rawlings, E. (2004) *Secrets of the Classroom*, 4th edn. UK. Smith House.

7 Fforde, P.J. (2002). How to get lost in a good book. In: Bennett, E. and Rochester, E. (eds) *Reading and Language Theories*. Bath, UK. Sensibility Press, pp. 415–430.

8 Edwards, H. (1999) *What Really Happens Before Broadcasts.* [WWW] Available from: http://www.newsreports.co.uk/NRaC/template.cfm&contentID=3051955/report.pdf [accessed 12 October 2004].

9 Coleman, C. and Skelton, F. (2009) Summer schools: the inside story. *The University Journal*, 7(5), 45–52.

10 Sparrow, J. (2002) The difficulty in finding rum. In: Turner, E. (ed.) *Pirates and Their Idiosyncrasies*. Portland. Caribbean Press. pp. 187–214.

11 Coupland, P. (2008). A review of post-modern social observations. *Writing and Society*, 9(2), 453–459. [WWW] Available from: :http://www.randomhousepublications.co.uk/was/query.rwod?cmd=Retrieve&db=Publist_uids=195423&jht=Citation [accessed 12 May 2009].

. . . .

Chapter 16

Exercise 16.1: example questions—where have they got marks?

Question: what is the difference between classical and operant conditioning (6 marks)

Answer A: 1/6

Classical conditioning is association and operant conditioning is reward and punishment. Pavlov did an experiment with dogs to see if they learned to link the bell with the food while Skinner did an experiment with rats and gave them electric shocks or food.

This answer is far too short and fundamentally does not answer the question. While it accurately states what classical and operant conditioning are there is no real detail given and no comparison of the differences at all. The student has given some details about the original studies which, while accurate, are not described in the context of the answer given and neither example is linked appropriately to a type of conditioning. This is definitely not what you should aim for in a 6 mark question.

Answer B: 3/6

Classical conditioning was studied by Pavlov and states that two unrelated stimuli can become associated together if they are presented at the same time repeatedly. Pavlov rang a bell every time he gave dogs some food and found that the dogs started salivating when they heard a bell rather than when they were presented with food. Operant conditioning was studied by Skinner and states that stimuli are learned through reward and punishment. Skinner gave rats 2 levers to choose from, one gave an electric shock and one gave food. The rats quickly learned to avoid the electric shock lever and only push the food lever.

This answer is a little better. There is an accurate (if a little brief) description of both classical and operant conditioning, but there is no actual comparison between the two types of conditioning. The student has described the original studies which is not appropriate. What they have written is accurate but because it is not required by the question no marks can be given. Hopefully you didn't give this one full marks!

Answer C: 6/6

Classical conditioning states that learning occurs when 2 previously unrelated stimuli are associated together though frequent appearance at the same time. The unconditioned stimulus (such as appearance of food) produces an unconditioned reflexive behaviour (such as salivation), while the neutral stimulus (for example ringing a bell) is presented at the same time. This neutral stimulus (the bell) eventually produces the same reflexive behaviour (salivation) and becomes known as the conditioned stimulus (the bell). The reflexive behaviour is now known as the conditioned response (salivation). In contrast to this slower method of learning, operant conditioning is a much quicker method of learning in that it relies on the immediate effects conferred by rewards and punishments. If an action is followed immediately by a negative event (such as an electric shock) then the action is no longer produced. However if the action is immediately followed by a favourable event (such as the production of food) then it is repeated.

This answer is the best of the three and gets full marks. There is an accurate and detailed description of both classical and operant conditioning, plus there is the crucial comparison. This answer is by no means perfect, the student does waffle a little and the comparison itself could be more detailed, but they have done enough to answer the question fully (including mentioning the magic word here—learning!) and so is awarded full marks. The biggest difference with Answer B here is that the student does not describe the original studies as part of the question. Instead they use the key aspects of the studies as their examples for each element of the types of conditioning.

Index

A

abbreviations 92–3
abstracts, *see* laboratory reports
academic staff 34–35
    lecturers, as source of help 34, 176, 180
    personal tutors 35
    tutors 16, 22
acronyms 92–4
American Psychological Association
    (APA) 139, 145, 149
APA (format of referencing) 139
apostrophes, *see punctuation*
appendices, *see* laboratory reports
arguments 75
    developing an argument 75–77, 79,
        82, 106–109
asking questions 19–20
assessment criteria 36–40
    specialist criteria 38–41
    standard criteria 38–40
assessments 36–41
assignments (*see also* assessments)
    56–57, 95

B

blogs 29–31
British Psychological Society (BPS) 121,
    139, 153
brainstorming 98, 108, 192

C

collusion 131–132
colons, *see* punctuation
commas, *see* punctuation
communication 1–2, 27–35
    communication skills 1–2
conclusions
    as part of abstract 113–114
    in essays 101–104
    in journal articles 66, 67
    in laboratory reports 127
    in posters 165–170
contractions 92–93
critical analysis 50–51, 73–76
critical thinking, *see* critical analysis

D

data
    interpretation of 65–66
    qualitative 112–113, 128–130

quantitative 112–113, 128, 130
design (of experiments) 65–66
diaries 6–7
discussion sections, *see also* dissertations,
    laboratory reports
    interpreting 66
discussion boards 31–32, 34–35
dissertations 172–180
    discussion section 175
    introduction section 175
    methods section 175
    structure of 177–179

E

eating 195
empirical project 172–175
essays 95–110, 191–192
    drafts of 100
    essay plans 98, 100
    essay titles, interpretation of 96–99,
        108
    feedback on 41–42
    structure of 95–96, 100–104,
        107–108
    using evidence in 109–110
ethics 121
evaluation
    of information 45, 54–56, 70–77, 105
    of textbooks 45–49, 70, 77, 93, 96–97,
        99–100, 105, 191
evidence 75–76
    of understanding 37–38, 101
    use of 40, 51, 56, 104–106
exams
    coping with stress during 192–193
    essay questions in 191–198
    multiple choice questions in
        188–189
    past papers of 187–189
    revising for 11–13, 181–188
    short answer questions in 189–191
    tips for 194–195

F

Facebook 31
feedback 41–44
figures
    in journal articles 63–65
    use of in lab reports 122
    use of in posters 157–158
flash cards 184–185
full stops (use of), *see* punctuations

G

Google (Scholar) 53, 60
grammar 80–81, 197
    personal pronouns 90–91, 110
graphs 123–124

H

hand-outs 18–19
    preparation of 160–162
Harvard (system of reference) 139,
    149–151
holidays 5
    making good use of 9–13
hypotheses
    constructing 116–117
    interpreting 60–62
    in posters 166, 167
    types of 116

I

independent learning 3
Interaction (with others) 22
internet
    as source of information 51–54
    referencing content from 145–146
    use of in presentations 160
introduction (section)
    in dissertations 175
    in essays 98, 101–103
    in journal articles 60–61
    in laboratory reports 114–117
    in posters 165–167

J

journal articles
    abstracts in 60, 62
    as source of information 49–50, 176
    discussion sections in 66
    evaluating quality of 54–55
    hypotheses in 61–62
    interpreting 60–68
    locating 59–60
    referencing material from 144, 146, 150
    structure of 112
journals, *see* journal articles

K

keywords 60, 68, 98–99, 101
    in revision 184, 186

L

laboratory reports 112–129,
         172–179
    abstract 113–114, 179
    aim of 116
    appendices 127, 175, 178
    discussion 125–127
    figures in 122–132
    hypotheses 116–117, 125
    introduction 114–117
    methods section 118–121
    reference section 127, 165–166, 175
    results section 121–125
    writing style for 90
learning
    independent 23, 28
    directed 23–25
    offline 32–34
    online 27–32
    with others 29–32
lecturers, *see* academic staff
lectures 16–25

M

materials section (in laboratory reports)
         119–120
methods (section)
    evaluating 62–63
    in dissertations 175
    in journal articles 62–63
    in laboratory reports 118–121
        design 118
        ethical considerations 121
        participants 118–119
        procedure 120–121
    in posters 165, 168–169
    structure of 113
mind maps 183–185
multiple choice questions, *see* exams

N

note-taking 17, 23–24

O

objectivity 76, 106–108
office hours 34

P

paragraphs 82
paraphrasing 86, 131–134
PEE (point, evidence, evaluation) 99
peer review 49
personal tutors, *see* academic staff
plagiarism 131–137

using referencing to avoid 138–152
posters 164–171
    conclusion section 165–166, 169–170
    discussion section 165–167, 169–270
    hypothesis 165, 167
    introduction section 165, 166–167
    methods section 165, 168–169
    results section 165, 166, 168–169
    stating aim of work in 165, 167
    structure of 165–166
Powerpoint slides 154–162
presentations
    delivery style 162–164
    using Powerpoint slides for 154–162
primary sources 47–48, 147–148
private study, *see* learning
procedure (section) 120–121
psychological reports, *see* laboratory
         reports
punctuation 72, 82–89
    apostrophes 86–87
    colons 87–88
    commas 84–85
        inverted 85–86
    exclamation marks 89
    full stops 81, 87
    semi colons 87–88

Q

qualitative data 112–113, 128–130
quantitative data 112–113, 128, 130
question types 188–192
quizzes (for revision) 185–186
quotations 133–134
    in written work 105, 109, 140
    quotation marks 85–86
    referencing of 141

R

reading
    critically 53–56, 70–77
    further/directed 23–25
    of books and journal articles 45–49,
         59–60, 70–77
    your own work 40–42
reading lists 23–25, 28, 45, 105
references
    in books 48–49
    in journal articles 67–68
referencing 109, 127, 131–134, 138–154
    APA system of 139
    Harvard system of, 139, 149–151
    in-text 139–141
    of different information sources
         141–147
    primary referencing (*see also* primary
         sources) 147–148

secondary referencing (*see also*
         secondary sources) 148–149
relaxation 10, 192–193
results (*see also* laboratory reports)
    interpretation of 65–66
revision 181–196
    active 183–186
    flash cards 184–185
    mind maps 183–185
    passive 183
    past exam papers 187–189
    quizzes 185–186
    reward systems for 182
    scheduling of 12–13
    sticky note technique for 186
    time out from 192–193
    when to revise 181–182
    where to revise 182–183

S

search engines 53, 60
secondary sources 47–48
semi-colons, *see* punctuation
seminars 21–22
    feedback during 42
sentences, use of in writing 81, 87
short answer questions, *see* exams
sleep 194
slides (Powerpoint)
    lecture slides 18–19
    use of in presentations 155–160
small group teaching 21–22
social media 31
statistics
    descriptive 122
    inferential 122
stress, dealing with 192–195
studying
    for exams 181–193
    when to study 182–183
    where to study 181–182

T

teaching time 16–26
templates
    for posters 165
    for Powerpoint slides 155–156
tenses 90–91
textbooks
    as information sources 24, 45–49
    evaluation of 54–56
    referencing content from 141, 142
theses 172
    comparison with dissertation 177
    structure of 177–181
time management 3–15, 179,
         181, 192

timetables
    lecture 28
    revision 12–13
    producing your own 8
tutorials 21–22
tutors, *see* academic staff

U

understanding, demonstration of
        104–106

V

vacation, *see* holidays
Virtual Learning Environments (VLEs)
        18, 20–21, 24, 27–29, 187
    discussion boards in 31–32

W

wall planners 7
weekends 9

Wikipedia 51–52
wikis 29–31
writing
    of essays 95–111
    of laboratory (practical) reports
        112–130
    style 79–82, 90–94
writing style, *see* writing